HERITAGE, LANDSCAPE AND SPATIAL JUSTICE

HERITAGE, LANDSCAPE AND SPATIAL JUSTICE

New Legal Perspectives on Heritage Protection in the Lesser Antilles

AMANDA BYER

© 2022 Amanda Byer

Published by Sidestone Press, Leiden
www.sidestone.com

Imprint: Sidestone Press dissertations

Lay-out & cover design: Sidestone Press
Photograph cover: AllyDay Creative Projects Ltd.

ISBN 978-94-6428-039-5 (softcover)
ISBN 978-94-6428-040-1 (hardcover)
ISBN 978-94-6428-041-8 (PDF e-book)

The research leading to this dissertation received funding from the European research council (ERC) under the European Union's Seventh Framework Programme (FP7/2007-2013)/ ERC-Synergy project NEXUS 1492, grant agreement n° 319209.

This dissertation followed the Nexus Ethics Code and the Code of Conduct/ Ethics of Leiden University

Contents

Acknowledgments	7
Table of Legislation	9
List of Abbreviations	15
1. Introduction	17
1.1 Traditional Approaches to Cultural Heritage Law	18
1.2 The Caribbean Context	21
1.3 Legal Geography and Spatial Justice: Description of the Conceptual Framework	25
1.4 Legal Anthropology: Law's Role as Regulator of Society	30
1.5 Aims and Objectives	31
1.6 Methodology	32
1.7 Outline of Chapters	33
1.8 A Note on Legislation	34
2. Landscape: A Caribbean Perspective	35
2.1 The Origins and Demise of Landscape: Enclosure, Alienation and Empire	35
2.2 The Caribbean as Imperial Landscape	46
2.3 Landscape and Spatial Justice	64
2.4 Conclusion	66
3. Landscape in International Law	69
3.1 Introduction	69
3.2 Protection of Landscape in International Law	70
3.3 Regional Developments and Landscape Law	92
3.4 Conclusion	103
4. Antiquities and Heritage Legislation	105
4.1 Introduction	105

4.2 The Role of Heritage Legislation in the Caribbean and the Modern Concept of Heritage	106
4.3 Antiquities Legislation	107
4.4 Museum Legislation	114
4.5 National Trust Legislation	122
4.6 Conclusion	129

5. Planning Legislation — **133**

5.1 Introduction	133
5.2 The Industrial and Post-war Foundations of Planning Law in the Lesser Antilles	134
5.3 Heritage in the Planning Process in the Lesser Antilles	136
5.4 Conclusion	147

6. National Parks and Protected Areas Legislation — **149**

6.1 Introduction	149
6.2 The History of the English Commons	150
6.3 Challenges for Commons in Caribbean Parks Law: Exclusive Conservation and the Emergence of Colonial Reserves	151
6.4 National Parks Legislation in the Lesser Antilles	152
6.5 Conclusion	159

7. Examples of Conflicts over Landscape as Public Space — **161**

7.1 Introduction	161
7.2 Greyfriars Church of Scotland, Trinidad and Tobago	162
7.3 Saint Lucia National Trust and Maria Islands Nature Reserve, Saint Lucia	168
7.4 Lower Sauteurs EIA Process /St Patrick's Breakwater, Grenada	170
7.5 Argyle International Airport EIA Process, St Vincent and the Grenadines	174
7.6 Camerhogne Park Relocation, Grenada	177
7.7 Conclusion	185

8. Conclusion	**187**
Bibliography	**193**
Summary	**211**
Curriculum Vitae	**215**

Acknowledgments

Many people shepherded this research through the process of becoming a dissertation. I am indebted to my supervisor Prof. dr. Corinne Hofman, for accepting me into the PhD programme, for being open to an environmental lawyer's perspective on heritage protection, and for her generosity in supporting my academic development along the way. This research could not have been completed without the funding provided by the European Research Council (ERC-Synergy Project Nexus 1492) under the European Union's Seventh Framework Programme (FP 7/2007-2013)/ERC grant agreement no. 319209. I owe a special thank you to my friend and colleague John Angus Martin, who first made me aware of the Nexus 1492 research opportunity.

My co-supervisor Dr Amy Strecker has been both mentor and friend for the past five years. She first introduced me to landscape and spatial justice, the twin theoretical pillars of this dissertation. I am deeply grateful to Amy for her unstinting support throughout the twists and turns of the research process and her unerring guidance when I felt as though my draft was drifting away from me. I could not have asked for a better advisor.

I thank the members of the reading committee for their time and valuable feedback. I also want to acknowledge the Nexus1492 project management team – Maribel, Ilone, Tibisay and Arelis – for their kind assistance while I was present at the Faculty of Archaeology, Leiden University. The Faculty was a welcoming and supportive intellectual space to discuss heritage issues with other PhD candidates and engage with experts in the field. Thank you to Eldris, Csilla, Jana, Emma, and many others for the discussions, whether in the office or over coffee!

For insights that could not be gleaned from the pages of a text, I thank the Caribbean heritage stakeholders who agreed to be interviewed. Thank you also to Dr Jonathan Hanna for generously sharing his knowledge and resources on Grenada's prehistory and Ms Celia Toppin for the opportunity to attend the OAS Heritage Legislation Workshop.

For many others I have failed to mention, know that your contributions, support and friendship were truly appreciated. Finally, this research on Caribbean heritage has made me reflect on my own roots. My mother and my father led by example, instilling in me a love of learning from a very young age. I thank them for their love and encouragement, for nurturing and sustaining me, and my sister especially, my rock, for always believing in me.

Table of Legislation

National laws

Antigua and Barbuda
Constitution of Antigua and Barbuda 1981
    Environmental Protection and Management Act 2014
    National Parks Act 1984
    Physical Planning Act 2003

Barbados
Constitution of Barbados 1966
    Museum and Historical Society Act 1933
    The National Trust Act 1961
    Town and Country Planning Act 1985

Dominica
Constitution of the Commonwealth of Dominica 1978
    National Parks and Protected Areas Act 1975
    Physical Planning Act 2002

Grenada
Constitution of Grenada 1973
    Grenada National Museum Act 2017
    National Parks and Protected Areas Act 1990
    National Trust Act 1967
    Physical Planning and Development Control Act 2016

Saint Lucia
Constitution of Saint Lucia 1978
    Physical Planning and Development Act 2005
    Saint Lucia National Trust Act 1975
    Saint Lucia National Trust Rules 1984

St Kitts and Nevis
Constitution of Saint Christopher and Nevis 1983
    Development Control and Planning Act 2000
    National Conservation and Environmental Protection Act 1987
    The Saint Christopher National Trust Act 2009

St Vincent and the Grenadines
Constitution of Saint Vincent and the Grenadines 1979
    National Trust Act 1969
    National Parks Act 2002
    Preservation of Historic Buildings and Antiquities Act 1976
    Town and Country Planning Act 1992

Trinidad and Tobago
Constitution of the Republic of Trinidad and Tobago Act 1976
    Municipal Corporations Act 1990
    Town and Country Planning Act 1960, as amended
    Trinidad and Tobago National Museum and Art Gallery Act 2000
    The National Trust of Trinidad and Tobago Act 1991
    The National Trust of Trinidad and Tobago (Amendment) Act 2015

Other jurisdictions

The Bahamas
The Antiquities, Monuments and Museum Act 1998
    The Bahamas National Trust Act 1959, as amended

United Kingdom
Antiquities, Monuments and Museum Act 1998
    Civic Amenities Act 1967
    Listed Buildings Act 1990
    Monuments and Archaeological Areas Act 1979
    Museum and Galleries Act 1992
    National Parks and Access to the Countryside Act 1949
    National Parks (Scotland) Act 2000
    The Countryside and Rights of Way Act 2000
    The Wildlife and Countryside Act 1981

International and regional

African Union
African (Banjul) Charter on Human and Peoples' Rights, 27 June 1981, CAB/LEG/67/3 rev.5. Entry into force: 21 October 1986.

Council of Europe

Convention for the Protection of the Architectural Heritage of Europe, Granada, 3 October 1985. ETS 121. Entry into force: 1 December 1987.

European Convention for the Protection of the Archaeological Heritage (Revised), Valetta, 16 January 1992. ETS 143. Entry into force: 25 May 1995.

European Landscape Convention, Florence, 20 October 2000. ETS 176. Entry into force: 1 March 2004.

Framework Convention on the Value of Cultural Heritage for Society, Faro, 27 October 2005. ETS 199. Entry into force: 1 June 2011.

Recommendation No. R(95)9 of 11 September 1995 of the Committee of Ministers on the Integrated Conservation of Cultural Landscape Areas as Part of Landscape Policies.

Recommendation 79 (9) of the Committee of Ministers Concerning the Identification and Evaluation for the Protection of Natural Landscapes.

Recommendation No. R(89)6 of the Committee of Ministers of 13 April 1989 relating to the Protection and Enhancement of Rural Architectural Heritage.

Recommendation No. R (80) 16 on the Specialised Training of Architects, Town Planners, Civil Engineers and Landscape Designers. European Landscape Convention, Florence, 20 October 2000. ETS 176. Entry into force: 1 March 2004.

Organization of American States

American Convention on Human Rights, 'Pact of San Jose', Costa Rica, 22 November 1969. Entry into force 18 July 1978.

American Declaration of the Rights and Duties of Man, adopted by the Ninth International Conference of American States, Bogotá, Colombia, 1948.

Additional Protocol to the American Convention on Human Rights in the Area of Economic, Social and Cultural Rights ('Protocol of San Salvador'), 16 November 1999, A-52.

Convention on the Protection of the Archeological, Historical, and Artistic Heritage of the American Nations, Approved on June 16, 1976, through Resolution AG/RES. 210 (VI-O/76), adopted at the Sixth Regular Session of the General Assembly, Santiago, Chile.

Declaration of Commitment of Port of Spain, adopted 19 April, 2009, OEA/Ser.E CA-V/DEC.1/09.

Declaration of Mar del Plata 'Creating Jobs to Fight Poverty and Strengthen Democratic Governance', Mar del Plata, Argentina, November 5, 2005.

Organisation of Eastern Caribbean States

Revised Treaty of Basseterre Establishing the Organisation of Eastern Caribbean States Economic Union, signed 18 June, 2010.

Secretariat of the Convention on Biological Diversity

Akwé: Kon Voluntary Guidelines for the Conduct of Cultural, Environmental and Social Impact Assessments Regarding Developments Proposed to Take Place on, or which are Likely to Impact on, Sacred Sites, and on Lands and Waters Traditionally Occupied by Indigenous and Local Communities (2004).

Convention on Biological Diversity, Rio de Janeiro, 5 June 1992. 1760 UNTS 79. Entry into force: 29 December 1993.

United Nations

International Covenant on Civil and Political Rights, 16 December 1966, 999 UNTS 171. Entry into force: 23 March 1976.

International Covenant on Economic, Social and Cultural Rights, 16 December 1966, 993 UNTS 3. Entry into force: 3 January 1976.

Optional Protocol to the International Covenant on Economic, Social and Cultural Rights, 5 March 2009, A/RES/63/117.

The United Nations Declaration on the Rights of Indigenous Peoples, 13 September 2007, A/RES/61/295.

United Nations Economic Commission for Europe

Convention on Access to Information, Public Participation and Access to Justice in Environmental Matters, Aarhus, 25 June 1998. 2161 UNTS 447. Entry into force: 30 October 2001.

UN Economic Commission for Latin America and the Caribbean

Regional Agreement on Access to Information, Public Participation and Justice in Environmental Matters in Latin America and the Caribbean, Escazú, 4 March 2018.

United Nations Environmental Programme

Rio Declaration on Environment and Development, Rio de Janeiro, 14 June 1992, UN Doc.A/CONF.151/26.

United Nations Declaration on the Human Environment, Stockholm, 15 December 1972, A/RES/2994. A/CONF.48/14.

United Nations General Assembly

UN General Assembly, International Covenant on Economic, Social and Cultural Rights, 16 December 1966, United Nations, Treaty Series, vol. 993, p. 3.

2005 World Summit Outcome, GA res A/60/1, 15 September 2005.

United Nations Educational Scientific and Cultural Organization

Convention for the Protection of Cultural Property in the Event of Armed Conflict, The Hague, 14 May 1954. 249 UNTS 240. Entry into force: 7 July 1956.

Recommendation on International Principles Applicable to Archaeological Excavations (UNESCO, New Delhi, 5 December 1956)

Recommendation concerning the Safeguarding of the Beauty and Character of Landscapes and Sites, Paris, 11 December 1962.

Recommendation concerning the Preservation of Cultural Property Endangered by Public or Private Works, Paris, 19 November 1968.

Convention on the Means of Prohibiting and Preventing the Illicit Import, Export, and Transfer of Ownership of Cultural Property, Paris, 14 November 1970. 823 U.N.T.S. 231. Entry into force: 24 April 1972.

Recommendation concerning the Protection, at National Level, of the Cultural and Natural Heritage, Paris, 16 November 1972.

Convention on the Promotion and Protection of the Diversity of Cultural Expressions, Paris, 20 October 2005, 2440 UNTS 311. Entry into force 18 March 2007.

Convention for the Protection of the World Cultural and Natural Heritage, Paris, 16 November 1972. 1037 UNTS 151. Entry into force: 17 December 1975.

Convention for the Safeguarding of the Intangible Cultural Heritage, Paris, 17 October 2003. 2368 UNTS 1. Entry into force 20 April 2006.

Convention on Wetlands of International Importance especially as Waterfowl Habitat, Ramsar, 2 February 1971, 996 UNTS 245. Entry into force: 21 December 1975.

Declaration concerning the Intentional Destruction of Cultural Heritage, Paris, 17 October 2003.

List of Abbreviations

ACHR	American Convention on Human Rights
CARICOM	Caribbean Community
CBD	Convention on Biological Diversity
CCD	Convention to Combat Desertification
CESCR	Committee on Economic, Social and Cultural Rights
CITES	Convention on the International Trade in Endangered Species
CoE	Council of Europe
CSICH	Convention on the Safeguarding of the Intangible Cultural Heritage
EC	European Communities
ECHR	European Convention on Human Rights
ECJ	European Court of Justice
ECtHR	European Court of Human Rights
EIA	Environmental Impact Assessment
ELC	European Landscape Convention
ESCR	Economic, Social and Cultural Rights
EU	European Union
IAMCrtHR	Inter-American Court of Human Rights
ICCPR	International Covenant on Civil and Political Rights
ICCROM	International Council for the Conservation and Restoration of Monuments
ICESCR	International Covenant on Economic, Social and Cultural Rights
ICJ	International Court of Justice
ICOMOS	International Council of Monuments and Sites
IUCN	International Union for the Conservation of Nature
NGO	Non-Governmental Organisation
OAS	Organisation of American States
OECS	Organisation of Eastern Caribbean States
RAMSAR	The Convention on Wetlands of International Importance especially as Waterfowl Habitat, Ramsar (Iran)
SIDS	Small Island Developing States
UDHR	Universal Declaration of Human Rights
UN	United Nations
UNCLOS	United Nations Convention on the Law of the Sea
UNCTAD	United Nations Conference on Trade and Development

UNDRIP	United Nations Declaration on the Rights of Indigenous Peoples
UNEP	United Nations Environment Programme
UNESCO	United Nations Educational, Scientific and Cultural Organisation
UNFCCC	United Nations Framework Convention on Climate Change
WHC	World Heritage Convention
WTO	World Trade Organisation

1

Introduction

Heritage and place are intertwined, and yet the Caribbean has always been treated as a place with no human past, defined by its placelessness. Even the Antilles, the collective name for the Caribbean islands, is derived from Antillia, a non-existent island thought to have existed in the Atlantic Ocean in the fifteenth century.[1] Christopher Columbus expected to encounter Antillia when he crossed the Atlantic in 1492, a fact recounted in a 2017 tourist magazine.[2] The Caribbean was a paradise discovered and is forever being discovered, each new iteration representing a blank screen upon which foreigners can project their definition of what it means to belong here.[3] It is not a place, and there are no people here, despite thousands of years of history, and a population of 40 million people of Amerindian, African, Asian, and European descent.

This context is significant for the protection of the region's cultural heritage. A sense of belonging is often linked to a physical place, and the protection of the landscape, that embodiment of the relationships between communities and their environment, is necessary for anchoring a sense of identity, national pride and communal ties. It is that perceived lack of cultural identity that served as the pretext for justifying 'civilisation' via colonisation. The Caribbean in particular has witnessed the rupture of these relationships, the displacement of peoples and cultural erasure, as Amerindian peoples were extirpated, and enslaved Africans and later indentured Asians were brought to develop and maintain plantation agriculture when the islands were converted to colonies for various European empires. Central to the colonial project was the consolidation of land to promote European interests, at the expense of humanity. Law is a key instrument for allocating land for these purposes, withdrawing resources and granting them to others, defining conquered spaces and inventing new places. Protecting a common heritage, history and identity is rendered difficult when communities have very little access to the source of identity, the very landscape that records the past practices, ri-

---

1 Malachy Tallack, 'Off the Charts', *High Life* magazine (June 2017) 62, discussing his book *The Un-Discovered Islands* (Polygon 2016).
2 Ibid.
3 Mimi Sheller, in *Consuming the Caribbean: From Arawaks to Zombies* (Routledge 2003) 1 summed it up thus: Displaced from the main narratives of modernity, the shores that Columbus first stumbled upon now appear only in tourist brochures, or in occasional disaster tales involving hurricanes, boat-people, drug barons, dictators, or revolutions. Despite its indisputable narrative position at the origin of the plot of Western modernity, history has been edited and the Caribbean left on the cutting room floor.

tuals, memories and livelihoods of a specific local community, collectively known as cultural heritage.

This is problematic for the Caribbean's future. As the region faces existential threats today in the form of climate change, globalisation and other drivers of unsustainable development, societies are in danger of destabilising when economic livelihoods are extinguished to make room for exclusive resorts and marinas, cultural practices are eroded as emigration increases, and visions for the future are undermined by the prospect of sea level rise, increased natural disasters and food and energy insecurity. Cultural heritage is the ballast that keeps societies on an even keel, because it represents the repository of traditional knowledge and community memory that defines existence and informs a community's values. Protecting landscapes protects these practices associated with geographically specific cultural and natural resources.

More than ever, realising sustainable development requires an understanding of how and why communities value natural resources they interact intimately with, across the diversity of ecosystems, since very often this interaction is the key to ecosystem integrity and by extension quality of life in society.[4] Any intervention that attempts to protect cultural heritage must sustain the landscape and by extension the communities that ensure the evolution of that landscape. Law is implicated in this endeavour, because locally appropriate cultural heritage law plays an important role in the preservation of such resources.

Landscape is therefore a particularly relevant concept for analysing the formation of place and sustainability of heritage in the Caribbean. Landscape is the prism through which the deficiencies of heritage law might be revealed; by examining the 'placelessness' of heritage law, the extent to which heritage law is effective can be assessed. The more place-based heritage law is, tethered to the community definition of a place, the less likely it is to fail to recognise social linkages to heritage resources, which would then contextualise its enforcement mechanisms in ways that are locally appropriate, relevant and sustainable. The aim of this research therefore is to conduct a legal geographical analysis of heritage laws in the Lesser Antilles with the intention of exposing the aspatialities, if any, that lead to inappropriate, inadequate and ineffective protection of cultural heritage. This requires a deep dive into the formation of the law itself, to explain the existing mechanisms and conventions produced to protect heritage.

1.1 Traditional Approaches to Cultural Heritage Law

Cultural heritage law varies from jurisdiction to jurisdiction, but in general has evolved in response to the changing concept of cultural heritage itself. Traditionally, heritage was defined as physical property, which does not incorporate concepts of duty to preserve and protect and was characterised by ownership.[5] Exploration of the past was driven by archaeology and its underlying curiosity about ancient civilisations, which also aligned with the impulses to exploit and dominate during the period of colonial

---

4   Janet Blake, *International Cultural Heritage Law* (Oxford University Press 2015) 129.
5   Blake, *International Cultural Heritage Law* 128; Lyndel Prott and Patrick O'Keefe, "Cultural Heritage' or 'Cultural Property'?' *International Journal of Cultural Property* 1(2) (1992): 307-320, 307.

expansion.⁶ This was exacerbated by the antiquarian movement, which influenced some of the first heritage legislation in the United Kingdom.⁷

Archaeological monuments within one's territory were considered valuable historical documents, national property to be protected by the state. The aim of excavations was to find and study these monuments so as to explain historical development, social relations, development of culture, and relations with other people.⁸ The emergence of UNESCO, an intergovernmental body with a General Conference comprised of delegates of national governments, has seen the development of cultural heritage law in the form of Recommendations and Conventions that influences cultural heritage protection globally.⁹ Law has thus developed from application of general law on finds and treasure trove to specific protective legislation on relics, sites and information to more holistic laws on cultural management.[10]

This is due to the Cultural Turn movement of the 1970s, during which insights from cultural anthropology led to shifts in thinking about meaning and representation, so that culture has assumed a wider meaning.[11] By extension, manifestations of cultural heritage can include almost anything made or given value by human beings that 'witnesses the history and affirms the validity of a particular view'.[12]

As Janet Blake observes, cultural heritage is thus a portmanteau term, with myriad meanings and interpretations. Today, it is the 'predominant term of art'[13] in cultural heritage law, because it encompasses notions of protection and preservation.[14] But while there is a clear conception of the subject matter, the legal definition remains a challenging one for legal scholars.[15] The definition of 'culture' appears to relate to the concept of shared values as expressed in a society's language, practices, objects,[16] and places, while 'heritage' is an inheritance received from the past, to be held in trust by the current generation to be handed down in at least as good a state to the next generation.[17] 'Property' is an inadequate term for these resources held in common, but continues to impact heritage protection.

Law's role in protecting cultural heritage has traditionally involved providing the regulatory framework for identifying heritage, especially via inventories, and the recording and making of lists and schedules. Preservation and protection of heritage through the prevention of damage has been articulated in law through systems of designation or by regulating development; the philosophy of conservation in place, in-

---

6   Patrick O'Keefe and Lyndel Prott, *Law and the Cultural Heritage. Volume 1: Discovery and Excavation* (Professional Books Ltd. 1984) 33.
7   O'Keefe and Prott, *Law and the Cultural Heritage* 37.
8   Ibid, 232.
9   Ibid, 74.
10 Ibid, 80.
11 Clifford Geertz, *The Interpretation of Cultures: Selected Essays* (Basic Books 1973).
12 Craig Forrest, *International Law and the Protection of Cultural Heritage* (Routledge 2010) 2.
13 Blake, *International Cultural Heritage Law* 1. Blake notes that there are instances where cultural property is the more appropriate term, such as in the settling of disputes concerning the trafficking of cultural objects.
14 Prott and O'Keefe, "Cultural Heritage' or 'Cultural Property'?' 307.
15 Blake, *International Cultural Heritage Law* 6, and Lyndel Prott, 'Problems of Private International Law for the Protection of the Cultural Heritage', *Recueils des Cours* V (1989): 224-317.
16 Forrest 2.
17 Blake, *International Cultural Heritage Law* 7 and Forrest 3.

cluding attitudes to restoration and reconstruction can be addressed in legal standards; and appropriate sanctions against breaches of the law and the means – coercive or otherwise – to encourage compliance can be laid down in regulations. The integration of cultural preservation with other governmental policies such as planning and land use; financial aspects – sources of funding, tax regimes and economic development programmes; the specific powers and duties of government and non-governmental agencies in respect of heritage; and education and training in heritage-related fields are also areas in which legal intervention can be made.[18]

At the national level, many types of cultural heritage law exist, such as specific legislation pertaining to an artefact or site. These laws may be divided between laws establishing rights and responsibilities for the heritage resource, and the administration for that resource via the creation of heritage institutional actors such as antiquities commissions, National Trusts, historical societies, museums and cultural foundations. Rules of property law also apply to heritage law, such as finders' law, and the law of treasure trove. Laws establishing national parks and protected areas can also contain archaeological sites. Land use planning and environmental laws also relate to heritage because heritage resources include the physical environment such as sacred sites and geological features. Other laws that apply include taxation laws, import and export regulations, and coronial legislation (relating to human remains).[19]

Absent in this framework is any acknowledgment of *where* the law is being applied, and whether this matters in the effectiveness of implementation. Spatial considerations, such as the geographic location, can be relevant to the content and application of such laws. In order to investigate how (where and why) legal or spatial practices, meanings or tactics are producing places or events, the various spatial, legal and/or social strands have to be untangled in order to identify what work law and spatiality are doing at any particular place and time.[20] These investigations tend to adopt one or more of three conceptual structures and points of concern, beginning with, how do spatial settings affect legal implementation and drafting, and vice versa? Secondly, what is the role of law in constituting place, and thirdly, how do lawyers and geographers engage with notions of jurisdiction and scale?[21] I focus on the first and second modes of inquiry. The first mode assesses the extent to which location influenced legal intervention. In most legal geographic studies, this requires an understanding of historical, social and spatial specificity of the location. The second mode focuses on how place-making mechanisms such as private property are legally implemented.[22] Given the complex present day realities of the Caribbean, as post-colonial societies and small island developing states, how this context influences the relationship between law and heritage deserves attention.

---

18   John Carman, *Archaeological Resource Management: An International Perspective* (Cambridge University Press 2015) 54 and 67.
19   O'Keefe and Prott, *Law and the Cultural Heritage* 108.
20   Luke Bennett and Antonia Layard, 'Legal Geography: Becoming Spatial Detectives.' *Geography Compass* 9(7) (July 2015): 406-422, 409.
21   Bennett and Layard 410.
22   Ibid, 411.

1.2 The Caribbean Context

The Organization of American States (OAS) conducted a region-wide survey of heritage-related legislation in the Caribbean in 2013. The overall analytical goals of the survey were to determine the extent and effectiveness of cultural heritage laws and policies in the region and particularly in the participating member states; to make an initial inventory of the skills, funding sources, and training capacities of all the regional cultural heritage sectors and each of the participating member-states; to document the stakeholders' responses regarding current sectorial performance, programmes, and particular challenges faced; and to make an initial analysis of the areas of gaps, overlaps, and potential for capacity sharing and to prioritise possible capacity-building projects in the region to meet these needs.[23]

The survey did not explicitly define cultural heritage but made reference to UNESCO instruments, most notably the World Heritage Convention.[24] There is reference to the 'collective memory and shared identity that cultural heritage embodies'[25] as well as the 'government's role in the protection of the historic landscape, artifacts, and archival records and its role in safeguarding time-honored art forms, crafts, and intangible traditions'.[26] Where heritage legislation is concerned, the analysis noted that laws protect '31 specific heritage types across four major categories: immoveable heritage (i.e. buildings, sites, and landscapes), moveable heritage (i.e. artifacts, documents, and archival material), intangible cultural heritage (i.e. performing arts, traditions, and rituals), and natural heritage'.[27] These categories align with UNESCO's classification system.

Findings concluded that the existing body of heritage legislation is ineffective, and that specific causes of ineffectiveness range from lack of political will, lack of capacity to carry out the law, and the deficiency of existing laws as currently drafted. An analysis of the responses indicated that there is no legislation that provides for an integrated approach to all heritage: moveable, immoveable, intangible, and natural. The rule across the region seems to be a compartmentalisation of specific legislation for each of these types of heritage resources, leaving the bureaucracy to manage potential inconsistencies, redundancies, overlaps, and gaps.[28] Nevertheless, the survey's findings, while useful, were not intended to overhaul the imposed legislative framework for heritage protection in the region. The survey was ultimately designed to identify legal, institutional and capacity obstacles to the promotion of heritage tourism, and assessed the heritage value of potential tourism attractions using external heritage benchmarks. It neither identified nor centred endogenous approaches to heritage protection in its analysis or recommendations.

---

23   OAS, 'Enhancing the Socio-economic potential of Cultural Heritage in the Caribbean: Caribbean Heritage Survey Analysis – Regional Needs and Opportunities to Support Cultural Heritage Protection.' Prepared by Coherit Associates, May 2013, 6.
24   Convention Concerning the Protection of the World Cultural and Natural Heritage, Paris, 16 November 1972, in force 17 December 1975, 1037 UNTS 151; 27 UST 37; 11 ILM 1358 (1972).
25   'OAS Caribbean Heritage Survey Analysis' 4.
26   Ibid, 7.
27   Ibid, 8.
28   OAS 'Caribbean Heritage Survey Analysis' 27.

1.2.1 Cultural Heritage in the Caribbean

The findings of the OAS survey demonstrated the challenges of regulating heritage resources where the concept is defined in isolation from the cultural reality. In this research, cultural heritage is taken to be indistinct from the natural environment in which it is embedded. Traditional classifications such as underwater and moveable are not emphasised, and neither is the distinction between tangible and intangible, as this is in many ways impossible.[29] Much of the physical environment that we know today (with the exception of the extremely rare wilderness sites) has been moulded by human activities. Many human, social and cultural practices have developed in response to the physical environment. Moreover, environmental elements – be they mountain ranges or desert landscapes – also serve as symbols for national cultural identity. The cultural heritage and the natural environment are highly inter-related.[30]

This is especially true for small islands. Their limited landmasses both constrain and enrich the interactions of its inhabitants who depend on natural resources for their very survival. Practically speaking, communities have intimate knowledge of their natural resources and the scarcity of land means sites are often re-engaged: it is no great exaggeration to consider an island a network of overlapping heritage sites. Seeing the island as palimpsest is practical because of the way in which land has been used over time, each historical period being overlaid by another.

This is also a trend that is likely to continue. As David Lowenthal has observed, the notion that nature can and should be left to look after itself is no longer a tenet of ecology, given that humanity is dependent on agriculture, architecture, antibiotics, water resources and sewage systems.[31] Nature untouched is an impossibility, as manipulation of the environment is critical to our survival. It is simply a question of 'meddling more carefully.'[32] The relationship between human societies and their physical environment – the 'environmental media' of air, water, sea and land – is a complex one that has been built up over millennia of mutual impacts and interactions. For this reason, to separate cultural heritage protection from environmental concerns is to create a false dichotomy. Cultural heritage practitioners also reject the 'hands off' approach as impractical as well as historically inaccurate.[33] Legal responses to heritage protection will therefore be influenced by rules regulating land use, specifically planning law, and environmental law (parks and protected areas legislation). These are the laws analysed in this research along with formal heritage protection legislation.

1.2.2 State of the Art in Caribbean Cultural Heritage Research

Scholarly studies on landscape protection in the Caribbean have emerged in the last decade, and have considered the landscape's role in influencing perceptions of land resources and land use (agriculture), but not its relationship with cultural heritage or

---

29 See Blake, *International Cultural Heritage Law* 10 and Forrest 28.
30 Janet Blake, 'UNESCO/World Heritage Convention- Towards a More Integrated Approach.' *Environmental Policy and Law* 43(1) (2013): 8-17, 8.
31 David Lowenthal, 'Natural and Cultural Heritage.' *International Journal of Heritage Studies* 11(1) (2005): 81-92, 89.
32 Ibid.
33 Ibid.

the legal system.[34] Investigating the Caribbean's pre-colonial history has also generated a wealth of research and literature.[35] Nevertheless, very often communities are not emphasised, except as audiences in public archaeology initiatives, rather than heritage actors and creators, which would centre them in the heritage discourse.[36] Re-examining the role of enslaved Africans in plantation life and their contributions to Caribbean society is an equally rich vein of research.[37] Here the role of these communities has been considered in terms of challenging conventional approaches to power on the plantation, but not in the context of the legal system or cultural policymaking today.

Sustainable strategies for heritage protection often focus on linking heritage protection to heritage tourism[38] and law is only addressed incidentally.[39] Colonialism as an environmental project is recognised, but legislation is not examined; where it is, the relationship with cultural heritage resources is not highlighted.[40]

The most comprehensive analysis of heritage protection in the Caribbean inclusive of legislation is Siegel and Righter's volume *Protecting Heritage in the Caribbean*.[41] Here heritage is broadly conceived as objects, processes, built environment and landscapes, in a region that is acknowledged in all its diversity, ranging from independent nation states to colonial territories, and reflecting a vast array of heritage strategies as a result. Challenges with legislation in terms of coverage of heritage resources and heritage actors, and gaps in addressing the activities of development projects, enforcement and public engagement are stressed. Siegel and Righter include contributions from practitioners in these islands to provide local, technical and insider perspectives on the state of heritage protection as well as current Caribbean heritage preservation challenges. However, emphasis is on heritage management rather than the role of law in heritage protection per se, and the contributors are not legal scholars or legal practitioners.

This research brings together these various strands of cultural heritage and landscape research by examining the relevant legislation using a spatial justice lens. This is the first comprehensive study of cultural heritage legislation in the Lesser Antilles to do so.

---

34 Jefferson Dillman, *Colonizing Paradise: Landscape and Empire in the British West Indies* (The University of Alabama Press 2015); Laura Hollsten, 'Controlling Nature and Transforming Landscapes in the Early Modern Caribbean.' *Global Environment* 1(1) (2008): 80-113; Jill Casid, *Sowing Empire: Landscape and Colonization* (University of Minnesota Press 2004).

35 William Keegan and Corinne Hofman, *The Caribbean before Columbus* (Oxford University Press 2017); Scott Fitzpatrick and Ann Ross (eds), *Island Shores, Distant Pasts: Archaeological and Biological Approaches to the Pre-Columbian Settlement of the Caribbean* (University Press of Florida 2010); Basil Reid, *Myths and Realities of Caribbean History* (University of Alabama Press, 2009).

36 Alissandra Cummins, Kevin Farmer and Roslyn Russell (eds), *Plantation to Nation: Caribbean Museums and National Identity* (Common Ground Publishers 2013).

37 Mark Hauser and Douglas Armstrong, 'The Archaeology of Not Being Governed: A Counterpoint to a History of Settlement of Two Colonies in the Eastern Caribbean'. *Journal of Social Archaeology*, 12(3) (2012): 310-333; Lydia Marshall (ed), *Archaeology of Slavery: Toward A Comparative Global Framework* (Southern Illinois University Press 2015).

38 Leslie Ann Jordan, 'Managing Built Heritage for Tourism in Trinidad and Tobago: Challenges and Opportunities.' *Journal of Heritage Tourism* 8(1) (2013):49-62. ·

39 Patricia Green, 'Caribbean Cultural Landscape: the English Caribbean Potential in the Journey from 'Tentative Listing' to being 'Inscribed'.' *Journal of Heritage Tourism* (2013) 8(1): 63-79.

40 Richard Drayton, *Nature's Government: Science, Imperial Britain, and the 'Improvement' of the World* (Yale University Press 2000); Richard Grove, *Green Imperialism: Colonial Expansion, Tropical Island Edens and the Origins of Environmentalism, 1600-1860* (Cambridge University Press 2005).

41 Peter Siegel and Elizabeth Righter, *Protecting Heritage in the Caribbean* (University of Alabama Press 2011).

Figure 1 Map of the Modern Circum-Caribbean Region. Source: https://commons.wikimedia.org/wiki/File:Caribbean_general_map.png

Figure 2 Map of the eight Lesser Antillean nations analysed in this study. Source: https://commons.wikimedia.org/wiki/File:Caribbean_general_map.png

1.2.3 The Caribbean Study Area Defined: The Lesser Antilles

The word 'Caribbean' reflects a diverse network of countries, ecosystems, populations and identities (see figure 1). Because this is a legal analysis, I have limited my attention to one legal system. The independent states of the English-speaking Caribbean share the common law tradition as a result of their status as former colonies of the British Empire.[42] I confine my study to the Lesser Antillean archipelago, the islands of which were historically governed together, and traditionally subdivided into the Windward islands (Dominica, Grenada, Saint Lucia, Saint Vincent and the Grenadines, Trinidad

---

42   Keegan and Hofman, *The Caribbean before Columbus* 5.

and Tobago) and the Leeward islands (Antigua and Barbuda, and Saint Kitts and Nevis), with Barbados as the outlier (figure 2).

1.3 Legal Geography and Spatial Justice: Description of the Conceptual Framework

Using the discipline of geography to examine the law is a form of socio-legal scholarship. While cultural heritage law has relied on a traditionally positivistic 'black-letter' approach to law, in which legal provisions are solely authoritative, this is no longer the dominant methodological paradigm.[43] Socio-legal research examines how law, legal phenomena and/or phenomena affected by law and the legal system occur in the world, interact with each other and influence those subject to this interaction. The 'socio' aspect addresses the societal context or impact of law and legal phenomena, rather than law in books. The 'legal' is more broadly defined than the text of the law.[44]

Considering law in isolation from society, politics and morality impairs our understanding of law itself. The socio-legal method, by situating law in its broader context, identifies a range of theoretical approaches available to garner new insights about the function of law, its processes and consequences, of which law and geography (legal geography) is but one.[45]

Legal geography draws attention to space in ways that can have significance for the former colonies in the Lesser Antilles. Law's neutrality treats space as vacuous, which can have devastating consequences for a way of life. This can be applied in colonial contexts – for instance, legal assumptions of terra nullius, justifying the granting of land to some people and the exclusion of others. This is very relevant to the Lesser Antilles, given that its peoples were displaced and dispossessed of their resources as a result of this narrative. Understanding how the geographical concept under investigation – be it space, territory, place, networks or mobility – is being conceptualised by legal actors can explain decisions more fully, rather than focusing on highly abstracted legal doctrine alone, which prioritises 'legally relevant' rules and facts and disguises the realities of those decisions.[46] Understanding how abstract legal rules are applied in a colonial setting to deprive local communities of their resources, has implications for the way those resources are managed today, and explains why vulnerabilities of the population are exacerbated by continued adherence to law that is seen as impartial and universal in scope. Law, even when it is the subject of legal reform in the Lesser Antilles, aligns closely with the doctrinal tradition and for this reason may not deliver effective results. Legal geography challenges the so-called neutrality of these rules that assumes effectiveness and fairness. The law is not always neutral – it can be 'spatially blind.'[47]

---

43   Naomi Creutzfeldt, Marc Mason and Kirsten McConnachie (eds), *Routledge Handbook of Socio-legal Theory and Methods* (Routledge 2019) 3.
44   Creutzfeldt, Mason and McConnachie (eds), *Routledge Handbook of Socio-legal Theory and Methods* 59.
45   Peter Cane and Joanne Conaghan (eds), *The New Oxford Companion to Law* (Oxford University Press 2008) at <http//www.oxfordreference.com> accessed 15 November 2019.
46   Antonia Layard 'Reading Law Spatially' in *Routledge Handbook of Socio-legal Theory and Methods* 233.
47   Antonia Layard, 'What is Legal Geography?' (University of Bristol Law School Blog, 11 April 2016) <http://legalresearch.blogs.bris.ac.uk/2016/04/what-is-legal-geography/> accessed 21 June 2017.

Legal concepts and rules thus do not exist in a vacuum, and have a geographical significance, as they determine the territorial boundaries of homes, courts, and nation states – law makes national, regional, local and private spaces.[48] Legal concepts such as property, jurisdiction, sovereignty and domicile all have a spatial (geographical) referent. Legal rules can be used to create space, delimiting geographic/normative areas within which people enjoy relative freedom to act, or by establishing relationships that give rise to obligations.[49]

The impact that law's complex interaction with space, through either attentiveness to, or dismissal of spatiality, has on the co-production of places, is the focus of legal geography. Legal geography investigates this co-constitutive relationship of people, place and law, or the social, spatial and legal dimensions of existence.[50] Spatial settings are not always relevant; what is critical is whether aspatiality, or the absence of geography, 'is a defeat for citizens, localities, and place'[51], giving rise to spatial injustice, which is an important project within legal geography.[52] In such situations, legal localisation must occur – law must make room for local conditions, or forms of regulation must be rooted in local conditions of existence.[53] This aims to reverse the 'placelessness' in law, which has never been addressed in the Lesser Antilles before. Locational analysis of the law therefore contributes to the improved delivery of efficient legal services, and justice, by exploring the social and cultural elements of legality.[54] In this section, I highlight the milestones in the evolution of legal geography as an interdisciplinary approach, and summarise its key concepts and modes of inquiry.

While Luke Bennett and Antonia Layard note that scholars in the past have observed that cultural factors can influence certain legal provisions, what changed in the 1980s was the idea that law, people and places are intertwined, and that the impact of law is both felt and made locally. This co-constitutive approach 'became the leitmotif of legal geography',[55] and Wesley Pue's article on law's 'spatial blindness'[56] was the 'opening salvo of what was to become the legal geography project',[57] because it identified the research gap that academics had been circling for decades. In a notable case, Pue critiqued the judgment for ignoring the spatial setting – a raft on the high seas – as insignificant to the circumstances in which the crime occurred.[58] He saw this

---

48 Ibid.
49 Kim Economides, Mark Blacksell and Charles Watkins, 'The Spatial Analysis of Legal Systems.' *Journal of Law and Society* 13(2) (1986): 161-181, 167.
50 Bennett and Layard 'Legal Geography: Becoming Spatial Detectives' 406, referring to WW Pue, 'Wrestling with Law: (Geographical) Specificity vs (Legal) Abstraction.' *Urban Geography* 11(6) (1990): 566-585.
51 Layard, 'What is Legal Geography?' (University of Bristol Law School Blog, 11 April, 2016)
52 David Delaney, 'Legal Geography II: Discerning Justice.' *Progress in Human Geography* 40(2) (2016): 267-274.
53 Jane Holder and Caroline Harrison (eds), *Law and Geography* (Oxford University Press 2003) 4.
54 Economides et al 171.
55 Bennett and Layard 408.
56 Wesley Pue, 'Wrestling with Law'; Layard, 'What is Legal Geography?'
57 Bennett and Layard 406.
58 The case was *R v Dudley & Stephens* (1884), 14 QBD 273, which proved to be one of the most contentious legal decisions in English legal history. The courts ruled that the killing and eating of a cabin boy by these sailors was a crime under English Law, even though the sailors would have died had they not done so, as they drifted helplessly aboard a lifeboat in the South Atlantic, 1600 miles off the Cape of Good Hope. See Bennett and Layard 406.

as evidence that the law treated location (space) as immaterial and that law's abstract logic was anti-geographic.[59] Pue argued that geography could demonstrate that the presumed rationality of law is in fact acontextual, such that legal relations and obligations are frequently thought of by the courts and other legal sources as existing in a purely conceptual space, with little recognition of the diversity of spatial definitions or the local material contexts within which law is understood and contested.[60]

In fact, law and geography are linked, as their categories are socially constructed. Law and space are relational, acquiring subjective meaning through social action.[61] Law and space influence the way power and social life are manifested, including the corresponding problematic and oppressive patterns that characterise them.[62] Space is not a backdrop to political and social action, but rather a product of such action.[63] Law configures space in ways that have consequences for justice and injustice in the world because it shapes relations of power. Injustice here relates to unnecessary social suffering, which may be distinguished from other forms of suffering that are not social or unjust.[64]

Legal geography examines these systemic asymmetries of power – domination, exploitation, and marginalisation both in the world and with respect to access to law. Contexts include racism, colonialism, homelessness and environmental justice.[65] The legal geographical perspective is therefore indispensable for revealing the workings of power that conventional spatial blindness obscures and for 'identifying the whys, how and wheres of injustice that are otherwise invisibilized and legitimized'.[66] As Robyn Bartel et al have noted, ignorance of geography has political consequences, for if we do not ask questions about the location of law's impact, and therefore also who it impacts on, then its effects, such as environmental destruction or the dispossession and genocide of indigenous peoples, may be ignored.[67] This presents legal geography with a significant opportunity to contribute to the decolonisation of law.[68] These are all themes integral to the development of post-colonial states in the Lesser Antilles.

Legal geography has been further developed over the years, notably by Nicholas Blomley.[69] He sees the task for legal geography as threefold: identify and explore the fixed legal and spatial representations and their implications, expose the social construction (and thus non-objectivity) of these representations, and analyse the material conditions under which challenging such dominant representations can contribute to progressive social change.[70]

---

59 Bennett and Layard 407.
60 Nicholas Blomley and Joel Bakan, 'Spacing Out: Towards A Critical Geography of Law.' *Osgoode Hall Law Journal* 30(3) (Fall 1992): 661-690, 663-664.
61 Blomley and Bakan 666.
62 Ibid, 669-670.
63 Ibid, 669.
64 Delaney, 'Legal Geography II' 268.
65 Ibid, 268.
66 Ibid, 273.
67 Robyn Bartel, Nicole Graham, Sue Jackson, Jason Hugh Prior, Daniel Francis Robinson, Meg Sherval and Stewart Williams, 'Legal Geography: An Australian Perspective.' *Geographical Research* 51(4) (November 2013):339-353, 341.
68 Bartel et al 344.
69 Ibid, 341.
70 Blomley and Bakan 690.

The aim of legal geography is to expose the 'concealed, forgotten or prohibited connections between peoples and places.'[71] Legal geography is not just about bringing a geographical perspective to formal legal systems. So-called 'formal' laws interact with informal customs and lore, social conventions and norms, religion and dogma, as well as the economy, and in fact this formal law may derive much of its (often silent) ideology and values from pre-existing systems of lore and norms that are spatially located, influencing its development and implementation.[72] Attending to material conditions, limits and connections, legal geography is necessarily also attuned to historic context. For example, although the histories of many lands and nations colonised by Anglo-Europeans in the seventeenth century share important political histories, they also have, in geographical terms, very different material histories.[73] This is why the colonies of the Lesser Antilles in the Caribbean are dissimilar from Australia or India or those in Africa, despite inheriting the common law tradition from England. By situating law in space, that is, within its physical conditions and limits, legal geography embeds place-based knowledge in law's foundations – this requires a paradigm shift, from 'the alienation of people and place in law and geography to their necessary connection'.[74]

The role of law in prescribing people-place relations is central to the success or failure of any society. As Layard writes, understanding and exposing the spatial assumptions inherent in law that are presented as neutral and abstract can introduce new possibilities regarding the production of more geographically sensitive and representative (spatially just) legal rules and practices.[75] For the small islands of the Lesser Antilles, this is necessary to their survival. Placelessness has suppressed the growth of these societies throughout their history, lack of cultural identity serving as its indicator and rendering inhabitants in need of 'civilisation'. Landscapes reveal the opportunities and limits of our connection with the world; recognising this dynamic in law's operation by integrating material conditions and consequences embraces sustainability of place and survival of its inhabitants.[76]

1.3.1 Distinguishing Space and Place in the Law

Space is a geographical location,[77] and spatiality is the state of existing within or having some relationship with space. Legal geographers seek to investigate spatiality by showing how legal provisions and practices relate to space.

Legal geography brings specific attention to space and spatiality, to the interrelationships between people and environments, analysing how these operate across and between humans, places and non-humans, as well as core geographical concepts of place, networks, mobility, scale, relationality, distance and temporality.[78]

---

71 Bartel et al 343.
72 Ibid, 346.
73 Ibid, 349.
74 Ibid.
75 Layard, 'Reading Law Spatially' 241.
76 Nicole Graham, *Lawscape: Property, Environment, Law* (Routledge 2010) 206.
77 Layard, 'What is Legal Geography?' (University of Bristol Law School Blog)
78 Layard, 'Reading Law Spatially' 232.

Place is a specific geographic location to which meaning has been ascribed, produced by the interaction of human relations, activated by movements, actions, narratives and signs.[79] Law can construct and stabilise places through the accumulation of property rights, contract law, planning law and natural resource law.[80] But in doing so, law can also alter and even extinguish place.[81] Law's oxymoronic character in both creating and dissolving place therefore underpins this analysis.

1.3.2 Landscape: Focusing Legal Geographical Analysis

Many terms are used to describe the foundational conceptual devices legal geographers employ in their analysis of place.[82] The 'splice' was introduced by Nicholas Blomley,[83] which is similar to Nicole Graham's 'lawscape'[84] and Andreas Philippopoulos-Mihalopoulos' 'nomosphere.'[85] These terms refer to instances or moments where legally informed decisions and actions take place (in the sense of both being performed as a legal event and of being spatially located and embodied). They are 'locally enacted encodings, which weave together spatial and legal meanings'.[86]

For the purpose of this research, landscape is the device used to represent such encodings, and to assess the formation, function, impact and effectiveness of heritage legislation. As defined by geographer Kenneth Olwig, landscape is generated through the practices of human residence and occupation, laid down as custom and law upon the physical fabric of the land.[87] These place-based rights give individuals a sense of identity and role in the community. Belonging is therefore couched in spatial terms.[88] Community identity arises from collective memory, historically associated with and emanating from the land, and the cultural sense of place identity also gives rise to legal rights and political institutions to represent and protect these rights. Historically then, landscape functions as the rubric for the relationship between land, law and people, and was 'constituted as an enduring record of – and testimony to – the lives and works of past generations who have dwelt within it, and in so doing, have left there something of themselves'.[89] Landscape therefore is the locus of heritage.

Landscape is particularly linked to the common law of Great Britain and its former colonies, as customary law adjudicated by representative legal assemblies is a tradition

---

79 Bartel et al 340; Bennett and Layard 409; William Mitchell (ed) *Landscape and Power* (2nd edn, University of Chicago Press 2002) x.
80 Luke Bennet, 'How does Law Make Place? Localisation, Translocalisation and Thing-law at the World's First Factory.' *Geoforum* 74(2016): 182-191, 189.
81 Ibid, 189-190.
82 Layard and Bennett 415.
83 Nicholas Blomley, *Law, Space, and the Geographies of Power* (Guilford Press 1994).
84 See Graham, *Lawscape*; Andreas Philippopoulos-Mihalopoulos, 'Introduction: in the lawscape' in Andreas Philippopoulos-Mihalopoulos (ed), *Law and the City* (Routledge-Cavendish: 2007) 1-20.
85 David Delaney, *The Spatial, the Legal and the Pragmatics of Place-making: Nomospheric Investigations* (Routledge 2010).
86 Layard and Bennett 410.
87 Kenneth Olwig, *Landscape, Nature and the Body Politic: From Britain's Renaissance to America's New World* (University of Wisconsin Press 2002) 226.
88 Michael Herzfeld, 'Spatial Cleansing: Monumental Vacuity and the Idea of the West.' *Journal of Material Culture* 11(1/2) (2006): 127-149, 128.
89 Tim Ingold, 'The Temporality of the Landscape.' *World Archaeology* 25(2) (1993): 152-174.

still found in the English legal system: the customary rights and regulation of such rights were originally shaped by the material landscape to ensure its sustainability.[90]

Because landscape embodies both the interaction between people, land and law, and provides evidence of that interaction, geographers from Blomley to Olwig have demonstrated that any landscape interested in justice has to pay close attention to theory, history and struggles over property.[91] As addressed earlier, the history and size of the geographic land masses that comprise the Lesser Antilles are factors shaping the physical environment. There are very few areas of unspoiled wilderness in the Caribbean due to the intensity and scale of plantation agriculture during colonialism, so access to land (which accompanied the dispossession of local peoples) and property law discussions also anchor the analysis of heritage law.

1.4 Legal Anthropology: Law's Role as Regulator of Society

Anthropology and the law share a close relationship. Law is a core cultural element for anthropologists,[92] and has been embedded in cultural anthropology since its founding.[93] Anthropology has also been concerned with the themes of territory, boundaries, place, and landscape as these bear on questions of culture and, in this sense, it is the field that most closely relates to legal geography.

Legal anthropology, like legal geography, challenges law's centralist and formalist orientation, which is predicated on the state's exclusive authority to write and enforce laws. This is especially relevant where law is imposed as a tool of imperial authority, as was the case in the Lesser Antilles. Through its use of ethnography, attention to law in non-Western cultures and law in everyday life, legal anthropology expands understanding of what law is beyond doctrinal and statist conceptualisations, and where it is to be found, grounding law in society and its relationship to culture.[94] As Kirsten McConnachie put it, 'A simpler way of describing the relationship might be to say that anthropology asks a question that is often never considered by lawyers: what is law? And to what extent can the label of law be applied to non-formal normative orders?'[95] Legal anthropology argues for a more expansive use of the term law to encompass those uncodified cultural and customary elements of dispute resolution that possess 'norm-setting and norm sanctioning powers'.[96] Legal pluralism thus challenges legal centralism, or the belief that law is in the exclusive control of the nation-state

---

90 Olwig, *Landscape, Nature and the Body Politic*, 232; Kenneth Olwig, 'Virtual Enclosure, Ecosystem Services, Landscape's Character and the 'Rewilding' of the Commons: the 'Lake District' Case.' *Landscape Research* 41(2) (2016): 253-264, 256.
91 Don Mitchell, 'Cultural Landscapes: Just Landscapes or Landscapes of Justice?' *Progress in Human Geography* 27(6) (2003): 787-796, 793.
92 John M Conley and William M O'Barr, 'Legal Anthropology Comes Home: A Brief History of the Ethnographic Study of Law.' *Loyola of Los Angeles Law Review* 27(1) (1993): 41- 64, 44.
93 Irus Braverman, David Delaney, Nicholas Blomley, and Alexandre Kedar (eds), *The Expanding Spaces of Law: A Timely Legal Geography* (Stanford University Press 2014) 10.
94 Creutzfeldt et al, *Routledge Handbook of Socio-legal Theory and Methods* 122.
95 Kirsten McConnachie, 'Law and Anthropology' in Creutzfeldt et al, *Routledge Handbook of Socio-legal Theory and Methods* 194.
96 Ibid.

by recognising that dispute resolution and order maintenance can occur outside the formal legal system via 'customary' and 'traditional' systems.[97]

Sally Falk Moore has identified three major approaches to law within legal anthropology: law as culture, law as domination, and law as problem-solver.[98] Legal anthropology, in investigating law's primary function as problem solver, explores cross-cultural, non-western and alternative methods of dispute or conflict resolution, and also engages in an analysis of the cultural dynamics at play within Western legal systems. Ultimately, the aim is to understand the general principles underlying the normative regulation of society, 'the social forces working to create and maintain ties of cohesion against the tidal pull of individual interests'.[99] How does society use law to heal divisions and resolve disputes? How does law order society and thereby facilitate control? Legal anthropology is qualitative in approach, discovering and describing the possibilities for ordering societies.[100] These tenets underpin the legal analysis herein.

1.5 Aims and Objectives

This research analyses the origins and implications of cultural heritage law by employing a spatial justice lens. This new approach to cultural heritage makes use of legal geographical and legal anthropological methods to challenge the traditional and colonial-era legal framework for heritage protection in the Lesser Antilles.

This aligns with the objectives of the Nexus 1492 project, of which this research was a sub-project. Nexus 1492 was a transdisciplinary project that investigated the impacts of colonial encounters in the Caribbean, the nexus of the first interactions between the New and the Old World. Nexus 1492's objectives were to provide a new perspective on the Columbian and subsequent colonial invasions by focusing on the histories and legacies of the Indigenous Caribbean, and to raise awareness of Caribbean histories and legacies, striving for practical outcomes in future heritage management efforts with implications for local communities, island nations, the pan-Caribbean region, and globally.[101]

These objectives are addressed in this research. Landscape and spatial justice offer new perspectives on cultural heritage protection, by reframing the impacts of colonialism as spatial, and considering the implications for heritage protection because heritage is place-specific. This research also considers how these insights can shape approaches to heritage, by ensuring that local communities that are the heritage creators are centred in strategies to protect heritage. This incorporates considerations of ownership and identity as integral to a functioning, thriving and resilient landscape. The task of the legal sub-project was to undertake an examination of legislation as a practical tool for heritage management, by examining colonialism's impact on Caribbean heritage legislation and practices. Geopolitical, historical, and contemporary factors were to

---

97 Ibid.
98 Sally Falk Moore, 'Certainties Undone: Fifty Turbulent Years of Legal Anthropology, 1949-1999.' *The Journal of the Royal Anthropological Institute* 7(March 2001):95-116.
99 James M Donovan, *Legal Anthropology: An Introduction* (AltaMira Press 2008) vii.
100 Conley and O'Barr 63-64.
101 Nexus 1492 project, Leiden University <https://www.universiteitleiden.nl/nexus1492> accessed 2 January 2019.

be considered to identify cross-cutting issues that would improve the integration of policies at local and regional levels through the application of best practices and capacity building. Specific attention was to be given to issues of cultural ownership and identity of Caribbean communities.

This legal diagnostic was one of two legal sub-projects; the other project addressing the role of international law in confronting the colonial past, specifically in relation to land rights, cultural heritage and restitution.[102] Other projects conducted under the aegis of Nexus 1492 addressed heritage education, community approaches to the environment, and the role of modern Caribbean museums.[103]

The main research question underpinning this dissertation is the extent to which the law is an effective instrument in the protection of cultural heritage in post-colonial societies of the Lesser Antilles. A number of sub-questions address the mechanisms available in international law for the protection of landscape; how the Caribbean landscape has influenced the perception and protection of cultural heritage; the key features of heritage law in the Lesser Antilles today and their relationship with spatiality; and finally, how locally specific strategies can be embedded to transform the present framework.

1.6 Methodology

In the absence of case law dealing with heritage disputes in the Lesser Antilles, community challenges of the uses of public space provide evidence of conflict over ownership of heritage resources and landscape. This is useful for understanding the ways in which the public define, value and interpret these spaces, and demonstrate 'place-protective behavior'.[104]

To this end, the research has entailed a major review of primary and secondary sources, including legislation, treaties, historical records and journals, as well as interviews with heritage stakeholders in government and civil society. Heritage policies, plans, and project documents were consulted to supplement understanding of the effectiveness of heritage law implementation and enforcement, as they constitute evidence of cultural issues, public sentiment, and conflict over the use and access to heritage resources. Draft heritage legislation is also considered as evidence of the law's development, as well as underlying public policy. Planning and policy decisions are used to demonstrate how law balances competing discourses and values.[105] These

---

102 Amy Strecker, 'Indigenous Land Rights and Caribbean Reparations Discourse.' *Leiden Journal of International Law* 30(3) (2017): 629-646; Amy Strecker, 'Revival, Recognition, Restitution: Indigenous Rights in the Eastern Caribbean.' *International Journal of Cultural Property* 23(2) (2016): 167-190.

103 Csilla Ariese-Vandemeulebroucke, *The Social Museum in the Caribbean: Grassroots Heritage Initiatives and Community Engagement* (Sidestone Press 2018); Charlotte Eloise Stancioff, *Landscape, Land-Change and Well-Being in Small Island Contexts: Case Studies from St. Kitts and the Kalinago Territory, Dominica* (Sidestone Press 2018); Eldris Con Aguilar, *Heritage Education – Memories of the Past in the Present Caribbean Social Studies Curriculum: A View from Teacher Practices* (Sidestone Press 2020).

104 Robyn Bartel and Nicole Graham, 'Property and Place Attachment: A Legal Geographical Analysis of Biodiversity Law.' *Geographical Research* 54(3) (August 2016): 267-284, 276.

105 Deborah G Martin and Alexander Scherr, 'Lawyering Landscapes: Lawyers as Constituents of Landscapes.' *Landscape Research* 30 (3) (July 2005): 379-393, 382.

sources are investigated with an eye for how and when spatiality influences, frames or determines language, mechanisms and decisions. Which legal concepts recur, which gaps exist, and the interrelationships with other factors, are clues for understanding law's relationship with space and how this may impact heritage protection.[106]

1.7 Outline of Chapters

There are eight chapters in this dissertation, including this introduction. There are two chapters that set the context for understanding landscape and its relation to the law. They precede the legal analysis of Lesser Antillean heritage law, its content and implementation.

In Chapter Two, I investigate the historical origins of landscape as the foundational concept in legal geography, discussing the existence and transformation of landscape in pre-industrial Britain and the consequences for the common law. I then train this conceptual framework on the Caribbean landscape as the substrate of Caribbean cultural heritage, to examine environmental and demographic factors present in the colonies and the effects on the landscape and early heritage law. I discuss the emergence of heritage law in the Lesser Antilles in circumstances of cultural erasure and environmental devastation (eco-imperialism), which ultimately shaped the legal rules that apply to heritage resources today.

In Chapter Three, I chart the evolution of landscape protection in international law, from its soft law origins in cultural heritage law to its development as a distinct sphere of law in its own right. I explore the interactions in cultural heritage law with respect to landscape and communities that have transformed its elitist perceptions, and influenced other areas of international law, such as international environmental law and human rights law. I examine challenges surrounding implementation of international landscape law in these various fields, and consider opportunities for protecting landscape regionally in the Lesser Antilles.

Landscape in the current domestic legislation of the Lesser Antilles is considered in Chapters Four through Six. The laws that regulate or impact the regulation of landscape are found in heritage protection legislation, planning legislation and conservation legislation (parks and protected areas) and are assessed via a spatial justice lens.

In Chapter Four, I examine contemporary heritage legislation in the Lesser Antilles, which includes heritage protection legislation, laws establishing heritage institutions such as national museums and National Trusts, as well as antiquities laws. In Chapter Five, I turn to planning law, examining the historical association between land use and heritage and consider whether heritage is perceived as a legitimate land use. In Chapter Six, I review the laws governing national parks and protected areas as modern public spaces. Where appropriate, I reference policies and draft laws from around the region that give an indication of the ways in which governments in the Lesser Antilles prioritise heritage resources and any guidance for aligning the implementation of heritage laws, such as cultural policies.

The effectiveness of these laws is the subject of Chapter Seven. Chapter Seven shares examples from the Lesser Antilles of conflict over landscape as public space

---

106 Layard, 'What is Legal Geography?' (University of Bristol Law School Blog, 11 April, 2016).

that illustrate the ongoing challenges to represent community interests where private property is elevated in the law. Each example explores a facet of landscape protection, revealing common trends in application of heritage law. I conclude with key findings from the research and a discussion of the way forward in landscape and heritage protection in Chapter Eight.

1.8 A Note on Legislation

The law concerning Caribbean heritage is a dynamic and fast moving area. During the writing and publication of this dissertation, a number of laws were repealed and enacted.[107] The laws analysed herein were those in force as of December 2019. Where available, proposed (draft) legislation was also reviewed. These discussions have been retained as they give a fuller picture of the progressive development of the law. In addition, the shortcomings highlighted, even where a law has been repealed, reflect underlying structural challenges common to the regulatory framework for heritage in this sub-region and will be of continued relevance.

---

107 Grenada repealed its National Heritage Protection Act when it enacted new museum legislation in 2017; Barbados replaced its Town and Country Planning legislation with the new Planning and Development Act in 2020, and at the international level, the Escazú Agreement entered into force on 22 April 2021.

2

Landscape: A Caribbean Perspective

This chapter delves into the major historical events that have shaped the Caribbean landscape, with the aim of understanding how these factors influenced the development of Caribbean heritage law in the Lesser Antilles. An overview of the landscape foundational concept is first provided, employing Kenneth Olwig's work on legal geography, before addressing the Lesser Antillean context and finally the relevance to spatial justice and sustainable heritage protection.[108]

2.1 The Origins and Demise of Landscape: Enclosure, Alienation and Empire

2.1.1 Landscape as Place: A Nexus of Land, Law and People

The word 'landscape' is often associated with a view or scenery, a passive visual representation such as a landscape painting or a landscaped garden. 'It is well known', Denis Cosgrove tells us, 'that in Europe the concept of landscape and the words for it in both Romance and Germanic languages emerged around the turn of the sixteenth century to denote a painting whose primary subject matter was natural scenery.'[109]

While it is certainly true that the concept of landscape as scenery emerged at this time, the older political meaning of landscape pre-dated the pictorial version.[110] Geographer Kenneth Olwig has shown that landscape as scenery is landscape in its reductionist form, and masks the true meaning of the relationship between land, law and people. The following section borrows from Olwig substantially for the purposes of outlining the origins of landscape. Landscape was originally a historically constituted place with particular cultural practices, customs and legal traditions and forms of political representation,[111] a historical document containing evidence of a long process of interaction between society and its material environs.[112] At the heart of landscape and country as

---

108 Olwig, *Landscape, Nature and the Body Politic* 226.
109 Denis Cosgrove, *Social Formation and Symbolic Landscape* (Croom Helm 1984) 9.
110 Kenneth Olwig, 'Representation and Alienation in the Political Landscape.' *Cultural Geographies* 12(2005): 19-40, 23.
111 Olwig, *Landscape, Nature and the Body Politic* 62.
112 Ibid, 226.

polity and place is custom and customary law.¹¹³ Customary law serves an important role in the enactment of place,¹¹⁴ by defining place in terms of a community of overlapping, inherited qualitatively different rights of use.¹¹⁵ As communities were displaced, landscape lost its original meaning. Landscape ceased to be a historical outcome of custom, and its extinguished form became subject to artistic genres such as painting and painting of stage scenery, and began to merge with scene – a real or imagined prospect suggesting a stage setting.¹¹⁶

Landscape's etymology sheds light on its origins, particularly its history, formation, and function. The word landscape originated from the Germanic family of languages: Dutch *landschap*, Danish *landskab*, Swedish *landskap*, German *landschaft*¹¹⁷ and *landscipe* in the Old English spelling.¹¹⁸ It refers to the land, its character, traditions or customs.¹¹⁹ 'Landscape' is distinguished from land by the suffix -scape, which is equivalent in function to the more common English suffix -ship, and this suffix generates an abstraction.¹²⁰ Thus, as Olwig explains, there might be two friends, comrades or fellows in a room, both concrete beings, but between them they share something abstract and difficult to define: friendship, comradeship or fellowship; it is the suffix -ship that designates this abstract quality, the nature, state, or constitution of being a friend, and these qualities in turn are linked together by Olwig to draw attention to their concretised and institutionalised counterparts (nature, the state and a constitution).¹²¹

'Scape' also means shape, or character, constitution, as in giving character, constituting the land that is being shaped by people and vice versa.¹²² The power of this sense of shape lies in the dynamic relation between the meaning of shape as, on the one hand, an expression of -ship as an underlying nature, state or constitution that manifests itself through an active, creative, shaping process and, on the other, the material form which that process generates – its shape.¹²³ Because such abstractions can be abstruse, knowledge of what constitutes the abstract nature, state or constitution of being friends, citizens or landsmen belonging to a land and how this relationship functions was often institutionalised, represented in a more defined objective form such as a representative body, concretising the relationship and facilitating the process 'by which the land is shaped as a social and material phenomenon'.¹²⁴

As Olwig writes, the ancient Germanic name for the representative legal and political body of a land was the thing or moot – the root of the modern words 'thing' and 'meeting'.¹²⁵ It is the deliberation of the thing that builds the land as a polity or

---

113 Ibid, 223.
114 Don Mitchell, 'Go Slow: An Afterword on Landscape and Justice.' *Norwegian Journal of Geography* 60(1) (2006):123-127, 125.
115 Olwig, *Landscape, Nature and the Body Politic* 118.
116 Ibid, 62.
117 Ibid, 232.
118 Olwig, 'Representation and Alienation' 22.
119 Olwig, *Landscape, Nature and the Body Politic* 18.
120 Olwig, 'Representation and Alienation' 20.
121 Ibid.
122 Kenneth Olwig, 'Landscape' in *International Encyclopedia of the Social & Behavioral Sciences* (2ⁿᵈ edn) 2015, 224-230, 225.
123 Olwig, 'Representation and Alienation' 21.
124 Ibid.
125 Olwig, 'Representation and Alienation' 22.

res publica (transliterated 'public thing'), or landscape. This interplay between land, community practice and its institutionalised relationship thus renders the landscape a political one, and situates the power of the representative body in custom.[126]

Custom is an expression of community practice, from which the common law of the land emanates.[127] The seventeenth-century English jurist Edward Coke stated that custom is 'defined as a law or right not written; which, being established by long use and the consent of our ancestors, hath been and is daily practised'.[128] It is because custom is rooted in this 'common usage' from 'time out of mind' that 'custom lies upon the land'.[129] As Olwig has explained, the word law derives from the Old Norse *liggja*, meaning to lie, and is akin to the plural of *lag*, meaning 'due place, order'.[130] The law, this suggests, was 'laid down, layer-like, through practice, thereby establishing a sense of emplaced order – the lay (out) of the land'.[131] In this way, customary rights in the land, such as rights in the commons, created a sense of belonging to, and having a place in, the land.[132]

Olwig indicates that these emplaced rights were typically part of a complex structure in which the rights of the differing estates (the nobility, the clergy, the burgers, the farmers and the prince or king) worked together, or opposed each other, in a creative (or destructive) tension that often involved representative legal and political bodies.[133] Even under oppressive conditions, customary rights, particularly in the commons, could form the basis for a moral economy that acted to protect the poor.[134] Though the commoners were individually weak, numerically they were a majority, and in exercising and defending their rights, they could ensure their voices were heard, challenge threats to their way of life, and generally appeal to balance, democracy and equality.[135] Customary rights were therefore inherently tied to notions of social justice.

Representative bodies both influence and are influenced by the features of the landscape, and this relationship is formalised in the law they enact. The law, Olwig observes, does not just lie upon the land; it shapes the land, and that shape will in turn have an effect upon the law, creating the nature, state, or constitution of the land as the embodiment of a res publica or commonwealth.[136] Olwig cites the example of the creation of dykes under the customary law of a Friesland Landschaft polity.[137] The dependency of the Landschaft commonwealth upon those dykes shaped that community, its customs and laws, and led to the writing down of its by-laws and the institutionalisation of the power of the bodies that manage the dykes and use the water.[138] The

---

126 Ibid.
127 Ibid.
128 Cited in Olwig, 'Representation and Alienation' 22.
129 Olwig, 'Representation and Alienation' 22.
130 Ibid.
131 Ibid.
132 Olwig, 'Representation and Alienation' 23.
133 Ibid.
134 Ibid.
135 Olwig, 'Representation and Alienation' 23.
136 Ibid.
137 Ibid.
138 Olwig, 'Representation and Alienation' 23.

corpus of law generated by those bodies will continue to influence the landscape over time, and it is this dynamic process that is responsible for the formation of place. It is not simply the physical natural resources in the land, or the community inhabiting the environs that are relevant, but the relationship between community and land as they continue to influence each other over time, reflected in the institutionalisation of that relationship through their laws, practices and structures.

As observed in Chapter 1, the historical concept of landscape in the primary substantive sense of place and polity, referring to lands 'scaped' or shaped according to customary law as adjudicated by representative legal assemblies, especially influenced English common law.[139] In such a polity, common customary law is primarily enforced through moral pressure and community control (the word 'moral' deriving from the Latin word for mores or customs), and a customary prescriptive use-right that is neglected or abused automatically extinguishes any moral right to it, and will be lost.[140] This principle ensured the functioning of a working community, and prevented the erosion of a shared-resource system by reinforcing rights held in common for the public good.[141] Sustainable resource management, representation and social justice characterised the working landscape.

This complex and indivisible relationship between land, law and people is a far cry from landscape as visual scenery, which originated in the Renaissance and Enlightenment with the rediscovery of Ptolemy's cartography.[142] Cartographical and surveying techniques were used to enclose land, and to create perspectival scenic representations of the spaces so enclosed.[143] This spatial and pictorial mode of representation would in turn influence related fields such as architecture, design, planning and engineering, which transformed the land.[144] A key figure in this process was the Italian architect Andreas Palladio, whose English protégé Inigo Jones nurtured and popularised this perception of landscape as an architectural style.[145] Inigo Jones took the Palladian ideal one step further in creating landscapes inspired by theatrical illusion, because he crafted 'natural' scenes out of countryside, which would eventually embody the natural landscape architectural ideal.[146]

This theatrical metaphor re-envisioned how the irregular visible surface upon which we live might be structured by regular behind-the-scene laws of perspective, paralleling how places represented on a globe are geometrically structured by invisible lines of latitude and longitude.[147] These behind-the-scene laws emulated God, the framer of the universe, whose vision was made manifest in nature.[148] As a result, Olwig writes that core concepts retained only the visual aspect of their meaning: landscape merged

---

139 Olwig, 'Virtual Enclosure' 256.
140 Ibid.
141 Ibid.
142 Kenneth Olwig, Chris Dalglish, Graham Fairclough and Pete Herring, 'Introduction to a Special Issue: the Future of Landscape Characterisation, and the Future Character of Landscape – between Space, Time, History, Place and Nature.' *Landscape Research* 41(2) (2016): 169-174, 170.
143 Olwig et al, 'Introduction to a Special Issue: the Future of Landscape Characterization' 170.
144 Ibid.
145 Ibid.
146 Olwig, *Landscape, Nature and the Body Politic* 116.
147 Olwig, 'Virtual Enclosure' 257.
148 Ibid.

with the idea of nature, so that by the mid-eighteenth century nature lost its original meaning of 'inherent character' and became 'natural scenery', while landscape came to mean 'natural inland scenery'.[149]

2.1.2 Enclosure

The popularity of the natural landscape ideal was no accident; it facilitated the enclosure movement in Britain, which created private property,[150] and ushered in the agricultural/industrial revolution, transforming the country into rural and urban spaces, wilderness and culture, and country and city.[151] Scenic perspectival representation transformed perception not just in the literal sense, in terms of the way the world was perceived, but also in the more figurative sociocultural sense of perception.[152] It thus created a new way of conceptualising and thinking about landscape that was based on an individual's point of view, rather than on the experience of a local community sharing the land.[153] 'Landscape is both site and sight'[154] and 'such scopic reframings are complicit with forms of domination. Landscape can distance us from the world in critical ways. Western ways of seeing 'enframe' the world and conceal this process as an ordering device.'[155]

This point of view culminated in the iconic English landscape garden, itself born of the increasingly sophisticated methods of representing landscape character for use in landscape planning, and representing the point of view of the owner of the privatised land who commissioned that garden.[156] These methods reframed the countryside as a bucolic paradise, inspired by a nostalgic notion of a fading rural Britain as heritage that would inform the protection efforts of a highly urbanised Britain in the early twentieth century.[157] The process of concealing enclosure was thus complete.

The paradoxical view of nature that had arisen by the mid-nineteenth century was characteristic of the underlying philosophy of enclosure: nature is both a realm of natural resources available for man's use, and an environment that determined man's character.[158] Landscape is altered through economic exploitation as well as re-designed to be more aesthetically pleasing, the latter representing the true hallmark of civilisation. Nature hereafter is visual space, albeit amenable to improvement.[159]

The cartographic techniques of perspective landscape representation were compatible with and facilitated the demarcation of land of the Renaissance state in terms of its

---

149 Ibid.
150 Nicole Graham dates the conceptual origins of modern property law to the enclosure of the commons. Customs or law of the commons were locally specific and responsive to geographic capacities and limits as defined by forests, marshes, wetlands and so on. These local limits were regarded as irrelevant to the development of an abstract law of private property. Enclosed land is privately owned land, excluding the interest of all but the owner. The land and its fruits were alienable, transferable and tradeable by the owner at their discretion. See Graham, *Lawscape* 51.
151 Olwig et al 170.
152 Ibid.
153 Ibid.
154 Blomley, 'Landscapes of Property.' *Law & Society Review* 32(1998): 567-612, 574.
155 Ibid, 575.
156 Ibid.
157 Ibid.
158 William Taylor (ed), *The Geography of Law: Landscape, Identity and Regulation* (Hart 2006) 7.
159 Ibid.

physical property, as well as the subdivision of that land into smaller properties under the control of a propertied class or estate.[160] Landscape as scenery thus informed the ideology of enclosure, or the desire to enclose and transform land as property.[161] New laws emerged to buttress the ambitions of this propertied class. The Enclosure Acts of 1760-1830 extinguished rights of common passage and usage.[162] The transformation of landscapes formerly associated with traditional patterns of rural life was instigated by historical events, and associated economic concerns raised by the so called improvement of fencing of common fields and pastures.[163]

With the Glorious Revolution, England overthrew James II, and installed a new monarch who would accept parliamentary rule, enabling an alliance between the court and bourgeois members of the Whig parliament.[164] The Old Whig ideology, in which the country was both source and seat of the customary rights and obligations from which the ancient constitution had sprung, now receded.[165] Left in place as figurehead was the mere image of the English countryside, preserved in the form of the country seat or estate, while the ancient country way of life that had been regulated by custom was dismantled to accommodate agricultural improvement and commerce.[166] Lost in this class conflict were the rural lower classes.

The legerdemain of enclosure is responsible for the rupturing of the biogeography of Britain, forever changing the relationship between people and their environment. Enclosure transformed landscape into property, eliminated the scaffolding of community and erased the local character. The original land laws of peasant economy, the customs that were locally developed, were relevant because they were sensitive to various local geographic conditions.[167] Providing highly specific limits or conditions to those rights in providing rights of access, use and enjoyment of land and other local resources had been an early form of natural resource management, observed over centuries.[168] The pre-enclosure local representative councils, and the corpus of customary law they established, shaped the land, thereby forming a 'substantive landscape' or polity, in which 'substantive' means 'real rather than apparent' and 'belonging to the substance of a thing', in the legal sense of 'creating and defining rights and duties'.[169]

---

160 The art historian Samuel Edgerton argues that the use of surveying and maps to demarcate geometrically measurable parcels of private property fitted in well with the growing mercantile economy of the age, as did the use of the same techniques to visualise and objectify the land as scenery. In such an economy, the abstraction of money reduced the exchange value of goods to the measure of a monetary-economic common denominator, measured according to the physical common denominator of an abstract unit of weight or space (as in the case of land) which was quite different from the equivalency of use values that characterised barter. The continuing erosion of medieval strictures against the alienation and sale of land made it possible, in practice, to transform land into property, even if this violated mores sanctioned by ancient custom. Quoted in Olwig, 'Representation and Alienation' 27 and 28.
161 Olwig, 'Representation and Alienation' 28.
162 Taylor (ed), *The Geography of Law* 9.
163 As a result of Napoleon's blockades and the American Revolution, which led to loss of overseas food sources, food security now relied heavily on local production. See Taylor (ed), *The Geography of Law* 9.
164 Olwig, *Landscape, Nature and the Body Politic* 102.
165 Ibid.
166 Ibid.
167 Graham 53.
168 Ibid.
169 Olwig, 'Virtual Enclosure, Ecosystem Services' 256.

Customary law was thus the formalisation and ritualisation of habits and practices, reinterpreted as required over time, and forming a bank of cultural memory and common identity.[170] The suppression of these customary rights of common people was not the result of an intrinsic failure, or collapse, but effected through legal seizure of lands via enclosure.[171] Custom ossified into tradition, and was interpreted as heritage because people, driven from the land, resurrected the memory of that extinguished community no longer powered by living custom.[172] Landscape was polity rooted in local community and custom, but 'landscaping' the countryside was used as a way to erase memory of the actual community and its relationship with the land.[173] Now solely existing in law, landscapes had one imposed spatial definition as private property. The transition to a spatial definition of land as property had distorted the substantive conceptualisation of landscape.[174]

2.1.3 Alienation

The consequences of enclosure were devastating for local communities. This may be best explained by alienation, which, as with many of the aforementioned concepts, is multi-faceted. In its original sense, alienation means the transferal, and hence loss, of rights in the land, and as Olwig explains, where one has a sense of belonging to the land, as the place of one's family, community and heritage, such loss is also psychologically alienating.[175] 'One becomes estranged from the land to which one belongs – an alien is a foreigner or a stranger, and alienation literally means to be made foreign, to be estranged.'[176] The loss of rights to the land effectively makes one an alien, or foreigner, in the land.[177]

Olwig notes that when the land is commodified as property and visual scenery, it is reduced to a physical thing, material land, and is estranged from its substantive social meaning, the land of a people as res publica.[178] 'Substantive' is used once more to mean real rather than apparent, belonging to the substance of a thing as used in the legal sense of creating and defining rights and duties.[179] Real is defined in terms of the things in law, realis, which determine what is real in a social and political context; alienation is the loss of the real through the reification of the rights in land that are the foundation of the res publica.[180] This means that power is now derived from the statutory right of property as a thing, rather than the customary right of use that defines things in law, and thus the real.[181] 'The social reality defined by shared rights in land is here transformed into private realty and its accompanying scenic landscape backdrop.'[182] Olwig

---

170 Olwig, *Landscape, Nature and the Body Politic* 58 and at 60.
171 Graham 54.
172 Olwig, *Landscape, Nature and the Body Politic* 60 and 223. See also David Lowenthal, *The Heritage Crusade and the Spoils of History* (Cambridge University Press 1998).
173 Olwig, *Landscape, Nature and the Body Politic* 114.
174 Olwig, 'Virtual Enclosure, Ecosystem Services' 256.
175 Olwig, 'Representation and Alienation' 20.
176 Ibid.
177 Ibid, 30-31.
178 Ibid, 34.
179 Ibid.
180 Ibid.
181 Olwig, 'Representation and Alienation' 35.
182 Ibid, 28.

explains that whereas the term 'estate' had once referred to one's place in the polity, landed property itself now became known as an estate, the seat of one's status in the countryside and nation; one's place in the country was thus effectively defined in terms of the possession of a country place.[183]

Those who were landless, not propertied, were therefore voiceless. They were disenfranchised as citizens, as they no longer could participate in representative legal bodies.[184] Land previously held in common was alienated from the commoners, as it now belonged to individuals as property over which the owner had exclusive rights.[185] As Olwig notes, this alienation also had psychological and social effects, because for the poor, enclosure not only eliminated their rights in common land, but reduced their resource base, leaving them much more dependent upon the property owners, and also estranged them from their sense of having a place in the land as a polity.[186] Rights of passage were now associated with vagrancy and mendicancy, and commoners were now outliers, at odds with lifestyles that promoted individual, physical and financial security.[187]

Alienation is the response to the severance of people from the landscape, the material aspects as well as the cultural aspects of landscape, 'thereby breaking the living bonds of custom that motivate sustainable use'.[188] The source of this alienation is the shared loss of common rights via the conversion of common land to private property during enclosure, and reification of the commons as the 'scenic backdrop, and ideological mask', for the purpose of the propertied class.[189] The role of landscape representation in objectifying and distancing people from their environment is alienating, via the repressive social conditions alienation creates.[190] Having been expelled from the landscape, commoners lose their way of life, their rights, their community, and their identity, which were all based on place attachment. They are 'displaced' in the truest sense of the word.[191]

However, the idea of common land never truly disappeared. The British labour movement of the early twentieth century drew upon these earlier notions of shared resources and regulatory regimes embodying participatory forms of governance rooted in custom, when it agitated for access to the countryside.[192] As Olwig has noted, they emphasised the working class's unjust loss of rural rights in the land, likely influenced by members of their audience who may well have been descendants of commoners.[193] This movement also included organisations such as Lord Eversley's Commons, Forests and Footpaths Society (now known as the Open Spaces Society), and would effectively use English common law to argue for the preservation of common land as

---

183 Olwig, 'Representation and Alienation' 29.
184 Ibid.
185 Olwig, 'Representation and Alienation' 28.
186 Ibid.
187 Taylor (ed), *Geography of Law* 10.
188 Kenneth Olwig, 'Globalism and the enclosure of the landscape commons.' In Ian Rotherham (ed), *Cultural Severance and the Environment – The Ending of Traditional and Customary Practice on Commons and Landscapes Managed in Common* (Springer 2013) 31-46, 31.
189 Olwig, 'Representation and Alienation' 35.
190 Ibid, 33.
191 Graham 52.
192 Olwig, 'Representation and Alienation' 29.
193 Ibid.

parks, particularly in urban areas, across Britain.[194] The idea that cities and nations ought to have shared landscapes, to which the larger citizenry has rights of access, had descended from these ancient practices concerning shared rights to common land.[195]

Pressure from various interest groups culminated in the enactment of legislation following World War II. The National Parks and Access to the Countryside Act was passed in 1949 to placate rambling associations, conservation groups, and those similarly concerned with rights of public access to the countryside.[196] The Act required the mapping of all local rights of way, the establishment of national parks, and the delegation of power to local authorities to secure access to open country areas.[197] The movement did not restore landscape. However, some aspects of customary law in the form of public rights of access were given statutory basis.[198] National parks were therefore not exclusive in the manner of private landscape parks created by estate owners, on typically enclosed common land.[199]

Landscape as scenic space was defined by cartographers and other experts and promoted the idea of the world as space, divided into bounded, privately or publicly owned properties.[200] Nevertheless, this masks the tension between property and community and place-centred landscape values identified with the common lands of the unenclosed landscape that preceded enclosure.[201] Such values can be seen in the form of social and legal practices of community governance, identity and even as working commons today.[202]

Alienation, as the loss of customary rights in land that comprise the foundation of the res publica, displaces people and renders them homeless, alien and foreign.[203] The substantive landscape, to which people become attached through working practice, is presented in diminished form, a visual scene artistically represented, 'legitimating the surveyed and planned space of the propertied'.[204] Olwig describes imperial landscape as a creature of the enclosure process, wherein alienation is the driving force of a particular notion of progress that justifies displacement by making 'social and material loss the source of economic and spiritual liberation.'[205] It was therefore necessary 'to reduce the living and changing social and legal force of custom to picturesque tradition and costume, and thereafter obliterate it, often with disastrous social and ecological consequences.'[206] Human beings become collateral damage in the imperial landscape. Thus enclosure was accompanied by 'the construction of parks which transformed working commons (shaped by practice and custom) into ideal pastoral landscape scenes, while literally alienating the commoners from the land.'[207]

---

194 Olwig, 'Representation and Alienation' 30.
195 Ibid.
196 Annika Dahlberg, Rick Rohde and Klas Sandell, 'National Parks and Environmental Justice: Comparing Access Rights and Ideological Legacies in Three Countries.' *Conservation and Society* 8(3) (2010): 209-224, 217.
197 Ibid.
198 Olwig, 'Representation and Alienation' 35.
199 Ibid, 30.
200 Olwig et al, 'Introduction to a Special Issue: The Future of Landscape Characterization' 172.
201 Ibid.
202 Ibid.
203 Olwig, 'Representation and Alienation' 34.
204 Ibid, 35.
205 Ibid.
206 Ibid.
207 Ibid.

2.1.4 Empire: Virtual Enclosure and Alienation Writ Large

Following enclosure, the country of England was no longer defined via historical custom but in terms of scenery, of its geographical body.[208] Landscape became a visualising technique, a way to render the country in particular scenic, spatial terms,[209] which was by no means a neutral activity. This scenic illusion of landscape facilitated the belief that differently constituted polities and places could be collapsed within the unitary space of a body politic as embodied by a geographic body or land mass.[210] Surveying and mapping the techniques of design and painting landscape scenery could be used to define territory as a quantity of geometric space, and such techniques need not be limited to Britain.[211] Gardeners, legislators and colonisers preferred the preordained cartographic structure of abstract space to the physicality and particularity of place, because it could be controlled.[212] Graham explains that when standardised universal and measurable space could be grafted over place, the physicality and particularity of places became irrelevant.[213]

Acts of enclosure in Great Britain carried the implicit assumption that unbounded lands were under-utilised and therefore largely unoccupied.[214] The underlying philosophy was simple: those who best used land and labour had the right to control both.[215] Improvement therefore depended upon the knowledge of plants and soils, and so science as the pursuit of environmental knowledge was joined to private property.[216] British imperialism over the long term was a campaign to extend this ecological regime, premised on the virtues of sedentary agriculture, husbandry, private property, production for exchange and ultimately manufacture.[217]

Such thinking was inevitable given that the wealth of the new powerful Whig oligarchy was derived from the expanding global agricultural, industrial and trading interests of imperial Britain, not the country of little England.[218] In order to retain legitimacy, this new class aligned itself with the English country ideal, even as it was transcending the country way of life that was regulated by custom, because it hindered agricultural improvement and commerce.[219] As Olwig notes, the country was "English' in aspect but British in its ability to manage a world imperium from a country seat in a united Britain.'[220] Hence the 'aura of country legitimacy transferred from England of custom to Britain of Empire'[221] and landscape as private property kept the commoners at bay through eviction, urban migration and transportation to the New World.[222]

---

208 Olwig, *Landscape, Nature and the Body Politic* 62.
209 Ibid, xxxi.
210 Olwig, *Landscape, Nature and the Body Politic* 218.
211 Ibid, 118.
212 Graham 66.
213 Ibid.
214 Taylor (ed), *Geography of Law* 11.
215 Drayton, *Nature's Government* 229.
216 Ibid, 52.
217 Ibid, 229.
218 Olwig, *Landscape, Nature and the Body Politic* 102.
219 Ibid.
220 Ibid.
221 Ibid.
222 Graham 52.

Newly discovered territory thus became wilderness as tabula rasa. 'Wilderness was a space bereft of all but natural resources, awaiting transformation under the improving hand of mankind'.[223] However, Graham points out that British colonists never believed the lands to which they travelled were unpopulated, just uncultured – terra nullius signified the absence of agricultural use of those lands, not the absence of indigenous peoples.[224] British sovereignty was thus asserted on the basis that Indigenous peoples had not demonstrated the capacity for proprietorship, justifying the grant of land to non-indigenous individuals on the condition that it was 'improved'.[225] This narrative thus 'mythologized conquest and imperialism as improvement and progress'.[226] Improvement was carried out via enclosure, landscape gardening and colonisation.[227] This form of land use secured the foundation for colonial property rights.[228]

Spatialising place reframed the appropriation of land as a rational and constructive process of discovery and exploration rather than a political and destructive process of dispossession and exploitation.[229] The concept of space and spatial technologies such as cartography were instrumental to enclosure and the ordering of place both conceptually and physically.[230] The 'irrelevance and absence of place thus underwrote the legitimacy of enclosure and colonialism because constructing a monolithic space allowed the British Empire to hierarchise the use of space to its own advantage'.[231]

Enclosure facilitated the transition from community to nation and from nation to empire.[232] The rationale of enclosure (and colonisation) is that cultural progress can only be measured by the improvement of nature.[233] Improvement, from a French word for profit, is associated with a particular form of land use for monetary gain.[234] But the improvement of nature is not a neutral activity, as it is achieved via the eviction, transportation and dispossession of native peoples, which physically displaces and 'deplaces' people.[235] The tabula rasa view of wilderness and beliefs in terra nullius enabled the assessment of the 'otherness' of foreign territories and their indigenous inhabitants, 'who were confronted and more often than not, disregarded'.[236]

This process of enclosing new territory outside of Britain may be described as a form of 'virtual' enclosure. According to Olwig, virtual enclosure transcends the strict definition of physical enclosure, which is historically associated with Britain and the Enclosure Acts.[237] As Olwig explains, virtual enclosure occurs whenever the character of landscape is 'pre-defined according to an assumed spatial logic that comprehends nature as a bounded scenic property, reinforcing ideas about privatization, priva-

---

223 Taylor (ed), *Geography of Law* 11.
224 Graham 95.
225 Ibid, 90.
226 Ibid, 95.
227 Ibid, 65.
228 Ibid, 90.
229 Ibid, 66.
230 Ibid.
231 Ibid.
232 Graham 60.
233 Ibid, 52.
234 Raymond Williams, *Keywords* (Fortuna 1976) 160-161 as cited in Graham 56.
235 Graham 52.
236 Taylor (ed), *Geography of Law* 13.
237 Olwig, 'Virtual Enclosure' 253.

te property and management control'.²³⁸ What is relevant is that enclosure reduces environmental diversity through spatial consolidation and spatial enclosure.²³⁹ This shifted landscape from a system that reflected the diversity of the land's environmental topography, to one of agricultural specialisation, in which common resources are no longer relied upon.²⁴⁰

Subjugating landscape to imperial ambitions was accomplished by obliterating ways of life, masked as rhetoric and the practice of 'improvement'.²⁴¹ The landscape installed was a new expression of the relationship between land, law and people, and was exported throughout the British Empire, mimicking the earlier physical and legal enclosure in England. This representation of the landscape objectifies and distances people from the land; it is alienating because of the oppressive social conditions in which legal rights are taken away.²⁴² Place ceases to exist and becomes geometric space to be surveyed and mapped. People are erased, either from existence or by dehumanising their existence based on their status as uncultured savages or human chattel. Landscape reaches its ultimate form of reification with the dehumanisation required for the establishment of Caribbean slave colonies, to which we now turn.

2.2 The Caribbean as Imperial Landscape

2.2.1 The Amerindian Landscape and the Environmental Consequences of 1492

The year 1492, in which Christopher Columbus made landfall in the Caribbean, is taken as the watershed event precipitating European colonial expansion in the region. It is important to note that Columbus did not 'discover' primitive isolated tribes but rather socially complex and ethnically heterogeneous Indigenous societies.²⁴³ Between the fourth and first millennia BC a new wave of immigrants from the South American mainland established large and relatively permanent settlements on the islands between Trinidad and Puerto Rico, and in the space of a few centuries the entire Lesser Antillean archipelago became a dynamic landscape with peoples moving between the islands and the mainland shores. The diversity of ecosystems and the complex social relationships informed a dynamic, highly interconnected island world, ranging from local groups to hierarchical societies that consolidated and shifted over time.²⁴⁴ Nevertheless, this dissertation is concerned with the impact of the law on the Caribbean heritage. The common law is a key instrument of the empire project, responsible for reordering and reframing the landscape in what would become the British Caribbean. Columbus' arrival (and Spain's entry into the New World as a European coloniser) therefore sym-

---

238 Ibid.
239 Ibid, 254.
240 Ibid.
241 Mitchell, 'Just Landscapes or Landscapes of Justice' 788.
242 Olwig, 'Representation and Alienation' 32 and 36.
243 Reid, *Myths and Realities of Caribbean History* 100. See also Lennox Honychurch, *Carib to Creole: A History of Contact and Culture Exchange* (The Dominica Institute 2000).
244 Corinne Hofman, 'Indigenous Caribbean Networks in a Globalizing World' 58. In Christopher De Corse (ed), *Power, Political Economy, and Historical Landscapes of the Modern World* (SUNY Press 2019).

bolically presages the destruction of the Amerindian landscape and the emergence of the imperial landscape.[245]

It is difficult to understand colonialism without reference to environmental factors that illustrate the physical transition of landscape to space.[246] Europeans transformed the New World, what Alfred Crosby has termed the greatest biological revolution since the Pleistocene area, shaping the land and histories of extensive areas by raising plants on extensive plantations.[247] This was carried to an extreme on the Caribbean islands, where the entire land mass became devoted to plantation agriculture. This distinguishes these islands from the settler states and conquered territories in other parts of the British Empire and explains the spatial and demographic dimensions of the Atlantic slave trade and Caribbean plantations.[248]

This is not to say that the Caribbean islands were in an untouched state prior to colonialism. Amerindian populations certainly modified their environment. The data suggest that earlier foraging/fishing Archaic groups who used a stone tool and shell technology and transported few, if any non-indigenous plants or animals, still impacted island landscapes as evidenced by bird and sloth extinctions. They were followed by more advanced ceramic making horticulturalists who engaged in forest clearance, overexploitation of both terrestrial and marine resources, and growing populations, but it was not until Europeans arrived and population centres grew that intensive and widespread degradation of island landscapes and resources occurred.[249] Indigenous agriculture made use of high earth mounds that produced agricultural staples.[250] There was small-scale logging for construction and introduction of plant species.[251] House gar-

---

245 See Dillman, *Colonizing Paradise: Landscape and Empire in the British West Indies* 174-175 and at 179. Dillman's thesis is that the Caribbean landscape has undergone successive iterations, first viewed through European eyes as paradise (beginning with Christopher Columbus, the first explorer to record his visual impressions), then a pastoral idyll for settlement, a reordered natural canvas to restore paradise, and finally a mask to hide the reality of the brutal conditions surrounding slavery and plantation agriculture. He notes that colonial landscape tropes remain salient today as the British Caribbean became reimagined as a paradise to attract tourists.
246 William Beinart and Lotte Hughes, *Environment and Empire* (Oxford University 2007) 8. See also Alfred Crosby, *Ecological Imperialism: the Biological Expansion of Europe* (Cambridge University Press 1986); Henry Hooghiemstra, Thomas Olijhoek, Menno Hoogland, Maarten Prins, Bas van Geel, Timme Donders, William Gosling and Corinne Hofman, 'Columbus' Environmental Impact in the New World: Land Use Change in the Yaque River Valley, Dominican Republic.' *Holocene* 28(11) (2018): 1818-1835; Alvaro Castilla-Beltrán, Henry Hooghiemstra, Menno Hoogland, Jaime Pagan Jimenez, Bas van Geel, Michael Field, Maarten Prins, Timme Donders , Eduardo Herrera Malatesta, and Jorge Ulloa Hung, Crystal McMichael, William Gosling and Corinne Hofman, 'Columbus' Footprint in Hispaniola: A Paleoenvironmental Record of Indigenous and Colonial Impacts on the Landscape of the Central Cibao Valley, Northern Dominican Republic.' *Anthropocene* 22 (2018): 66-80.
247 Alfred Crosby, *The Columbian Exchange: Biological and Cultural Consequences of 1492* (Greenwood Press 1972) 66.
248 Beinart and Hughes 9.
249 Scott Fitzpatrick and William Keegan, 'Human Impacts and Adaptations in the Caribbean Islands: An Historical Ecology approach.' *Earth and Environmental Science Transactions of the Royal Society of Edinburgh* 98 (2007): 29-45, 29.
250 Corinne Hofman, Jorge Ulloa Hung, Eduardo Herrera Malatesta, Joseph Jean, Till Sonnemann and Menno Hoogland, 'Indigenous Caribbean Perspectives: Archaeologies and Legacies of the First Colonised Region in the New World.' *Antiquity* 92(361) (2018): 200-216.
251 David Watts, *The West Indies: Patterns of Development Culture and Environmental Change since 1492* (Cambridge University Press 1990) 75.

dens were cultivated with various crops grown in small quantities, while more intensive farming was practiced in the conucos or fields some distance from the village.[252] There was deforestation, and intensive agricultural practices such as slash and burn and slope agriculture altered the environment.[253]

In the Lesser Antilles, arable land was used for horticulture, and marine resources exploited, and there was land clearance resulting in significant environmental change.[254] But no Amerindian communities in 1492 had developed the concept of private ownership of land; land was a communal resource, to be utilised fully within the limits of their technology and with an eye to sustainability, for the long-term conservation of food security. With the advent of colonialism, and the acquisition of land, the relationship between Amerindian communities and their environment was drastically altered. The diversity of agricultural practices was also suppressed as more and more land was absorbed by the colonisers. Their productive conuco agricultural systems were to be dismantled and replaced by Spanish settlements, and most of their populations eliminated, at least in the Lesser Antilles.[255]

After some early efforts to enslave indigenous peoples in the Americas, which were later condemned by Spain and the papacy, the Spaniards relied on the encomienda, a semi-feudal system of tributary labour initially applied to the conquered Moors in Spain. Theoretically, the main justification for ruling the Amerindians was to convert them to Christianity and a Christian way of life, so the system required a Spanish master, or encomendero, to protect and slowly Christianise a small community of Amerindians in exchange for tribute. The tribute could be in the form of crops, personal service, or work in underground mines. In actuality, not only did the Spaniards continue to enslave some Amerindians, but encomenderos made large fortunes by exploiting Amerindian workers.[256] The imposition of the encomienda system marked the consolidation of domination, and was the springboard for destruction of Indigenous societies. Because of its economic importance, the encomienda structured the existence of indigenous and European individuals, as well as their social and economic positions in the colonial environment. Domination transformed the individuals into colonial subjects, with specific roles in the social and productive spheres. For indigenous individuals it meant being Indian, changing their language, appearance, creed, and identity, and being assigned a lower place in the social echelon.[257] The encomienda system helped to destroy native populations in the Caribbean. Demographic devastation explains the rapid clearance of land in the Americas and the limits of the local labour force.[258]

---

252 Keegan and Hofman 250.
253 Ibid, 198.
254 Ibid, 210-211.
255 Watts 77.
256 David Brion Davis, *Inhuman Bondage: The Rise and Fall of Slavery in the New World* (Oxford University Press 2008) 97.
257 Roberto Valcárcel Rojas, *Archaeology of Early Colonial Interaction at El Chorro de Maíta, Cuba* (University Press of Florida 2016) 332; see also Karen Anderson-Córdova, *Surviving Spanish Conquest: Indian Fight, Flight, and Cultural Transformation in Hispaniola and Puerto Rico* (University of Alabama Press 2017); Luis Arranz Márquez, *Repartimientos y Encomiendas en la Isla Española* (Fundación García Arévalo 1991); Carlos Esteban Deive, *La Española y La Esclavitud del Indio* (Fundación García Arévalo 1995) and Jorge Ulloa Hung and Roberto Rojas Valcárcel (eds) *Indígenas e Indios en el Caribe: Presencia, Legado y Estudio* (Instituto Tecnológico de Santo Domingo 2016).
258 Beinart and Hughes 33.

As early as 1516, two witnesses to the horrors of the New World, Licenciado Zuazo and Bartolomé de Las Casas, 'protectors of the Indians,' called for the sparing of Amerindian lives, especially in the mines, by importing Africans to serve as slave labour. For twenty-five years Las Casas saw the importation of Africans as the 'solution' for the Spaniards' oppression of Amerindians. This substitution of African peoples for Amerindians became a common pattern.[259] Unlike the indigenous inhabitants, most West Africans were familiar with large-scale agriculture, organised labour, and making iron/steel tools. Indigenous peoples, now restricted on small islands, had been decimated by enslavement and disease, and were no longer a viable labour source.[260] Racial slavery thus became an intrinsic and indispensable part of New World settlement.[261] As the British and then French Caribbean began producing sugar, molasses, rum, and coffee for an international mass market, the West Indies became the true economic centre of the New World, a point confirmed by the fact that imperial powers immediately sent their navies to protect or capture Caribbean colonies upon the outbreak of a war.[262]

2.2.2 Landscape as Plantation I: The Environmental Consequences of Plantation Agriculture

Colonialism's philosophical underpinnings are imperialist, and so concern the acquisition of land, whether by conquest, settlement or exploitation. The colonies of Africa, India and Spanish America were conquered, often retaining their peoples and cultures, while the United States and Australia were colonised for settlement.[263] The Caribbean colonies were colonised ultimately for exploitation, relying on a new form of slavery, the chattel slavery of West Africans, to develop plantation monoculture.[264]

The ecosystems of the Caribbean were central to the region's transformation into slave colonies. Sugar and many other key plantation crops could not be grown in Europe, so demand for these commodities coupled with unique environmental factors shaped the evolution of the Atlantic plantation system. This accelerated the growth of the slave trade, and sustained empires, especially in Britain.[265] Since sugar gradually became one of the first luxuries consumed by the masses in Western societies (along with slave-produced coffee, tobacco, and eventually chocolate), it also became the

---

259 Brion Davis 98.
260 Hofman, 'Indigenous Caribbean Networks in a Globalizing World' 55. In De Corse (ed) *Power, Political Economy, and Historical Landscapes of the Modern World*.
261 Brion Davis 102.
262 Ibid, 112.
263 George Beckford, 'Institutional Foundations of Resource Underdevelopment in the Caribbean.' *The Review of Black Political Economy* 2, 3 (Spring 1972): 81-101, as cited in George Beckford, *Persistent Poverty: Underdevelopment of Plantation Economies in the Third World* (Oxford University Press 1972) 8.
264 Kenneth Kelly and Meredith Hardy (eds) *French Colonial Archaeology in the Southeast and Caribbean* (University of Florida Press 2011) 3; Kenneth Kelly, 'Archaeology, Plantations, and Slavery in the French West Indies' 19 in Kenneth Kelly and Benoit Bérard (eds) *Lesser Antilles Plantation Archaeology* (Sidestone Press 2014).
265 Beinart and Hughes 26 and 22.

principal incentive for transporting millions of Africans to the New World.²⁶⁶ The consequences of these events were imprinted upon the Caribbean landscape.²⁶⁷

Sugar is not native to the Caribbean and it was not until the Crusades that Europeans came into contact with the crop itself.²⁶⁸ A cultivar from New Guinea, sugar cane spread along migration routes to India, where it hybridised, and was first processed to develop crystals, which could provide an intense concentrated sweetener that could be stored.²⁶⁹ Sugar swiftly replaced honey as an effective preserver of fruit and as it was also quickly soluble, its consumption became linked to newly appreciated sweetened beverages, coffee and tea.²⁷⁰ As sugar's popularity skyrocketed, attempts were made to cultivate sugarcane. Initial experiments in the Mediterranean during the medieval period failed, as sugar requires abundant water, and production was plagued by widely fluctuating temperatures.²⁷¹ In the fourteenth century, Spain grew sugar in the Canary Islands, yet while the crop thrived, available land was limited in such mountainous terrain.²⁷² Portuguese colonisers experienced similar success when they grew sugar in the previously uninhabited Atlantic islands, but once again, the quantity of suitable soil inhibited production.²⁷³

The exploratory forays to cultivate crops in these islands also revealed that sugar production demanded much more skill and labour than originally envisaged.²⁷⁴ Effective sugar production requires on site processing, as cane, once cut, loses its sucrose content rapidly.²⁷⁵ Mills were therefore established on or close to canefields, which necessitated permanent labour, not only for the seasonal harvesting, but for a wide range of agricultural tasks and work in the mills.²⁷⁶ Initially, European indentured labour had been used, but they were susceptible to disease and the supply diminished rapidly after the English Civil War ended in 1660.²⁷⁷ Enslaved Africans, though expensive, were purchased for life, had no rights, were immune to European diseases and were exploitable as proved elsewhere.²⁷⁸ The Portuguese introduced sugar cultivation to Brazil, advantageously located near the West coast of Africa; until the French and British appeared in the 1600s, Brazil was the undisputed titan in the sugar market, the Portuguese having finally perfected the formula for land, access to slave labour, and

---

266 Brion Davis 107.
267 Such settlement patterns reflect the power dynamics of the plantation. See James Delle, 'The Habitus of Jamaican Landscapes' 130 in James Delle, Mark Hauser, Douglas Armstrong, and Ainsley Henriques, *Out of Many, One People: The Historical Archaeology of Colonial Jamaica* (1st edn, The University of Alabama Press 2011).
268 Carrie Gibson, *Empire's Crossroads: A New History of the Caribbean* (Macmillan 2014) 83.
269 Beinart and Hughes 24.
270 Ibid, 25.
271 Ibid, 26-27 and Gibson 84.
272 Dan Hicks 'The Garden of the World': An Historical Archaeology of Sugar Landscapes in the Eastern Caribbean* (Archaeopress 2007) 8.
273 Beinart and Hughes 26-27.
274 Gibson 91.
275 Beinart and Hughes 24.
276 Ibid.
277 Ibid, 35.
278 Ibid.

climate.[279] Sugar production's particular reliance on agriculture and manufacture had created the plantationscape.[280]

Plantations had been attempted in West Africa, the preferred location, as the region was suitable for growing tropical commodities. However, European settlement and supervision was greatly hampered by high rates of death due to mosquito-borne diseases such as yellow fever and malaria.[281] But it was not only the problem of disease. Local populations could not be displaced and local political authorities prevented the alienation of land.[282] African political systems were entrenched and difficult to overwhelm militarily, and it also proved challenging to transform internal social relations, thus requiring negotiations to acquire slave labour.[283] These enslaved Africans acquired for local African plantations were an improvement on European labour, but they could easily escape; this was much more difficult on tiny Caribbean islands completely reduced to plantation agriculture, where slaves were essentially trapped, and full colonial political control had been established.[284] African labour was therefore ideal, just not in Africa.

While African rulers themselves never developed plantation agriculture, they did supply the great bulk of slaves for the external trade as their capacity for resisting colonial intrusion gave them the ability to regulate the market.[285] With the potential for sugar plantations in the Americas amply demonstrated by the Portuguese in Brazil in the sixteenth century along with this ready supply of slaves from Africa, the two poles of the triangular Atlantic trade[286] became established, in no way hampered by an alternative geographic location for plantations.[287]

The Caribbean was an attractive alternate location because climatic, geographical and environmental conditions were ideal for sugar cultivation.[288] The Caribbean colonies, as islands, were surrounded by sea, and also had surface water such as rivers, so plantations could be sited very near water, which was the cheapest way of moving goods.[289] The environmental factors necessary for establishing a sugar plantation, such as soil not prone to flooding, and a hot climate with plenty strong sunlight, but not too dry an atmosphere, were present.[290] Plantations require extensive land, and the sparsely inhabited coastal tropical lowlands where Amerindians practiced shifting cultivation were not permanently settled in the sense that Europeans were accustomed to.[291] By

---

279 Gibson 85.
280 Ibid, 24.
281 Ibid, 28.
282 Ibid, 19.
283 Ibid, 30.
284 Ibid.
285 Beinart and Hughes 32.
286 European goods – firearms, textiles, iron and copper bars – were taken to Africa and traded for slaves, who were shipped on the southerly routes to the Americas. Plantation commodities were then loaded for the return northerly voyage to Europe. See Beinart and Hughes 32.
287 Beinart and Hughes 32.
288 Mark Hauser, 'A Political Ecology of Water and Enslavement.' *Current Anthropology* 58(2) (2017): 227-256, 229, 233-34.
289 Beinart and Hughes 23.
290 Gibson 89.
291 Beckford 34.

absorbing as much land as possible, the plantation soon transformed the open resource situation of the Caribbean islands.[292]

The plantation system in the New World initially was established by grants of land from the imperial crowns to European citizens.[293] This was bestowed directly to individuals or indirectly through charter companies.[294] As noted earlier, this facilitated the overpowering of the Amerindian population, who could not withstand the onslaught of European colonisers given their numbers and style of semi-nomadic shifting cultivation.[295] 'Sugar crushed an earlier landscape as well as hundreds of thousands of lives,'[296] enabled by the process of virtual enclosure, which transformed the local ecology, upended a communal resource system and entrenched a system of law that relied upon private property and slave labour.[297] The philosophy that cultivating land improves it, underpinned England's hierarchical land use system, and so provided justification for taking untilled fields in the New World from native peoples.[298] Europeans had little understanding of the Amerindians' sophisticated agricultural systems, perceiving them as slothful and incompetent for not 'using' these tracts of land.[299]

Private property is thus introduced with colonisation of the Caribbean, as the entrenched land laws and succession practices in African countries stymied attempts to establish plantations on that continent.[300] European elites exercised power over the European masses by means of private, revenue-producing land – exemplified by the landlord-tenant relationship. By contrast, West African land was 'owned by the state as a corporation,' and thus the main symbols of private wealth and success were large numbers of slaves.[301] However, the nature of slavery in these islands was unique with regard to its relationship with the land and the law and diverged substantially from African practices.

Caribbean slavery was uniquely place-based; restricted to the plantation for the duration of their lives, and hemmed in on all sides by the ocean, slaves were physically, legally and socially limited in their mobility and in their access to space. This demonstrates that colonialism in the Caribbean is a form of spatial injustice, because it aimed to prevent the establishment of communities, access to community resources and denied people a sense of belonging, which is spatially located.[302]

---

292 Hicks 42.
293 Beckford 88.
294 Ibid, 89.
295 Ibid, 90.
296 Beinart and Hughes 38.
297 See Mark Hauser and Dan Hicks, 'Colonialism and Landscape: Power, Materiality and Scales of Analysis in Caribbean Historical Archaeology' 253 in Dan Hicks, Laura McAtackney and Graham Fairclough (eds) *Envisioning Landscape: Situations and Standpoints in Archaeology and Heritage* (Routledge 2007).
298 Hicks discusses improvement in the Lesser Antillean plantation context at 48.
299 On the theory of land use, see John Locke, *Two Treatises of Government* (1821) 213, as cited in Gibson 122.
300 Beinart and Hughes, and see Gibson 99.
301 Brion Davis 89.
302 Herzfeld 129.

2.2.3 Landscape as Plantation II: Racial Chattel Slavery, Natal Alienation and Caribbean Slave Societies

Plantations are deeply rooted in the natural environment.[303] They create relationships between people and the land and determine how people live on the land and interact with one another.[304] The racial demography of the Caribbean was thus transformed, as Africans displaced Amerindians and European indentured servants as plantation labour. Disease patterns, driven by ecological upheavals, helped to shape the conquest and peopling of the Americas.[305] Colonialism was also driven by conceptions and misconceptions of land, property and slavery, which transformed Caribbean islands into chattel slave societies.

Europeans did not understand that land in Africa was not held privately, but in common, and slaves, not land, were the source of wealth. Europeans also failed to understand the distinctions and traditions of African slavery, which could involve various dimensions, such as being captured as prisoners of war, serving in slave armies, or being treated as members of the family.[306] There were enormous cultural differences between African and European enslavement. In Africa, many slaves were treated much like peasant farmers, and some served as administrators, soldiers, and even royal advisers, while others provided a labour supply for mines or were ritually used for human sacrifice.[307] Chattel slavery predated Atlantic slavery, and slave societies certainly predated Caribbean slave societies. Indeed, Greece was probably the first genuine 'slave society', where city states were totally dependent on slave labour, as distinct from the many societies that simply possessed slaves.[308] But slavery in the ancient world can be distinguished from the racial slavery that came to pervade the New World. For instance, Romans imported slaves from countless countries and all directions, including blond, blue-eyed slaves from northern Europe, highly educated and professional slaves from Greece and northern Africa, as well as sub-Saharan Africa.[309]

David Brion Davis observes that chattel slavery is the most extreme example not only of domination and oppression but of human attempts to dehumanise other people.[310] He sees this inhuman bondage as an attempt to bestialise human beings, and believes chattel slavery takes on a unique brutality in the New World.[311] From its inception, New World slavery was focused on Native Americans, and then transitioned to black Africans – in both cases to people who were strikingly different in physical appearance as well as in cultural background from the white colonists.[312] The racial element is thus a significant distinction.

Traditional definitions of slavery have stressed that the slave person is the chattel property of another man or woman and subject to sale and other forms of transfer; that the slave's will is subject to the owner's authority, and that the slave's labour or

---

303 Beckford 5.
304 Ibid, 8.
305 Beinart and Hughes 36.
306 Gibson 99.
307 Brion Davis 89.
308 Ibid, 40.
309 Ibid, 46.
310 Ibid, 2.
311 Ibid, 3.
312 Ibid, 3.

services is obtained through coercion.[313] The concept of chattel property is very relevant to landscape analysis of heritage law in the Caribbean, as it provides evidence of the imperial landscape. Both the terms 'chattel' and 'property' have legal meanings of abstraction, wherein humanity is abstracted out of these people, who are divested of their culture, traditions, land, just as landscape was turned into property. Chattel as in chattel slaves, do not belong to the land; they are chattels personal, items of tangible movable personal property (such as livestock) not permanently connected with real estate.[314] Chattel property is a legal term tying slavery to a system of law: slaves are denied their humanity, as they are reified as things, paralleling the denuding of landscape of its substantive cultural, natural and community qualities.[315] Slaves have no heritage when they belong to the law rather than the land, which confirms their dehumanisation, displacement and powerlessness. 'The reality of slavery demanded an abrogation of the past.'[316]

Planters drew slave supplies from African people of different linguistic, cultural and social backgrounds, which aided cultural assimilation and erasure in the New World.[317] Because enslaved Africans were so far removed from their places of origin, they were truly 'natally alienated,' to use Orlando Patterson's term;[318] people who are natally alienated have no identity, and enslaved Africans had no connection to the Caribbean islands or the plantations in which they laboured. They were alienated from their 'homeland', and as strangers, had no natural relationship their new environments, truly foreign as noted in Olwig's discussion of the alienation of legal rights. Natal alienation is therefore best understood as alienation from land.[319] This is the 'double injustice inherent in the slave-based plantation system: the denial of ownership of the land and the resulting denial of an identity, of a self, of an existence in the world.'[320]

The particular confluence of slavery, chattel status and dehumanisation based on perceived racial differences, has never occurred elsewhere contemporaneously. Slavery in the Caribbean is also place-based as well as race-based; slaves are imported and brought to small islands where they cannot escape. Planters and whites dominate and move freely within the same space that Amerindians and Africans cannot – they possess spatial privilege. Space is constructed when legal actors designate boundaries between public and private spaces, or consider questions of personal mobility or spatial equality. Space, like law, is not an empty or objective category, but has a direct bearing on the way power is deployed and social life constituted, which may follow problematic and oppressive patterns.[321]

---

313 Ibid, 30.
314 'Chattel' *Oxford English Dictionary* (11th edn, Oxford University Press 2006) 240.
315 Cf Olwig 'Representation and Alienation' 34.
316 Gibson 105.
317 Beckford 38.
318 Orlando Patterson, *Slavery and Social Death: A Comparative Study* (Harvard University Press 1982) 21-27; Brion Davis 94.
319 Olwig, *Representation and Alienation* 20.
320 Malcom Ferdinand, 'Ecology, Identity, and Colonialism in Martinique: The Discourse of An Ecological NGO (1980-2011)' in Chris Campbell and Michael Niblett (eds.), *The Caribbean: Aesthetics, World-Ecology, Politics* (Liverpool University Press 2016) 174-188, 180.
321 Blomley and Bakan 669-670.

This is why it is important to distinguish between colonies, such as those located in Africa and Asia, where colonised populations retained their land, and settler societies where British and other European immigrants became demographically dominant.[322] Caribbean slave colonies are the only countries in which the entire land mass was dedicated to plantation agriculture driven by African slave labour.[323] This was not the case in Brazil or the American South. As Davis explains, although British Caribbean planters initially borrowed their sugar-making technology from Dutch and Portuguese Brazilians, the political culture of their slave plantations was wholly different from that in Brazil, where the wealthiest mill owners at least maintained the appearance of being patriarchs and community leaders, though they too were capitalists.[324] There were no such illusions with British planters, who made plain the fact that they were entrepreneurs whose primary goal in life was to make money, not 'resident seigneurs'.[325] The British sugar plantation had evolved into its own creature, 'a purely capitalistic enterprise, not a quasi-seigneurial community with religious and social services that stimulated a surrounding economy'.[326] Agriculture and commerce characterised slavery, not community and custom.

Where colonisation is a process of bringing territory and people under new and more stringent forms of control, the plantation can be a central instrument of colonisation.[327] In a plantation society or economy, several plantations monopolise most of the arable land in a country that is predominantly agricultural.[328] Plantations are established for external trade, hence their location on or near coastal land.[329] The plantation is designed for pure exploitation, which distinguishes it from other agricultural settlement institutions such as manors or haciendas that adopt a pastoral and patriarchal image. Religion, family, social status are irrelevant for the enslaved.[330] Davis observes that when the proportion of slaves in a given colony exceed ninety percent or more, this can blur the usual boundaries of human society, as the society becomes oriented to the twin goals of lowering production costs and increasing output. In most of the Caribbean, there were no sectors of society that were truly independent from sugar production.[331] The plantation and the island merged into one, and the landscape was now a 'plantationscape'.

Barbados illustrates this very well, as it was the premier sugar colony in the British Empire by 1680. From a broad base of nearly 40,000 enslaved Africans, the hierarchical pyramid society moved upward to 2,300 white servants, 1,000 small planters, and 175 big planters at the top.[332] The small planter elite, in the words of the historian Richard S Dunn, 'held the best land, sold the most sugar, and monopolised the best

---

322 Beinart and Hughes 20.
323 Beckford 12.
324 Brion Davis 115.
325 Ibid, 116.
326 Ibid.
327 Beckford 30.
328 Ibid, 12.
329 Ibid, 32.
330 Ibid, 33.
331 Brion Davis 121.
332 The population of Barbados still included some 20,000 whites, more than any British-American colony except Virginia and Massachusetts. See Brion Davis 115.

offices. In only one generation these planters had turned their small island into an amazingly effective sugar-production machine and had built a social structure to rival the tradition-encrusted hierarchy of old England.'[333]

However, the population disparities concerned the white elite, who were surrounded by captive black labour. These underlying fears were responsible for the most successful planters practicing absenteeism in the eighteenth and early nineteenth centuries.[334] In their place they hired ambitious and upwardly mobile men as professional 'book-keepers' (managers) and overseers to manage their estates, who were determined to maximise plantation profits in order to escape the region and retire home in Britain. This reinforced the perception that the region was considered 'uninhabitable', as there were no 'reassuring social and psychological boundaries of traditional societies'.[335]

Public authorities entrenched the power of the plantocracy, because their sole function was to perpetuate the plantation system, which included regulation of life and work on the estates, and to ensure above all else that the enslaved population never challenged the status quo.[336] Legislation could not maximise profitability of plantation production and ensure the welfare of plantation labour at the same time.[337] It was thus antithetical to the survival of the slave colonies for legislation to recognise the humanity of the slaves. 'The common law of England is the common law of the plantations,' wrote the Admiralty's legal counsel, Richard West, in 1720.[338]

Political scientist George Beckford has examined the power dynamics of Caribbean plantations, noting that in all societies, the distribution of real political power echoes the patterns of distribution of economic and social power.[339] Popular participation was limited when political power was monopolised by the planter, because his authority was the only unifying element on the plantation.[340] The planter class was based on white supremacy, which was characterised by extreme individualism and a lack of social responsibility, resulting in an undemocratic social structure.[341] Plantation economies are stunted because these societies were strictly for exploitation.[342] It was in the plantocracy's interest to keep the slave population from forming any semblance of a civilised society.[343] Rigid control of the labour supply was essential and involved control over movement of slaves in space and status – illiteracy was thus strictly enforced because it was believed that education would encourage insurrection.[344] It was easier to con-

---

333 Brion Davis 115.
334 Hicks 43-44.
335 Brion Davis 115.
336 Beckford 40.
337 Ibid.
338 Richard West, 'On English Common and Statute Law in Settled Colonies,' June 1720, in Frederick Madden and David Fieldhouse(eds), *Select Documents on the Constitutional History of the British Empire and Commonwealth*, 4 vols. (Westport, Conn, 1985), 2:192, as cited in Eliga Gould, 'Zones of Law, Zones of Violence: The Legal Geography of the British Atlantic, circa 1772.' *The William and Mary Quarterly* 60(3) (July 2003): 471-510, 497.
339 Beckford 79.
340 Ibid, 76.
341 Ibid, 208-209.
342 Ibid, 210.
343 Ibid, 77.
344 Ibid, 64.

trol people who are brought into a strange environment than a resident population. Child labour was used when slave labour became too expensive, and only then were large families encouraged.[345] As a source of labour supply for plantations, enslaved and indentured labour created new societies descended from these trafficked and transplanted peoples, influenced by the plantation's requirements that determined the racial and sex composition of the population, the social structure and social organisation.[346]

Slavery demanded violence, and colonial societies were shaped by rebellions and the impact of runaway slaves.[347] This was due to the increased supply of enslaved Africans, which outnumbered Europeans on the islands, making them rely on increasingly inhumane means to maintain control of their plantations and slave societies.[348] Slaves were herded together as an undifferentiated mass in compounds of a village character. As slaves came from different cultures, a lingua franca was necessary to facilitate chain of command, and creoles were born as African language speakers adopted the English language.[349] Plantation culture was built around production of the crop, and this is the chief bond governing interaction between the enslaved labourers.[350] The only skills acquired and disseminated were generally related to the requirements of plantation production, and so considerable technical knowledge was amassed but in relation to one crop only.[351] Common cultural features in the Caribbean related to similar peasant crops, production techniques and marketing arrangements; cuisine, music and dance, folklore, religious cults and a series of traditions, attitudes and beliefs derived from the common experiences of enslaved ancestors and the pervasive influence of the plantation at the centre of their existence.[352]

While it is important to note that varying degrees of agency can be ascribed to the enslaved population, who challenged the plantation power dynamic throughout the period of slavery, there were near insurmountable obstacles to the development of a strong and well-defined local community in the Caribbean as the result of colonialism and the plantation system.[353] The decimation of Amerindians in the region (socially and politically) precluded any possible aboriginal basis for local community life, and the transferred population of enslaved Africans from diverse tribes and nations were unable under conditions of slavery to form sustainable communities.[354] Plantations monopolised land, which was not efficiently utilised yet the general labour force was prevented from accessing fertile land.[355] The enslaved Africans were allowed to practice subsistence cultivation on unwanted backlands only during periods when their

---

345   Ibid, 59.
346   Ibid, 37.
347   Gibson 120.
348   Ibid.
349   Beckford 63.
350   Ibid.
351   Ibid, 207.
352   Beckford 18. On the environmental legacy of plantations and foodways, see also Sarah Oas and Mark Hauser, 'The Political Ecology of Plantations from the Ground Up.' *Environmental Archaeology* 23(1) (2018): 4-12.
353   Hauser and Hicks 258 and Charles Wagley, 'Recent Studies of Caribbean Local Societies' in Curtis Wilgus (ed), *The Caribbean: Natural Resources* (Gainesville 1961) 199 as cited in Beckford *Persistent Poverty* 77.
354   Beckford 77.
355   Ibid.

labour was not required for the plantation crop.[356] This 'proto-peasantry' developed on islands with mountainous interiors, such as Jamaica, and the Windward islands such as St Vincent and the Grenadines, Saint Lucia, Dominica and Grenada.[357] The low productivity of the peasantry following abolition and emancipation was due to limited access to fertile land and capital.[358] A sharecropper system was developed following emancipation to secure the labour of ex-slaves. However, as noted by Beckford, it did not provide any firm guarantee to the sharecropper of his rights of possession, security of tenure, or a clear claim to a share of the crop.[359]

The Royal Commission noted that the labour intensive practices of sugar monoculture rendered a large number of people unfit for any other form of agriculture, since there were no transferable skills, knowledge and habits for sustainable land management.[360] This can be traced directly to the effect of environmental change on the insular Caribbean, which has been overwhelmingly negative and is unique.[361] Tropical habitats were misunderstood and poorly managed, and had little chance to recover from the intensity of plantation agriculture, such was the scale and speed of colonisation that encouraged both ecological dislocation and general environmental instability in the quest for profit.[362]

The societies that were created to support plantation economies were also unique. Beckford observes that within plantation society, tradition, values, beliefs and attitudes are shaped by paternalism and indifference to development.[363] Studies on plantation agriculture in the Caribbean and Latin America have observed that people reject nature as a viable partner, reject innovation, co-operation and long-range planning.[364] Indeed, Olwig has observed that when the natural heritage is shaped by brutal subjugation of both man and nature, it is very difficult to mobilise as a common source of identity, especially where there is no ancient class of farmers, rooted in the land, upon which to build that national identity.[365] This is the legacy of colonial exploitation, which severs people from landscape.

---

356 Ibid, 90.
357 Jean Besson, 'History, Culture and Land in the English-speaking Caribbean' in Allan Williams (ed), *Proceedings of the Conference on Land in the Caribbean: Policy, Administration and Management in the English-speaking Caribbean* (Land Tenure Centre, University of Wisconsin-Madison 2003) 31-60.
358 Beckford 180.
359 Ibid, 91.
360 Watts 516.
361 Ibid, 533.
362 Ibid, 536.
363 Beckford 206. Recent scholarship does suggest however, that the plantation space was decidedly more complex. When enslaved populations contested in both subtle and express ways prescribed uses of the landscape, which was in effect challenging planter control of plantation space, the plantationscape would respond to local circumstances as well as global influences. See Mark Hauser, 'The Infrastructure of Nature's Island: Settlements, Networks and Economy of Two Plantations in Colonial Dominica.' *International Journal of Historical Archaeology* 19 (3) (2015): 601-622; Hauser and Armstrong, 'The Archaeology of Not Being Governed'; Marshall (ed), *Archaeology of Slavery: Toward A Comparative Global Framework.*
364 Harry Hutchinson, 'Value Orientations and Northeast Brazilian Agro-Industrial Modernization', *Inter-American Economic Affairs (*Spring 1968) 88, as cited in Beckford 207.
365 Kenneth Olwig, 'Introduction: The Nature of Cultural Heritage and the Culture of Natural Heritage – Northern Perspectives on a Contested Patrimony.' *International Journal of Heritage Studies* 11(1) (2005): 3-7, 6.

2.2.4 Early Legal Intervention in the Protection of Caribbean Heritage

The cultural dimensions of ecological change have implications for the content and effectiveness of heritage law.[366] The British Empire, as an ecological regime radiating into domestic and colonial nature, sought to annihilate the local, and to include all people and territory in a single total system.[367] Thus the earliest legal interventions relevant to protecting heritage concern property law and environmental law, through the creation of reserves for the purposes of imperial ecology and botany.[368]

These practices reflect a 'dephysicalised'[369] concept of property.[370] Property law creates unsustainable people-place relations in such a way as to obscure its own effects, blind to the environmental and social chaos it instigated.[371] Because property law emphasises a right over a thing, it bases its legitimacy in power rather than place. The individual landowner has possession, power over the land. This may be contrasted with a custodian of the land, who belongs to the communal landscape. This custodial relationship is reversed when landscape becomes enclosed as private property.[372] If place is irrelevant to property, then property law can be seen as responsible for promoting a lack of care for place,[373] since it can erase land's specificities, the essence of landscape,[374] and, as noted earlier, the basis for a people's common identity or heritage.

Plantation agriculture in the Caribbean slave colonies resulted in a complete restructuring of the land and removal of native peoples, the importation of West Africans as slave labour, and the manipulation of natural resources in such a manner as to maintain the planter/slave power dynamic.[375] All land suitable for sugar cane was deforested, and in some cases this meant that the entire island was reduced to sugar cultivation.[376] Capital-intensive plantation agriculture that was based on slave labour

---

366 James Beattie, Edward Melillo, and Emily O'Gorman, 'Introduction: Eco-Cultural Networks and the British Empire, 1837-1945' in James Beattie, Edward Melillo, and Emily O'Gorman (eds), *Eco-Cultural Networks and the British Empire: New Views on Environmental History* (Bloomsbury Academic 2015) 8.

367 Richard Drayton, 'Imperial Science and a Scientific Empire: Kew Gardens and the Uses of Nature, 1772-1903'. PhD diss., Yale University, 1993, at 442.

368 Grove, *Green Imperialism*, and Drayton, *Nature's Government* address this topic.

369 Bartel and Graham, 'Property and Place Attachment' 272-273:
Legal discourse refers to property as dephysicalised because it succinctly describes and explains the oxymoron at the heart of modern property law – that it is not about land. Previously known as 'land law', modern property law no longer regulates the relationship between people and land; rather, it prescribes legal relationships between 'persons' with regard to their competing and relative 'interests' in various 'objects' using the language of 'rights'…Accordingly, land law became referred to increasingly as 'property law' because property can be, and is, about rights over any object, real things like land, or abstract things like shares – it does not matter. The point is that property law is not about any specific thing; rather, it is about legal rights in and of themselves.

370 Graham 133 and at 24: property originally linked people and place. What was proper to a person were the physical qualities so closely associated with that person that he could be identified with them. Today the secondary meaning is significant only in the scientific world e.g. what are the properties of hydrogen. The primary meaning pertains to abstract relations between people, rather than with or over physical things. Today the dominant feature of property is alienability not identity.

371 Ibid, xi.
372 Ibid, 205.
373 Ibid.
374 Ibid, 67.
375 Beinart and Hughes 37.
376 See also Watts.

promoted very rapid environmental change in terms of deforestation, soil erosion, flooding, gullying, local aridification and drying up of streams and rivers.[377] Empirical observations of the catastrophic effects of colonial plantation agriculture made it clear that plantation policies were causing environmental damage.[378]

Watts summarises that at the end of the plantation agriculture period (1665-1833) in the English-speaking Caribbean, the lowland environment had been deforested, depleted in nutrients and invaded by alien species.[379] This has profound effects on cultural evolution, which was guided by these alterations imposed on the environment, and by external economic and social pressure.[380] Sugarcane estates brought immense wealth to England and France, but this was only achieved at overwhelming cost to the Caribbean landscape.[381] The industry required new technology and structures in the form of mills and transport such as rail and shipping and associated port infrastructure. Deforestation, soil loss and decline in soil quality changed animal and plant communities forever.[382] The extreme land use and patterns of timber clearance made species recovery all but impossible, since their native habitats were being transformed into sugar plantations.[383] Watts notes that while a Caribbean-wide trend, these consequences dominated the ecosystems in the Lesser Antilles, where space for species survival was restricted, and cane agriculture at its most intense.[384]

Under the Peace of Paris, the constituent territories of the Grenada Governorate (Grenada, Dominica, St Vincent and the Grenadines, and Tobago), were ceded to Britain by France at the end of the Seven Years' War. The strategy for the Grenada Governorate involved rapid development of sugar plantations, which required deforestation and major allocation of land and transfer of ownership.[385] In Tobago, woodlands were to be preserved for the repair of fortifications and buildings, and to prevent drought from deforestation.[386] Soame Jenyns, writer and political commenter, believed that the forests on the ceded islands should be protected to enhance economic yields. Climate change was seen as a major threat to colonial economic projects.[387] Therefore the idea of improving the colonial landscape as he had done on his estate near Cambridge was very appealing.[388] One of the reasons deforestation was such a priority was the ecological and resource crisis experienced in nearby Barbados at the time of the signing of the Peace of Paris.[389]

By the mid-eighteenth century, over fishing and major reductions in catches were occurring around these increasingly populated islands. New conservation legislation

---

377 Richard Grove, 'The Island and the History of Environmentalism' in Mikuláš Teich, Roy Porter, and Bo Gustafsson (eds), *Nature and Society in Historical Context* (Cambridge University Press 1997) 150.
378 Grove, *Nature and Society* 153-154.
379 Watts 443.
380 Ibid.
381 Ibid, 447.
382 Ibid, 438.
383 Ibid.
384 Ibid, 447.
385 Grove, *Green Imperialism* 269.
386 Ibid, 271.
387 Ibid, 276.
388 Ibid.
389 Ibid.

was developed as a key instrument of colonial landscape control.[390] Before the 1760s, the effects of colonial economic globalisation were addressed on a piecemeal basis in order to protect local food, fuel, timber supplies, and what were already recognised as rare island species. However, in the mid-1760s, legal responses to deforestation in particular were influenced by Pierre Poivre's theory, linking deforestation to rainfall and regional climate change.[391] By the next century, new forest-reserve legislation responding to fears of deforestation-induced climate change could be found throughout the French, British, and Dutch empires.[392]

As early as 1764, a system of forest reserves and environmental legislation was set up in the ceded islands of St Vincent and Tobago. The relevant legislation addressing local climate change included the Grenada Governorate Ordinance of March 1764, the Barbados Land Ordinance of 1765 and the St. Vincent King's Hill Forest Act of 1791.[393] This led to resistance by the Kalinago[394] in certain islands, as the links between colonial forest control and control of indigenous peoples were firmly established. This was sanctioned by international law, which justified this oppression as a side effect of sovereignty.[395]

In the English-speaking Caribbean, The King's Hill Act constituted one of the earliest attempts at forest protection legislation in the English-speaking world based on climatic theory.[396] King's Hill bridged the gap between French physiocratic conservationism as developed on Mauritius by Pierre Poivre and evolution of a British colonial environmentalism.[397] The Act is an example of desiccation-based forest legislation, desiccationism being the prevailing theory that was developed in 1790, following observations that forest destruction could be connected to rainfall change, which led to an interest in tree-planting and afforestation.[398] Nevertheless, Richard Grove points out that the choice of St Vincent was expert-driven: the colony did not receive legislation because of its local conditions but because its island geography was deemed suitable for the imported technological assumptions of the available experts.[399] Desiccation-based forest legislation was attractive to Vincentian colonists because of concerns about supplies of ship timber, a problem prevailing throughout the empire at the time.[400]

Grove highlights that colonial conservation in the Eastern Caribbean was more about constructing a new landscape, since uncultivated forests represented wildness and lawlessness, and less about preservation of the primeval forests.[401] It was about claiming and consolidating territory, organising economic space, and subduing unruly peoples, and the creation of forest reservations was often followed by the forced resettlement of

---

390 See Vinita Damodaran, 'Environment and Empire: A Major Theme in Environmental History' in Mary Harris and Csaba Lévai (eds), *Europe and its Empires* (Plus-Pisa University Press 2008) 129-139 at 134.
391 Ibid.
392 Ibid.
393 Grove, *Green Imperialism* 266.
394 Historically referred to as the Caribs, which can be considered derogatory. See also John Angus Martin, *Island Caribs and French Settlers in Grenada 1498-1763* (Grenada National Museum Press 2013).
395 Grove, *Green Imperialism* 266.
396 Grove, *Nature and Society* 160.
397 Ibid, 161.
398 Ibid, 149.
399 Ibid, 157.
400 Ibid, 155.
401 Grove, *Green Imperialism* 280.

peoples, starvation and famine.[402] Conservation therefore involved the biological reconstruction of the forest environment to serve the interests of the Empire.[403] Law effected the transition from the Amerindian landscape to the imperial one, the creation of parks and reserves a typical feature identified by Kenneth Olwig following virtual enclosure and alienation.[404] 'A cultural confrontation between a land hungry colonial state and an indigenous culture' was inevitable once the state had developed a legal system that conferred annexation rights on those who cleared forests and cultivated land.[405]

Initially, the Kalinago of St Vincent did not accept the concept of private property implicit in the proposals laid out by the British,[406] as only those practicing settled agriculture could be considered legally entitled to claim sovereign rights over land. This land use ideology justified the expropriation and colonisation of native lands, since the Kalinago were semi-nomadic,[407] and believed in a common or clan perception of landscape.[408] In the parceling of land to planters, town dwellers, poor whites and slaves, no provision was therefore made for the indigenous Kalinago. Large tracts of land were designated forest reserves. As Grove notes, mapmaking took on an oppressive quality, for what was omitted was as important and what was represented: cartographically the Kalinago were excluded, and within twenty years ceased to exist as a separate population.[409]

Law's conservationist interventions were profoundly influenced by the eco-imperialist ambitions it served.[410] It is an exclusionary sort of conservation that preserves some threatened species, not the relationship between the natural resources and the needs of the local population.[411] The earliest environmental legislation in the English-speaking Caribbean developed forest and botanical reserves to support priorities of the British Empire. It had no local legitimacy.[412] Indeed, by the 1800s, the creation of colonial botanic gardens had become standard practice in the consolidation of new conquests of the British Empire.[413] The significance of this network of gardens lies in the fact that they were not simply clearing-houses for the transfer of economic crops, but the bases from which wide-ranging collecting missions were dispatched into surrounding territory.[414] Such botanical and scientific knowledge was necessary for maintaining imperial interests. Environmental watchwords, such as climate, deforestation and health were used to explain away the economic or political causality of

---

402 Ibid.
403 Ibid.
404 Olwig, 'Representation and Alienation' 35. See also Karen Fog Olwig and Kenneth Olwig, 'Underdevelopment and the Development of "Natural" Park Ideology.' *Antipode: A Radical Journal of Geography* Vol. II, no. 2(1979): 16-25.
405 Grove, *Green Imperialism* 265.
406 Ibid, 285.
407 Ibid, 286.
408 Ibid, 291.
409 Ibid, 283.
410 Beinart and Hughes 289.
411 Ibid.
412 Ibid.
413 Drayton, 'Imperial Science and a Scientific Empire' 151.
414 Ibid, 153.

imperialism even as laws established reserves to facilitate imperial expansion.[415] The masking of the landscape was therefore facilitated by the framework of these early conservation laws, supported by mapmaking, surveying and reserving techniques to enable implementation.

In colonising space in the Caribbean, the environment was socially constructed so that the 'tropics were invented as much as they were encountered'; the idea of the tropics as 'warm, fecund, luxuriant, paradisiacal and pestilential' was central to the constitution of British colonial knowledge and was a critical ingredient in the larger colonising process.[416] But this visualisation masked the violence and degradation of both people and land. The perception of oceanic islands as highly desirable 'Edenic' locations in European cultural traditions only served to highlight the shock of their rapid degradation, which had destabilising consequences for the transit of company ships relying on their watering and supply station roles. These were the circumstances in which the colonial governments of many small islands became environmentalist, if only to ensure their own survival.[417]

Colonial ideologies of improvement stressed the appropriation of lands from local residents and the transformation of imperial environments into sources of economic and moral value, and private property regimes conferred ownership rights to advance these objectives.[418] Colonial authorities facilitated the orderly exploitation and management of the environment through regulatory intervention, as the colonial state by definition and practice was designed to serve economic and political ends that were often at odds with the long-term interests of the colonised.[419] The legacy of colonial resource management policies continues today. When colonies obtained 'flag' independence, the environment they inherited was already severely damaged from years of exploitation by colonial administration.[420] The capacity of post-colonial states to internalise and enforce environmental norms is hobbled by the colonial ideology and its attendant administrative apparatus.

Humans modify their environments and 'grow in both understanding and misunderstanding of the natural world.'[421] This misunderstanding of nature is at the heart of the Caribbean understanding of the past, and manifests in continued inappropriate centralised government decision-making, and frequent reliance on cumbersome authoritarian modes of regulation that together disenfranchise communities closest to nature.[422] These practices were played out in the earliest types of conservation legislation drafted for the region. This conservation legislation conserved the 'plantationscape', in which the Caribbean landscape had been rearranged as scenery, in no small measure due to the use of topographic sur-

---

415 Georgina Endfield and Samuel Randalls, 'Climate and Empire' in Beattie, Melillo, and O'Gorman (eds) *Eco-Cultural Networks* 21-44, 25.
416 Damodaran 137.
417 Ibid, 131.
418 Beattie, Melillo, and O'Gorman, 'Introduction: Eco-Cultural Networks and the British Empire' in Beattie, Melillo, and O'Gorman (eds), *Eco-Cultural Networks and the British Empire* 3-21, 9.
419 Benjamin Richardson, Ikechi Mgbeoji, and Francis Botchway, 'Environmental Law in Post-colonial Societies: Aspirations, Achievements and Limitations' in Benjamin Richardson and Stephan Wood (eds), *Environmental Law for Sustainability* (Hart Publishing 2006) 413-443, 415.
420 Ibid.
421 John MacKenzie, 'Foreword' in Beattie, Melillo, and O'Gorman (eds) *Eco-Cultural Networks*, xv.
422 Richardson et al 'Environmental Law in Post-colonial Societies' 416.

veys, to re-envision and control the environment. The 'images and the processes involved in renaming, landmarking and resource assessment [led] to the establishment of colonial boundaries and colonial order' and allowed explorers, surveyors and cartographers to shape the way the Caribbean was visualised and interpreted.[423]

As land was treated as space rather than place, property law and environmental law were not rooted in the needs and capacities of these environments, and a lack of understanding of these ecosystems quickly led to their decline. Monoculture plantations faced collapse as a result of unsustainable patterns of resource exploitation. Plantation agriculture depleted soil nutrients and deforestation, causing erosion, and led to the calling for new practices and regulations.[424] The production of knowledge about environments coincided with their exploitation under imperial regimes. It was no wonder that the first forays into legislative protection of the natural heritage coincided with the erasure of cultural heritage – these laws wrote native peoples out of existence, erasing their identity, contributions and culture from the landscape, as well as dehumanising enslaved African labour so that no new communities could arise. This completed the creation of the imperial landscape, from which it is difficult to build a new narrative that interweaves cultural identity, ecological integrity and justice.[425]

2.3 Landscape and Spatial Justice

Landscape integrates environmental and cultural values and accommodates diverse non-proprietary interests in land besides private property and ownership.[426] These interests represent a multiplicity of spatial definitions, as people use space according to their own interpretations, layered experiences that give rise to cultural practices passed on from one generation to the next.[427] Spatial injustice can be created by reducing landscapes to abstract space such as private property, as was the case in the Caribbean, where the common or clan perception of landscape of the semi-nomadic Kalinago peoples was converted by the British to private property, resulting in the expulsion of these inhabitants from their homes and their access to these resources withdrawn.[428] This imperial landscape is thus both a defined geographic place and an intangible space in which a uniform meaning is imposed.

Space is a result of the struggle between different spatial definitions that co-exist and challenge one another. When more than one body seeks to occupy the same space at the same time, 'a conflict of bodies that will never be sated' occurs.[429] A way to negotiate this conflict is through a 'permanent state of oscillation', where the parties with their

---

423 Damodaran 135.
424 Beattie, Melillo, and O'Gorman, 'Introduction: Eco-Cultural Networks and the British Empire' in Beattie, Melillo, and O'Gorman (eds), *Eco-Cultural Networks and the British Empire* 3-21, 15.
425 Ferdinand 187.
426 Strecker 189.
427 Herzfeld 128 and 145.
428 Grove, *Green Imperialism* 282, 285-286, and 291.
429 Andreas Philippopoulos-Mihalopoulos, 'Geography, Justice and a Certain Fear of Space.' *Law, Culture and the Humanities* 7(2) (2011): 187-202, 199.

individual legitimate claims alternate in taking possession of the space and retreating from that claim.[430] Spatial justice thus 'demands a radical gesture of withdrawal'.[431]

The virtual enclosure found in the Caribbean colonies required a social and cultural evacuation of space in order to serve imperial interests, which was supported by a legal framework.[432] This is known as 'spatial cleansing', or the conceptual and physical clarification of boundaries, with a concomitant definition of former residents as intruders.[433] The move toward formal mapping of properties gave this legal weight, so that relationships defined in alternative terms were replaced by abstract description, enumeration and measurement.[434] Spatial cleansing ensures harmony between an imperial ideology and the physical environment.[435] The implications for heritage are profound, because with the extinguishing of communities and society at large, came the imperial narrative, which absorbed both native and enslaved populations, their memories, practices and identities.

By restricting access to space, legal frameworks can reform landscapes.[436] Through a focus on public safety and order, early colonial laws essentially bequeathed spatial privilege to the planter class – those who would enjoy full access to and benefits of private space through their economic standing. Simultaneously, loss of access and rights to space coincided with the denial of the humanity of the enslaved Africans. Thus, 'public space' becomes exclusionary rather than a common ground for all persons, and the landscapes of public spaces are to some degree 'cleansed' of social difference.[437]

Spatial complexity and recognition of place specificity alongside historical contexts can thus be important to the realisation of justice.[438] Deploying the spatial justice lens allows us to view conflicts over common resources not merely as challenges to government authority but 'as expressions of 'place protective' behavior, which arise through strong place attachment and locally specific views on how places should change (or not) over time.'[439] Herzfeld notes that belonging is couched in spatial terms, and local knowledge, rooted in lived experience, is resistant to the imperious claims of universalism and abstraction.[440] Resistance is therefore also spatial. 'People use space according to their own understandings, rather than by following the prescriptions of protocol, and the resulting configuration is almost always a palimpsest representing the many phases of struggle that is rarely conclusive in its results and that also rarely comes to a clearly defined end.'[441]

This means that the boundaries of place itself are subject to social negotiation, potentially disrupting the 'geographical complacency' that characterises the industrialised world, specifically our built environments and their natural settings.[442] This geographical complacency is a product of the colonial era, and a feature of the imperial landscape.

---

430 Philippopoulos-Mihalopoulos, 'Law's Spatial Turn', 201.
431 Philippopoulos-Mihalopoulos, 'Spatial Justice: Law and the Geography of Withdrawal.' *International Journal of Law in Context* 6 (3) (2010): 201-216, 202 and see Bengsten 81.
432 Herzfeld 132.
433 Ibid, 142.
434 Ibid.
435 Ibid, 129.
436 Bengtsen 90.
437 Martin and Scherr, 'Lawyering Landscapes' 380-381.
438 Dahlberg 220.
439 Bartel and Graham 276.
440 Herzfeld 129.
441 Ibid, 145.
442 Ibid, 129.

2.4 Conclusion

In this chapter, landscape's origins were explored, as were the historical developments that undermined customary law and reduced landscape to scene, space, property and ossified tradition or heritage. Transforming customary rights into common law private property rights through the erection of boundaries and fences changed the British landscape physically, and severed local communities culturally, as the exclusion of commoners led to the creation of the landless poor, who flooded urban centres. The subsequent rise in vagrancy saw increasing numbers transported to the New World. Law no longer protected the diverse rights and obligations of various and specific interests in particular localised resources; instead it protected the standardised rights and wealth of the private realm, independent of location.[443] This gave rise to the imperial landscape and was subsequently extended into the New World.

Britain's ability to manipulate indigenous polities and customs was a vital component of its growing dominance over the Atlantic. The philosophy of imperialism required a new set of structures, mechanisms and laws. Using these instruments and techniques, Caribbean ecosystems were completely reconfigured under colonialism, characterised by a total rearrangement of societies, demographics and the environment. The Caribbean landscape as plantation was spatially removed from its Amerindian origins and the very origins of landscape itself. Alienation of its inhabitants was extreme. Amerindian populations were removed, deported, killed, and expunged from the legal record, their 'savagery' excluding any consideration as civilised peoples and their management of land at odds with English property law. When enslaved Africans, who were alienated from their own landscapes, were introduced as foreigners to this new region, they lost their human qualities due to their race, and became 'things', dehumanised chattel appurtenant to the land, moveable property to be inherited and sold as the contents of an estate, with no way of life and no recognised attachment to the land. The slave was subject not only to an individual owner's will, but to the claims of creditors, heirs, other family members, and the state.[444]

What does this mean for identity, for history and collective memory, and ultimately Caribbean heritage? The British working class was able to lobby for a restoration, in a limited sense, of their access rights, in the form of the Countryside Act. But former slaves were unable to appeal to a way of life prior to the plantation system that they were born or introduced to, as they were denied a cultural heritage. Their status as chattel precluded their recognition as a people and polity with a relationship to the land. The consequences of plantation agriculture in the Caribbean further entrenched a system that is contextualised not by the environment but by the exploitation of that environment as 'improvement'. Where conservation was practised, it was to serve the imperial mission, not local needs. Knowledge of plants was needed to strengthen colonial botany, and maintain plantation agriculture. Spatial cleansing narratives entrenched the idea of evacuating space of social and cultural differences, and creating exclusive spaces for the elite.

---

443 Graham 60.
444 See Walter Johnson (ed), *The Chattel Principle: Internal Slave Trades in the Americas* (Yale University Press 2005).

This presents a challenge for law when a state's existence is premised on maintaining a divide between the land and its people. Repairing that divide requires the revelation of these hidden relationships with the land, to explore the ways in which historic patterns undermined management of heritage resources, and to empower communities to challenge this dynamic. Landscape in its substantive, political sense challenges imperial power, because it reflects the interests of its inhabitants, not the empire.[445] Law, especially property law, has been a strategic ordering device for imperialism, inspired by the pictorial and graphic techniques rediscovered during the Renaissance. Contested landscapes are about spatial justice, because landscape not only embodies the social and natural world, but how we position ourselves relative to the world. Nowhere is this clearer than in the postcolonial Caribbean landscape, where the physical environment is a reflection of the political landscape, bolstered by legally prescribed land uses, which implicate law in the destruction of landscape.

It is this legacy that heritage law must confront because protecting heritage in a sustainable manner requires protecting the place from which it is derived. How the legal framework for heritage protection addresses this challenge is discussed in the next chapter, beginning with the role of international law in landscape protection vis-à-vis nation states, and then focusing on domestic legislation in the Lesser Antilles in the chapters that follow.

---

445 Mitchell, 'Just Landscapes or Landscapes of Justice?' 788.

3

Landscape in International Law

3.1 Introduction

This chapter surveys the evolution of landscape protection via three main spheres of international law: international cultural heritage law, international environmental law, and international human rights law. Landscape first emerged in soft law instruments, becoming a cross-cutting concept of these three areas of law, and finally a distinct body of law in its own right.[446] In so doing, landscape demonstrates the potential of international law to shed its imperialist origins to buttress landscape in its entirety, not as an aesthetic backdrop to human activity but a place embodying the diverse relationships communities have with land.[447] This is due to a number of underlying factors: heritage assuming a more holistic definition to embrace anthropological aspects beyond individual artefacts, thereby considering culture as a way of life for communities; heritage law becoming more human-rights focused; and the influence of sustainable development on the management and preservation of natural resources for future generations (and the continuation of their communities).

This has particular relevance for the post-colonial states in the Lesser Antilles, which are parties to most of the international treaties discussed herein, so this overview considers the implications of these trends and developments in landscape from this perspective. The focus on international and regional law in this chapter reveals the partial transformation of international law from instrument of empire to perceived catalyst for change in relation to human rights, cultural heritage and the environment.

The most recent demonstration of international law's attempt to empower local communities can be seen in the plurilateral responses to landscape. These have contributed to the crystallisation of a nascent landscape law, namely through the European Landscape Convention and other initiatives discussed below. Regional arrangements are significant to the Caribbean post-colonial small island developing states (SIDS), which have created co-operative institutional frameworks for addressing development

---

[446] The definitive text relied on in this chapter is Amy Strecker's *Landscape Protection in International Law* (Oxford University Press 2018), which analysed the role of international and European law in the protection of landscape, mainly as expressed in cultural heritage law, environmental law and human rights.

[447] Amy Strecker, 'Landscape as Cultural Heritage' in Francesco Francioni and Ana Vrodljak (eds), *Oxford Handbook on International Cultural Heritage Law* (Oxford University Press 2020), 272-294, 272.

issues common to the region. The potential for a Caribbean approach to landscape using existing regional fora as a springboard is examined by analysing regional and sub-regional instruments such as the Escazú Agreement and the St George's Declaration to the Revised Treaty of Basseterre, the constituent treaty of the Organisation of Eastern Caribbean States (OECS), to which most of the Lesser Antillean states belong.[448]

3.2 Protection of Landscape in International Law

3.2.1 Soft Law

Landscape's entry into international law is via the soft law instruments promulgated by UNESCO and the Council of Europe in the 1960s. The UNESCO Recommendation concerning the Safeguarding of the Beauty and Character of Landscapes and Sites of 1962[449] highlighted the aesthetic beauty of the landscape as its defining feature and worthy of protection. As Amy Strecker has noted, the Recommendation introduced a number of cornerstone concepts characteristic of the traditional approach to landscape:

> *Terms such as 'virgin land' and 'dangers which threaten them' reflect the concern within the Recommendation of the acceleration of modern society and the effects of industrial and commercial development, but also of the misconception that landscape is predominantly a 'natural' construct, somehow external to human interaction.*[450]

The remaking of landscape into the pastoral ideal was addressed in Chapter Two, and the influence of this philosophy on cultural heritage law is discussed later in this chapter. In 1968, UNESCO adopted the Recommendation concerning the Preservation of Cultural Property Endangered by Public or Private Works.[451] With respect to landscape, cultural property was defined to include immovable heritage such as archaeological and historic or scientific sites, as well as their 'setting'.[452] The Recommendation outlined the general principles for the preventive and corrective measures aimed at protecting cultural property from public or private works likely to damage or destroy it, including the 'construction and alteration of highways which are a particular danger to sites or to historically important structures or groups of structures',[453] the 'construction of dams for irrigation,'[454] pipelines,[455] farming operations and afforestation.[456] As Strecker writes, the Recommendation promotes an innovative mechanism, the impact

---

448 Barbados and Trinidad and Tobago are not members.
449 UNESCO Recommendation concerning the Safeguarding of the Beauty and Character of Landscapes and Sites, adopted on 11 December 1962.
450 Strecker, 'Landscape as Cultural Heritage' 274; Art 1, UNESCO Recommendation concerning the Safeguarding of the Beauty and Character of Landscapes and Sites.
451 UNESCO Recommendation concerning the Preservation of Cultural Property Endangered by Public or Private Works, adopted on 19 November 1968.
452 Art 1(a).
453 Art 8(d).
454 Art 8(e).
455 Art 8(f).
456 Art 8(h).

assessment, when it called for the conduct of surveys prior to any public or private works.[457] The Recommendation notably identifies in situ preservation of cultural property endangered by public or private works as critical 'in order to preserve historical association and continuity'.[458]

The 1976 UNESCO recommendation concerning the Safeguarding and Contemporary Role of Historic Areas,[459] does not explicitly refer to landscape,[460] but emphasises the importance of historic areas in its preamble for the 'daily environment of human beings everywhere' which 'represent the living presence of the past which formed them,' [...] 'provide the variety in life's background needed to match the diversity of society, and that by doing so they gain in value and acquire an additional human dimension'.[461] As Strecker notes, this continues the theme underlying landscape in soft law that human interaction is secondary to the site's aesthetic value, hence the focus on preservationist and restorative measures.[462] There is little by way of participation and human rights concerns, but it is noted that plans to protect such areas should not disrupt 'the social fabric' and the poorest inhabitants should be compensated so that they can maintain their 'traditional living patterns and occupations, especially rural crafts, small-scale agriculture, fishing etc.'[463] Ultimately, this is meant to preserve the area as is, a backdrop to human existence. However, as Strecker writes, the 1976 Recommendation did advance the role of local, regional and national planning, as well as the responsibilities of citizens in landscape protection, and Article 13 in particular established the obligation to provide 'machinery for appeal against arbitrary or unjust decisions.'[464]

The Recommendation concerning the Protection, at National level, of the Cultural and Natural Heritage (1972) adopted by UNESCO at its seventeenth session to complement the World Heritage Convention, marked a departure in the development of the law by noting that 'the cultural and natural heritage forms an harmonious whole, the components of which are indissociable'.[465] This is the first time that the cultural dimensions are not divorced from the environment. In addition, the Recommendation recognised that the cultural and natural heritage should not be restricted to the monumental and iconic, and include vernacular facets of the heritage as well: 'cultural and natural heritage should be considered in its entirety as a homogenous whole, comprising not only works of great intrinsic value, but also more modest items.'[466] This is a retreat from the view that purely aesthetic aspects of the heritage are worthy of

---

457 Art 22. See also Strecker, 'Landscape as Cultural Heritage' 274.
458 Art 9.
459 Adopted on 26 November 1976.
460 Article 1(a) states that 'Historic [...] areas shall be taken to mean any groups of buildings, structures and open spaces including archaeological and paleontological sites, constituting human settlements in an urban or rural environment, the cohesion and value of which, from the archaeological, architectural, prehistoric, historic, aesthetic or socio-cultural point of view are recognized'.
461 See Preamble, Recommendation concerning the Safeguarding and Contemporary Role of Historic Areas.
462 Strecker, 'Landscape as Cultural Heritage' 275.
463 Art 46, Recommendation concerning the Safeguarding and Contemporary Role of Historic Areas.
464 Strecker, 'Landscape as Cultural Heritage' 275.
465 Preamble, Recommendation concerning the Protection, at National Level, of the Cultural and Natural Heritage, adopted on 16 November 1972.
466 Art 5, 1972 Recommendation, and see Strecker, 'Landscape as Cultural Heritage' 275.

protection. The duty to preserve cultural and natural heritage in order to hand it down to future generations incorporates considerations of sustainability in the protection of heritage, as this inter-generational component is a principle of the sustainable development approach.[467]

While ambitious in scope, the Recommendation nevertheless promotes measures that refer only to natural, not cultural, heritage, and they are in fact defined and categorised separately.[468] The text states that 'member states should develop short and long range plans, based on inventories of their natural heritage, to achieve a system of conservation to meet the needs of their countries'.[469] No mention is made of culture in the article on planning, reflecting the underlying perception observed by Olwig that rural landscapes had been reframed as pristine natural environments, devoid of manmade influence, the original wilderness.[470] This dichotomy was to be embedded in the World Heritage Convention.

3.2.2 Landscape in Cultural Heritage Law

The recognition of the value of cultural heritage to all of mankind was given prominent attention in the World Heritage Convention (WHC).[471] The WHC was conceived as a platform for the identification, recognition and protection of heritage with outstanding universal value. The States parties have the opportunity to submit an inventory of the most valuable cultural and natural property situated in their territories to the World Heritage Committee (the Committee). If the Committee recognises that the property has outstanding universal value, it adds it to the 'World Heritage List' (the List) and where that site is threatened, may include it on the 'List of World Heritage in Danger'.[472] The Committee has established certain criteria in the Operational Guidelines (Guidelines) to determine whether a property proposed for inscription should be included on the List.[473] The State Party, on whose territory the object is si-

---

467 Preamble.
468 Arts 1 and 2.
469 Art 37.
470 See also Strecker, 'Landscape as Cultural Heritage' 276 and discussion of the WHC below.
471 Convention concerning the Protection of the World Cultural and Natural Heritage (opened for signature 16 November 1972, entered into force 17 December 1975), 1037 UNTS 151 (hereafter World Heritage Convention).
472 WHC arts 11 (2) and (5). Paras 1 and 2 of the Operational Guidelines for the Implementation of the World Heritage Convention WHC.17/01 12 July 2017 state that: 1. The Operational Guidelines for the Implementation of the World Heritage Convention (hereinafter referred to as the Operational Guidelines) aim to facilitate the implementation of the Convention concerning the Protection of the World Cultural and Natural Heritage (hereinafter referred to as 'the World Heritage Convention' or 'the Convention'), by setting forth the procedure for: a) the inscription of properties on the World Heritage List and the List of World Heritage in Danger; b) the protection and conservation of World Heritage properties; c) the granting of International Assistance under the World Heritage Fund; and d) the mobilization of national and international support in favor of the Convention. 2. The Operational Guidelines are periodically revised to reflect the decisions of the World Heritage Committee.
473 Abdulqawi A Yusuf, 'Article 1: Definition of Cultural Heritage' in Francesco Francioni and Federico Lenzerini (eds), *The 1972 World Heritage Convention: A Commentary* (Oxford University Press 2008) 30.

tuated, has the duty to ensure its identification, protection, conservation, presentation and transmission to future generations.[474]

As Craig Forrest observes, the phrase 'cultural heritage' makes its international debut in the WHC text.[475] Widely considered a philosophical breakthrough, the reference to cultural heritage is a complete departure from predecessor treaties, which defined heritage as physical property.[476] While neither property nor heritage has been defined in conventional heritage law, it appears that cultural heritage 'is generally conceived of as a broader all-encompassing term of which cultural property forms a subsection'.[477] Using the term 'property' can commodify certain cultural aspects of life, which would be inappropriate for heritage resources that were never meant to be treated as goods in the marketplace, to be bought, sold or traded.[478]

This is chiefly as a result of the Cultural Turn, which first arose as a result of changes occurring at the end of the Second World War, and saw a retreat from the exclusive (and exclusionary) approaches to heritage protection. The movement originated in the humanities and social sciences and provided the impetus for deconstructing heritage in its elitist form and injecting into the concept the dynamism associated with anthropological understandings of heritage in its wider cultural context, relevant to livelihoods, identity and community.[479] International cultural heritage law began to mirror this development a few decades later, as UNESCO adopted an integrated perspective that incorporated intangible elements and traditional knowledge.[480]

The WHC thus pivots away from heritage as property dominated by private property rights and framed as economic in nature, towards recognition of a collective and public interest in the heritage.[481] Nevertheless, the scope of the treaty is limited to a subset of heritage, that which is of outstanding universal value.[482] Another constraint is that the way heritage was defined had troubling implications for landscape protection. While the WHC recognised both natural and cultural aspects of heritage as worthy of protection, building on the 1972 Recommendation, criteria for assessing these sites were separated according to the type of site i.e. as natural or cultural. Although no explicit mention was made of landscapes in the original text of the WHC, the Operational Guidelines referred to landscapes under the criteria for natural heritage, namely as examples of the 'interaction between man and his environment'.[483] Where an interrelationship between natural and cultural resources existed, the 'mixed sites' designation (though not expressly catered for in the WHC) was the preferred solution adopted by the Committee.[484]

---

474 WHC, arts 4 and 5.
475 Forrest 25.
476 Blake, *International Cultural Heritage Law* 128.
477 Blake, *International Cultural Heritage Law* 7 and 128.
478 Lucas Lixinski, *Intangible Cultural Heritage in International Law* (Oxford University Press 2013) 6.
479 Strecker, *Landscape Protection in International Law* 122; see also Geertz, *The Interpretation of Cultures* and Victoria Bonnell and Lynn Hunt, *Beyond the Cultural Turn* (University of California Press 1999).
480 Strecker, *Landscape Protection in International Law* 123.
481 Lixinski 7 and Forrest 25.
482 Yusuf, 'Article 1: Definition of Cultural Heritage' in *The 1972 WHC: A Commentary* 30.
483 Operational Guidelines for the Implementation of the World Heritage Convention, CC-77/CONF.001/8 Rev, para 10 ii(c).
484 Operational Guidelines WHC.17/01 13 July 2017, para 46.

3.2.2.1 The Mixed Sites Category: the Need for Recognition of Landscapes

A number of mixed sites on the List had been inscribed on the basis of natural heritage criteria (ii) and (iii), which referred to 'man's interaction with his natural environment' and to 'the combined works of nature and man' respectively.[485] However, mixed sites were not an appropriate designation for those sites in which cultural and natural elements could not be separated, or where neither culture nor nature predominated in the interactions of people and the environment.[486] Such landscapes were designated as natural sites because of the perceived absence of evidence of human interaction with the landscape.[487] This was deeply problematic. As Kathryn Whitby Last writes, properties nominated for both cultural and natural aspects were often accepted for one aspect only, rather than on a joint cultural/natural basis. Such was the case of the nomination of Yosemite National Park in the USA, which ultimately ignored the contributions of indigenous communities associated with the site in question as it was considered a natural site.[488]

The ease with which nature and culture had been decoupled in the WHC text is due to its drafting origins. The treaty text had been directly influenced by a US draft proposal for a World Heritage Trust, which included natural zones, cultural and historic sites and provided for voluntary contributions.[489] Though mention was made of historic sites, the US proposal was primarily focused on conserving areas of outstanding natural beauty or natural sites of exceptional importance such as Yellowstone Park, and the Grand Canyon.[490] Termed vast wilderness areas, they were, as with Yosemite, modified Native American landscapes.[491] This conceptualisation of landscape originates in England's destruction of the commons, reflecting the need to both mask and vindicate widespread enclosure practices, as discussed in Chapter Two.[492] As Kenneth Olwig's investigation into the origins of landscapes and their influence on England has shown, landscape as scenery was also transported to England's colonies in the Americas[493] where its uptake in the law can thus be seen in the drafting of the

---

485   Yusuf, 'Article 1: Definition of Cultural Heritage' in *The WHC: A Commentary* 48-49.
486   Kathryn Whitby Last, 'Article 1: Cultural Landscapes' in *The WHC: A Commentary*, 51-62, 60-61.
487   Last, 'Article 1: Cultural Landscapes' in *The WHC: A Commentary* 51-52.
488   Ibid, 54.
489   Raymond Goy, 'The International Protection of the Cultural and Natural Heritage.' *Netherlands Yearbook of International Law* 4 (1973): 117-141, 126.
490   Francesco Francioni, 'Thirty Years On: Is the World Heritage Convention Ready for the 21st Century.' *The Italian Yearbook of International Law Online* 12 (1) (2002):13-38, 16.
491   Olwig, *Landscape, Nature and the Body Politic,* 224 notes that with the expulsion of the Indian populace from Yosemite Park America was merely replicating practices in British landscaping, with imperial landscape garden parks that enclosed communal land and removed villages and commons.
492   Olwig, *Landscape, Nature and the Body Politic* 202.
493   Ibid.

WHC, which relied on a misrepresentation of indigenous landscape in defining and classifying natural heritage.[494]

While clearly innovative in its recognition of natural 'heritage', the WHC's concept is rooted in a restrictive understanding of the environment, given the role of communities in shaping and ensuring the survival of ecosystems.[495] The search for exceptional and untouched natural sites can therefore exclude heritage sites such as landscapes that are worthy of protection, by undervaluing the role of communities in the formation of these places. Strict observance of these categories meant sites were deemed too modified to be accepted as truly 'natural' sites, and too 'natural' to be accepted as cultural sites, because 'a convention uniquely designed to integrate cultural and natural perspectives on heritage singularly failed to make this all-important connection.'[496] It would take some developments for the WHC to incorporate a more inclusive approach to heritage. The development of the concept of 'cultural landscapes' through the revisions to the Operational Guidelines resolved the previously irreconcilable issue of aligning mixed sites with the definition of natural heritage in Article 2 of the WHC.[497]

3.2.2.2 Introduction of the Cultural Landscapes Category

The challenges associated with the mixed sites category, led the World Heritage Committee to request the formation of a taskforce with representatives from the IUCN, ICOMOS and the International Federation of Landscape Architects to develop appropriate guidelines for the identification and nomination of mixed natural and cultural sites.[498] A first meeting was held in 1985 and guidelines were drafted. The first test was the 1987 nomination by the United Kingdom of the Lake District as a potential mixed natural/cultural landscape.[499] The application revealed the limitations of the WHC criteria and the need to develop specific criteria for cultural landscapes.

In 1992, the first expert meeting on World Heritage cultural landscapes was held in La Petite Pierre, France.[500] Based on the meeting's recommendations, the Operational

---

494 Erasing Native American landscapes across the United States in order to facilitate the development of the national park system in the nineteenth century – Yellowstone Park in fact was created by the expulsion of the Crow and Shoshone peoples – echoed a long-held practice of displacing communities from common lands. On the 'natural and 'neutral' perceived values of parks, see also Karen Fog Olwig and Kenneth Olwig, 'Underdevelopment and the Development of "Natural" Park Ideology' at 17, and on Yellowstone and the universal logic of park development, Karen Fog Olwig, 'National Parks, Tourism and Local Development: A West Indian Case.' *Human Organization*, 39(1) (1980): 22-30 at 22 and 27. See also Adrian Phillips, 'The Nature of Cultural Landscapes – A Nature Conservation Perspective.' *Landscape Research* 23(1) (1998): 21-38.
495 Blake, *International Cultural Heritage Law* 129.
496 Phillips 29.
497 Last, 'Article 1: Cultural Landscapes' in the *WHC: A Commentary* 51-52.
498 Peter Fowler, World Heritage Papers 6. World Heritage Cultural Landscapes 1992-2002, (UNESCO World Heritage Centre, 2003) 66; Mechtild Rössler, 'UNESCO and Cultural Landscape Protection' in Bernd von Droste et al (eds), *Cultural Landscapes of Universal Value: Components of a Global Strategy* (Gustav Fisher Verlag with UNESCO, 1995), 42-49.
499 Last, 'Article 1: Cultural Landscapes' in *The WHC: A Commentary* 55.
500 Report of the Expert Group on Cultural Landscapes (La Petite Pierre, France, 24-26 October 1992). WHC-92/CONF.202/10/Add. See Strecker, 'Article 13 (d)(ii) – Respecting Customary Practices'; Last, 'Article 1: Cultural Landscapes' in *The WHC: A Commentary* 57; Mechtild Rössler, 'Linking Nature and Culture: World Heritage Cultural Landscapes', Cultural Landscapes: the Challenges of Conservation, World Heritage 2002, Shared Legacy, Common Responsibility; Associated Workshops, 11-12 November 2002 (Ferrara), 10.

Guidelines were subsequently revised to officially include 'cultural landscapes'[501] within the scope of the WHC, and were adopted by the sixteenth session of the World Heritage Committee.[502] Cultural landscapes were defined as:

> *'cultural properties representing the combined works of nature and of man designated in Article 1 of the Convention. They are illustrative of the evolution of human society and settlement over time, under the influence of the physical constraints and/or opportunities presented by their natural environment and of successive social, economic and cultural forces, both external and internal'.*[503] *[…] 'The term embraces a diversity of manifestations of the interaction between humankind and its natural environment'.*[504]

It was further noted that landscapes 'should be selected on the basis both of their outstanding universal value and of their representativity in terms of a clearly defined geo-cultural region and also for their capacity to illustrate the essential and distinct cultural elements of such regions.'[505]

As Mechtild Rössler writes, most of the world's landscapes are to a considerable extent human artefacts, representing countless generations of human activity and creativity, but have for the most part been ignored because they lack the monumental elements inseparable in the European mind from the traditional 'cultural heritage'.[506] Their omission on the World Heritage List had skewed the List, making it unrepresentative of the totality – and hence the universality – of human cultural development and achievement.[507]

The WHC further enhanced its Operational Guidelines to address landscape following the issue of the Kakadu natural and cultural landscape in Australia, home of the Mirrar people. Strecker notes that the Australian government developed plans to expand uranium mining into Kakadu without proper consultation, or the free, prior and informed consent of the Mirrar people, which led to protests. The Mirrar people eventually approached the World Heritage Committee in Paris, essentially by-passing the State. The World Heritage Committee held a single-item Extraordinary Session in Kakadu in July 1999 to address concerns about the serious threats to the living cultural heritage values of the Mirrar people and requested the Australian government to provide updates on actions to remedy the situation.[508] Ultimately, the project was abandoned due to financial challenges and consistent protest from the Aboriginal com-

---

501 Pioneered by cultural geographer Carl Sauer and the Berkeley School of Geographers.
502 Decision 16COM XIII. 1-3.
503 *Operational Guidelines for the Implementation of the World Heritage Convention*, 1999, 35, < http://whc.unesco.org/archive/opguide05-en.pdf> accessed 8 January 2018.
504 Ibid, para 37.
505 Ibid, para 36.
506 Mechtild Rössler, 'World Heritage cultural landscapes: A UNESCO flagship programme 1992 – 2006.' *Landscape Research* 31(4) (2006): 333-353, 349 and see Henry Cleere 'The Uneasy Bedfellows: Universality and Cultural Heritage', in Robert Layton, Julian Thomas and Peter Stone (eds), *Destruction and Conservation of Cultural Property* (Routledge 2001).
507 Rössler 349.
508 Third Extraordinary Session of the World Heritage Committee, 12 July 1999. WHC-00/CONF.205/5Rev.

munities. The Operational Guidelines now incorporate participation considerations where heritage is concerned.[509]

Three categories of cultural landscapes were incorporated into the Operational Guidelines:[510]

> *i. clearly defined landscapes designed and created intentionally by man. This embraces garden and parkland landscapes characteristically constructed for aesthetic, social and recreational reasons which are often but not always associated with religious or other monumental buildings and ensembles;*
>
> *ii. organically evolved landscapes resulting from an initial social, economic, administrative, and/or religious imperative and have developed their present form by association with and in response to the natural environment. Such landscapes reflect that process of evolution in their form and component features. They fall into two sub-categories:*

a. relict (or fossil) landscapes in which an evolutionary process came to an end at some time in the past, either abruptly or over a period. Their significant distinguishing features are, however, still visible in material form;
b. continuing landscapes which retain an active social role in contemporary society closely associated with a traditional way of life. They are continuing to evolve while, at the same time, exhibit significant material evidence of their historic evolution;

> *iii. associative cultural landscapes with definable powerful, religious, artistic or cultural associations with the natural element rather than material cultural evidence, which may be insignificant or even absent.*

The criteria concerning continuing and associative landscapes gave recognition to continuing tradition, customary practices and the associative dimension to landscapes. By doing so, the landscapes category was distinctive for 'the acceptance of communities and their relationship with the environment.'[511] As Amy Strecker writes, the inclusion of both continuing landscapes and associative landscapes were influenced by arguments raised by Indigenous Peoples in response to the 'natural' heritage nominations of well-known heritage sites in Australia and New Zealand, most notably Uluru and Tongariro National Park respectively.

UNESCO has promulgated cultural landscapes, with their traditional resource management supported by customary law, as living models of sustainable use of land and natural resources. Because they also illustrate the religious and cultural connections

---

509 See Strecker's discussion, 'Article 13: Respecting Customary Practices' in Lucas Lixinski and Janet Blake (eds), *Commentary on the 2003 Convention on Safeguarding the Intangible Heritage* (Oxford University Press 2020).
510 Defined in para. 39, 1999 Operational Guidelines for the Implementation of the World Heritage Convention.
511 Rössler, 'World Heritage Cultural Landscapes: A UNESCO Flagship Programme 1992-2006.'

indigenous peoples have with their natural environment,[512] landscapes have inspired UNESCO to use the category as a springboard for promoting international cooperation among nations and peoples.[513]

The inscription of sites as cultural landscapes on the World Heritage List has had major effects on the interpretation, presentation, and management of these properties. The nomination process led to awareness-raising among local communities, rekindled pride in their heritage, and rehabilitated and revived local traditions.[514] Sustainable land-use and community stewardship have stimulated the marketing of specific agricultural products or traditional arts and crafts. The introduction of cultural landscapes into the World Heritage field amplified the understanding of heritage beyond monuments and strict nature reserves – there are cultural linkages in time and space that make landscapes living repositories, and the concept is therefore exemplary for the evolution in protected area thinking and heritage conservation as a whole.[515]

3.2.2.3 Challenges with the Cultural Landscapes Category

The main point of contention however, is that landscapes are not in fact synonymous with protected areas or parks. World Heritage 'cultural landscapes' were intended to give recognition to the intangible and associative values attached to certain landscapes, to sustainable agricultural practices and to 'people and communities' – essentially the human dimension of landscape. But as Strecker notes, the WHC's inherent focus on 'outstanding universal value' means that a critical element of landscapes is not accounted for – that they are contested as reflective of the democratic character of the community, and not concerned with presenting a model that is fixed in time.[516] With respect to cultural landscapes, the Committee had adopted the following guidelines concerning their inclusion on the World Heritage List:

> *(i) the existing balance between nature and human activity may only be modified in a way which ensures the continuation of this special relationship and will exclude any major alterations to the appearance and function of the area…; (ii) legislative protection must exist as well as practicable mechanisms for bringing the relevant institutions together to ensure the preservation of the significant harmonious balance between nature and human activity in an evolving context; and (iii) the area nominated should be of such a size that these protective measures can seriously be expected to be effective.*[517]

Aplin notes that these suggested criteria and guidelines have potentially negative implications. The wording limits inscription of Cultural Landscape sites to those that

---

512 Graeme Aplin, 'World Heritage Cultural Landscapes.' *International Journal of Heritage Studies* 13(6) (2007): 427-446, 440.
513 Aplin 440 and see UNESCO World Heritage Centre, 'Cultural Landscapes: The Challenges of Conservation.' World Heritage Papers no. 7. Paris: UNESCO World Heritage Centre, 2003.
514 Rössler 337.
515 Ibid, 340.
516 Strecker, *Landscape Protection in International Law* 85.
517 Item 13 of the Provisional Agenda: Revision of the Operational Guidelines for the Implementation of the World Heritage Convention–'Elaboration of Criterion or Criteria for Cultural Landscapes'. WHC Document SC-91/CONF.002/11 (1991).

maintain 'traditional' forms of land use and evince little change over time. While this has the advantage of limiting the sites to those characterised by a well-established balance between human activities and the biophysical landscape, the implication is that to meet the definition of landscape, change is restricted. The relationship is frozen is time, and this is not 'natural, but, rather, an artificial or bureaucratic restriction on cultural evolution and development'.[518] Furthermore, maintaining such a balance may not be acceptable because it compels community members to live a lifestyle that may be physically challenging, demanding and economically static. The Rice Terraces of the Cordilleras in the Philippines illustrate this conflict well.[519]

The distinctive terraced mountain slopes were produced by the Cordillera tribes, who had developed their complex agricultural infrastructure and farmed entirely by hand for millennia. The Rice Terraces had been inscribed as a cultural landscape in 1995.[520] However, customs and traditional farming practices were increasingly under threat due to market forces, poverty, and environmental issues.[521] As a result of abandonment of terraces, dispossession of property rights and conflicts over resources, the Cordilleras were placed on the List of World Heritage in Danger in 2001.[522] After a number of fact-finding missions, benchmarks were set in 2006 by the World Heritage Centre and the advisory bodies ICOMOS and IUCN, giving consideration to local peoples' perceptions, local development aspirations of the communities, and functional governance mechanisms.[523] Following efforts by the state party to remedy the situation, the Cordilleras were withdrawn from the List of World Heritage in Danger in 2012. Nevertheless, Strecker notes that the case reveals the challenges of designating living landscapes, when outstanding universal value implies restrictions on the fundamental rights of its inhabitants such as development and self-determination, to be discussed later in the chapter.[524]

Landscapes are not by definition preserved in amber. Such thinking is at odds with the understanding of heritage as dynamic and evolving, and in fact heritage conservation itself, which is not about fossilisation or creating models to be emulated.[525] The WHC has made significant advances in its understanding of cultural heritage, by attempting to make the List 'more credible, representative and less Eurocentric' with the cultural landscapes category, but as the Cordilleras example shows, landscapes are not detached from local circumstances, and long held practices of a community regulating access, use and management evolve over time in response to economic, environmental and social stimuli.[526] Sensitivity to rather than insulation from local circumstances is critical to any effective heritage preservation strategy.

Recognition of a cultural place as a World Heritage site can intentionally or unintentionally marginalise certain groups, the unrecognised 'others' with a long, verifiable

---

518 Aplin 431.
519 Ibid, 432.
520 Decision 19COM VIII.C.1.
521 Strecker, *Landscape Protection in International Law* 69.
522 Ibid, 68.
523 Ibid.
524 Ibid, 69.
525 Lowenthal, *The Heritage Crusade* 88.
526 Strecker, *Landscape Protection in International Law* 71.

and dynamic inter-relationship with the place, and repeat the practice of excluding communities as exemplified by the design of US parks.[527] Landscape is more than park management by traditional communities, even though recognition of the associative cultural landscape values of traditional people as being worthy of World Heritage listing can empower these groups via new heritage tourism management arrangements.[528] Many listed sites did not receive protection until recognition by the WHC caught the attention of the wider public.[529] How the WHC relates to local implementation efforts to protect heritage is thus considered in the next section.

3.2.2.4 Lesser Antilles and WHC Implementation

With respect to the role of international law, the former British colonies of the Lesser Antilles have inherited the dualist doctrine of the common law, which requires implementing legislation to give the force of law to treaty obligations.[530] Legislative enactment of the treaty may take the form of pre-existing statute or treaty-specific enactments (implementation by enactment), or incorporation by reference, stating in a short statute that the treaties listed (sometimes in a schedule) have 'the force of law' in the country concerned.[531] Without this legislation, the executive (Cabinet) on signing the treaty, would be able to legislate without the legislature, and so usurp the role of Parliament – transposing international legal obligations into domestic law therefore ensures effective functioning of the executive and legislative branches of government.[532] Winston Anderson notes that in keeping with British practice, treaties are often signed and ratified, followed by a lag in the process to develop implementing legislation.[533]

Implementation by enactment is the traditional approach, which involves repeating verbatim or by paraphrase the substantive provisions of the treaty to which the State is party.[534] However, the technical capacity required of legislative drafters, in terms of familiarity with the nuances of international treaty law, and ability to translate

---

527 As Ben Boer points out, while the identification and delineation of the cultural and natural heritage as items of 'outstanding universal value' is a central obligation for States Parties to the WHC, the act of identification is complex, and often politically motivated. The process can potentially raise a number of cultural, social, political, economic, human rights, and religious issues in certain cases. There are often competing claims between the properties that a national government may want to protect and the properties that particular groups within a country may wish to protect through World Heritage listing. See Boer, 'Identification and Delineation of World Heritage Properties' in *The WHC: A Commentary* 86.
528 Ken Taylor and Jane Lennon, 'Cultural Landscapes: A Bridge between Culture and Nature?' *International Journal of Heritage Studies* 17(6) (2011): 537-554, 550.
529 Kerstin Odendahl and Mayte Peters, 'The Significance of Cultural Heritage for State Stability and its Protection by Public International Law', in Julia Raue and Patrick Sutter (eds), *Facts and Practice of State-building* (Brill 2009) 278.
530 Upheld by case law throughout the English speaking Caribbean; see *Natural Resources Conservation Authority v Seafood and Ting International Ltd* 58 WIR 269 (App Ct 1999) (Jamaica) concerning the absence of local legislation for CITES, and *Talisman (Trinidad) Petroleum Ltd vs Environmental Management Authority* Dec. EA3 Environmental Commission (2002) (Trinidad and Tobago) which considered the legal effect of the unincorporated Ramsar Convention.
531 Winston Anderson, *Principles of Caribbean Environmental Law* (Environmental Law Institute 2012) 36.
532 Malcolm Shaw, *International Law* (5th edn, Cambridge University Press 2003) 136.
533 Winston Anderson, 'Multilateral Environmental Agreements (MEA) Implementation in the Caribbean: Report and Guidelines' (UNEP 2000) 9.
534 Ibid.

soft law obligations into legislative rights and duties is often absent in this region.[535] In addition, the measures necessary for compliance with a specific treaty may be onerous, demanding the establishment of specific enabling administrative/institutional arrangements; public awareness and education initiatives; management measures; and regulation and enforcement.[536] The trend in the last two decades has been to provide support to these countries to develop the capacity to improve implementation of international treaties, via training for legislative drafters, focal points, grant-writers and policymakers, to create the enabling environment necessary to facilitate uptake of treaty obligations in the existing institutional framework and improve overall treaty governance. These practices are evident in the approach to implementation of the WHC in the Lesser Antilles.

The Lesser Antillean states (the subjects of this study) are all parties to the World Heritage Convention, and five countries have UNESCO listed sites: Antigua and Barbados each have a cultural site,[537] and there are three natural heritage sites in Dominica, Saint Lucia and St Kitts respectively.[538] However, no cultural landscapes have been designated, and this is interesting because the UNESCO listed sites all have cultural and historical significance to their populations as public spaces and symbols of patriotism. Two main initiatives with relevance to landscape protection, the UNESCO Small Island Developing States (SIDS) Programme[539], and the Training Course in the Management of Caribbean Cultural Resources in a Natural Environment: Sites of Memory and Participation of Local Communities[540] will be briefly discussed.

The SIDS were recognised as a distinct group of developing countries in June 1992, at the UN Conference on Environment and Development. The 29th session of the World Heritage Committee in 2005 adopted the World Heritage Programme for SIDS, and the SIDS have since become a point of focus for World Heritage identification and protection. The UNESCO SIDS Programme develops World Heritage activities in these areas, providing support for new nominations to the World Heritage List, and training in sustainable conservation and management practices for sites already inscribed. In 2014, the International Year of the SIDS resulted in the outcome document the Samoa Pathway,[541] for which a SIDS Action Plan was developed to implement its goals for sustainable development. Heritage is specifically referenced.[542]

Priority 4 of the SIDS Action Plan calls upon the international community to support SIDS in designing and implementing their own innovative cultural policies to strengthen heritage and creativity and leverage the economic, social and natural benefits of culture. It further reaffirmed that 'indigenous bio-cultural heritage recognises the deep connections among people, culture, knowledge and the natural environment, and

---

535 Ibid.
536 Anderson, 'Multilateral Environmental Agreements (MEA) Implementation in the Caribbean' 4.
537 Nelson's Dockyard, Antigua, and Historic Bridgetown and its Garrison, Barbados. See <https://whc.unesco.org/en/list/1499/> and <https://whc.unesco.org/en/list/1376/> accessed 19 September 2019.
538 Morne Trois Pitons National Park, Dominica <https://whc.unesco.org/en/list/814/>, Pitons Management Area, Saint Lucia <https://whc.unesco.org/en/list/1161/>, and Brimstone Hill Fortress National Park < https://whc.unesco.org/en/list/910/> accessed 19 September 2019.
539 Website at: <https://whc.unesco.org/en/sids/> accessed 8 October 2019.
540 See <https://whc.unesco.org/en/events/1000/> accessed 8 October 2019.
541 SIDS Accelerated Modalities of Action (SAMOA) Pathway, A/RES/69/15 at para 81.
542 UNESCO SIDS Action Plan (2016-2021) 199 EX/5.INF.REV, at para 7.

can meaningfully advance sustainable development'. In this context, protecting tangible cultural heritage, safeguarding intangible cultural heritage, promoting responsible sustainable tourism, boosting creative industries and transmitting traditional knowledge are crucial. This also implies adopting a holistic approach to the cultural heritage of SIDS in the specific context of the relationship of these human settlements to the land and the sea, which requires high levels of protection and whose potential for driving sustainable development is as yet relatively underexplored.[543]

As a subset of SIDS, the Lesser Antillean states benefit from these activities and initiatives. Two documents developed to support WHC implementation apply to these states: the Regional Work Plan for Culture in Latin America and the Caribbean 2016-2021, and the Action Plan for World Heritage in the Caribbean 2015-2019.[544] The Action Plan presents an operational framework to facilitate the implementation of the Latin America and the Caribbean plan in the specific context of the Caribbean, and proposes an updated Caribbean Capacity Building Programme for World Heritage, which had been previously developed in 2007 to build capacity in Caribbean countries to implement the WHC.[545] Objective 1 of the Action Plan concerns improving the conservation and management of the cultural and natural heritage. In order to consolidate institutional, policy and legal networks, actions should sensitise decision-makers about the value of cultural and natural heritage, promoting coordination and communication among different levels of government where laws and actions may interfere with the protection, conservation and heritage management, and integrate heritage into national development policies. The first action to achieve this outcome requires that '*cultural landscapes, industrial heritage, modern heritage, vernacular architecture*, marine and archaeological sites and *sites of memory* [be integrated] into heritage protection policies'.[546] Local communities are to be involved in heritage protection, conservation and management activities.

Objective 2 of the plan, which addresses the updating and harmonisation of heritage inventories, notes that cultural landscape designation constitutes a gap, in spite of the wealth of cultural landscapes in the Caribbean, particularly landscapes related to the Slave Route and Sites of Memory.[547] Also highlighted is the fact that States should be aware that the inscription on the World Heritage List is not an end by itself, but

---

543 Ibid.
544 UNESCO, 'Action Plan for World Heritage in the Caribbean 2015-2019'. Adopted in Havana on 28th November, 2014.
545 The Caribbean Capacity Building Programme (CCBP) offered a targeted response to the needs identified in the 'Latin America and the Caribbean Periodic Report', which showed that most of the Caribbean States Parties still lacked the capacity and expertise needed to enable full protection and management of present World Heritage sites, and to identify new sites. Within the CCBP over twelve expert meetings have been organised, and six training manuals focusing on the various aspects of management (application of the World Heritage Convention, tourism, historic centres, risks, cultural landscapes and natural heritage) have been published. See Green, 'Caribbean Cultural Landscape: the English Caribbean Potential in the Journey from 'Tentative Listing' to being 'Inscribed'.' *Journal of Heritage Tourism* 8(1) (2013): 63-79, 71, and *World Heritage Papers 38: Safeguarding Precious Resources for Island Communities*, UNESCO Paris, 2014, 20.
546 Action 1.27 (emphasis added).
547 A UNESCO programme that aims at providing recognition and protection to places that have a significant importance for local communities because of their sacred or symbolic values. See < http://www.unesco.org/new/en/social-and-human-sciences/themes/slave-route/> accessed 18 October 2019.

the continuation of a process to enhance the effective identification and protection of cultural heritage in the Caribbean.[548] Objective 4 is devoted to communities, and their traditional knowledge. While involvement and participation of communities is encouraged for heritage preservation and economic benefit, the objective does not address ownership by communities, or recognise them as heritage creators, and does not go so far as to centre these communities in heritage protection.[549] This is borne out by objective 5, which addresses the establishment of tourism itineraries at local, national and Caribbean levels, in particular related to the Slave Route, Indentured Labour Routes, Sites of Memory, fortifications, cultural landscapes and others, to further promote Caribbean heritage,[550] but does not make clear whether these sites have received community support as tourist attractions.

Under the auspices of the Caribbean Capacity Building Programme, established in 2007, workshops and supporting activities have been held to meet the CCBP's aims of strengthening capacities of Caribbean experts to implement the World Heritage Convention. Training includes six modules concerning the WHC itself, tourism, risk management, cultural landscapes, historic centres and natural heritage. In 2013, a workshop was held on Sites of Memory, which paid particular attention to the management of cultural resources in a natural environment, and the participation of local communities.[551] The subject under discussion concerned natural areas, which often include tangible and intangible cultural heritage that local communities value – this is landscape though not identified as such. It was noted that many of these spaces may be protected or contain natural resources, which may imply that external stakeholders from governmental and non-governmental entities, as well as private companies have management responsibilities, which could impact the capacity of local communities to continue benefitting from those cultural resources.[552]

It was recommended that States parties consider pursuing serial nominations based on shared history and heritage.[553] It was acknowledged that these concepts open the doorway to innovative approaches to heritage protection, but there were no attempts to link land use change to identity and heritage in any proposed strategies. Interestingly, there has been a study on Cultural Landscapes in the Pacific, but none on the Caribbean, where capacity building initiatives are ongoing and clearly need to develop community-oriented approaches to landscape in order to maximise the potential of UNESCO's heritage protection regime.[554]

---

548 Objective 2, Action Plan, World Heritage in the Caribbean 2015-2019, 8.
549 Objective 4.
550 Action 5.1.5.
551 'Management of Caribbean Cultural Resources in a Natural Environment: Sites of Memory and Participation of Local Communities' Concept Note, Barbados, 11-15 March 2013 at 1.
552 Concept Note 1.
553 Report of the Workshop: Management of Caribbean Cultural Resources in a Natural Environment: Sites of Memory and Participation of Local Communities, Barbados, 11-15 March 2013, at 12.
554 ICOMOS Thematic Study: Cultural Landscapes of the Pacific Islands (2007). See *World Heritage Series 38: Safeguarding Precious Resources for Island Communities*, at 22. The Caribbean Capacity Building Programme developed two activities with relevance to Caribbean landscapes: Module 4: Management of Cultural Landscapes (2008) and a Workshop on Management of Cultural Landscapes, as part of the Regional Meeting on Heritage, Biodiversity and Community (October 2008, Havana, Cuba). See *World Heritage Series 38: Safeguarding Precious Resources for Island Communities*, at 22.

3.2.3 Landscape in Environmental Law

In spite of environmental law's influence on the development of cultural heritage law,[555] the two spheres have had limited interaction on the subject of landscape. Originally, heritage sites were to be included at the 1972 UN Conference on the Human Environment to be held in Stockholm, but in order to accommodate parallel negotiations for the agreement that would be ultimately become the WHC, delegates refrained from direct mention of world heritage in the formal Declaration of the UN Conference on the Human Environment, and this appears to have defined the field's approach to cultural heritage issues until fairly recently.[556] Advancements in the law pertaining to parks and protected areas, as well as biodiversity conservation, have since brought landscape matters within the purview of the environment.

3.2.3.1 IUCN and Protected Areas

As a global environmental body, the IUCN has widened its ambit on nature reserves and national parks to now include a 'protected landscapes' category.[557] This is due in part to its prior involvement in the WHC process to include a 'mixed sites' category, and later the cultural landscapes category.[558] The protected landscapes category can be distinguished from other protected areas[559] by its recognition of a close relationship between people and nature, the physical environment as well as the associated social, cultural and traditional values. Protected landscape is defined as:

> *an area of land, with coast or seas as appropriate, where the interaction of people and nature over time has produced an area of distinct character with significant aesthetic, ecological and/or cultural value, and often with high biological diversity. Safeguarding the integrity of this traditional interaction is vital to the protection, maintenance and evolution of such as area.*[560]

---

[555] Janet Blake notes that the structure of the WHC emulates wildlife treaties such as the Convention on International Trade in Endangered Species of Wild Fauna and Flora, Bonn, 23 June 1979 in force 1 November 1983 27 UST 1087; and The Convention on Wetlands of International Importance especially as Waterfowl Habitat, Ramsar (Iran), 2 February 1971, in force 21 December 1975 996 UNTS 245, with a main treaty text and two or more lists requiring certain criteria be met for inscription. See Blake *International Cultural Heritage Law* 128.

[556] Catherine Redgwell, 'Article 2: Definition of Natural Heritage', in *The World Heritage Convention: A Commentary* 64-65.

[557] See IUCN *Management Guidelines for IUCN Category V: Protected Areas Protected Landscapes/Seascapes* (IUCN, 2002) < https://www.iucn.org/theme/protected-areas/about/protected-areas-categories/category-v-protected-landscapeseascape> accessed 6 October 2019.

[558] Strecker, *Landscape Protection in International Law* 67.

[559] The other five IUCN categories of protected areas include 'strict nature reserve/wilderness area', 'national park', 'natural monument', habitat/species area, and 'managed resource area'.

[560] The Management Guidelines also include the objective 'to support lifestyles and economic activities which are in harmony with nature and the preservation of social and cultural fabric of the communities concerned', 'to bring benefits to and contribute to the welfare of the local community'. *IUCN Management Guidelines* 23, 29.

Category V areas (protected landscapes) have been recognised by other regimes such as the 2003 African Convention,[561] the Man and Biosphere Programme (MAB),[562] and the International Tropical Timber Organisation Guidelines on the Conservation of Biological Diversity.[563]

3.2.3.2 Convention on Biological Diversity

The Convention on Biological Diversity recognised the symbiotic nature of the relationship between nature and culture when it acknowledged the role communities can play in the protection of biological diversity in Article 8(j) of that treaty:

> *States shall, subject to its national legislation, respect, preserve and maintain knowledge, innovations and practices of indigenous and local communities embodying traditional lifestyles relevant for the conservation and sustainable use of biological diversity and promote their wider application with the approval and involvement of the holders of such knowledge, innovations and practices and encourage the equitable sharing of the benefits arising from the utilization of such knowledge, innovations and practices.*

That this interaction between cultural diversity and biological diversity is expressed in practices and traditions linked to the land is also clear. The CBD established a working group on article 8(j) in 1998 at the fourth meeting of the Conference of the Parties (COP). In 2000, the COP agreed to enhance the role and involvement of indigenous and local communities in the achievement of the objectives of the CBD. As a result, the 'Akwé: Kon Guidelines for the Conduct of Cultural, Environmental and Social Impact Assessments regarding Developments Proposed to Take Place or which are Likely to Impact on Sacred Sites and on Lands and Waters Traditionally Occupied or Used by Indigenous and Local Communities'[564] were produced. This document has important ramifications for landscape protection, as it is intended to respect indigenous and local communities' land resources by integrating relevant criteria in the assessment of cultural, environmental and social impacts of proposed developments.

The Preamble to the Guidelines recognises the negative impacts of many developments on sacred sites and traditional lands of indigenous and local communities, and the corresponding loss of these communities' traditional knowledge, innovations and practices as a result. Governments are encouraged to engage in a legal and institutional review of all matters related to cultural, environmental and social impact assessment, and where possible incorporate the guidelines into national legislation, policies, and

---

561 African Convention on the Conservation of Nature and Natural Resources (revised Maputo 2003). Date of Adoption: March 07, 2017, Preamble and Article V.
562 The overarching objective of the biosphere reserve is 'sustainable development'. People are not excluded from the protected area, and are a defining component of the management and conservation of the area and its surroundings. See Strecker, *Landscape Protection in International Law* 68.
563 5 June 1992, 1760 UNTS 79; 31 ILM 818 (1992). Entry into force: 29 December 1993; see also Management Guidelines for IUCN Category V, 30.
564 COP 7 Decision VII/16. Secretariat of the Convention on Biological Diversity (2004). Akwé: Kon Voluntary Guidelines for the Conduct of Cultural, Environmental and Social Impact Assessment regarding Developments Proposed to Take Place on, or which are Likely to Impact on, Sacred Sites and on Lands and Waters Traditionally Occupied or Used by Indigenous and Local Communities.

procedures, 'bearing in mind that nothing in these guidelines should adversely affect biodiversity and the livelihoods of other communities, and that they should be implemented in a manner that is consistent with international law and with other international obligations.'[565]

The Guidelines acknowledge the unique relationship between the environment and indigenous and local communities and promotes where possible the incorporation of cultural and social considerations within any environmental impact assessment legislation or policies.[566] In determining the scope of a cultural impact assessment, possible impacts on continued customary use of biological resources should be considered, as well as possible impacts on the respect, preservation, protection and maintenance of traditional knowledge, innovations and practices, on sacred sites and associated ritual or ceremonial activities. The need for cultural privacy should be respected.[567]

Where social impact assessments are concerned, possible impacts on traditional uses of natural resources, traditional lifestyles, social cohesion and access to biological resources for livelihoods should be considered.[568] Protocols should be established where particular development activities will involve interaction with indigenous and local communities and the use of particular sites or resources.[569] Baseline studies can be used for assessing income and asset distribution, traditional systems of production and sharing natural resources, and views of the communities on the future, whether informally or formally articulated in community or government plans.[570]

The Guidelines emphasise that where cultural, environmental and social impact assessment processes relevant to indigenous and local communities are made an integral part of the environmental impact assessment process and incorporated into legislation, and the requirements for project/policy developers to find the most culturally, environmentally and socially sound, efficient options that avoid, reduce or mitigate adverse impacts are made explicit, this will prompt developers, at a very early stage, to use these tools to improve the development process prior to the project application or consent stage or in some cases, prior to screening procedures.[571] This has the potential to protect functioning landscapes and the communities that live in them.

The impact of changes to the landscape on communities has also been considered in the human rights context.

3.2.4 Landscape in Human Rights Law

3.2.4.1 The Significance of Human Rights to Landscape
Human rights law has increasingly become relevant to landscape protection as communities seek solutions to conflicts over the natural and cultural heritage in the absence of other forums to raise such challenges. There is no right to landscape in human rights law, as human rights are defined in terms of the individual, whereas landscape is a

---

565 Para 4.
566 Para 23.
567 Para 27.
568 Para 43.
569 Para 30.
570 Paras 44, 45, 51 and 55.
571 Para 67.

collective right. Nevertheless, Amy Strecker has noted that there exists a cultural rights dimension to landscape, if we consider landscape as the source of cultural heritage, the sum of practices which could be expressed materially in the environment and also represent a way of life as part of a people's collective identity.[572]

There is also a human rights dimension to landscape as expressed in the rights associated with environmental integrity, or rights to a healthy environment. Other rights are associated with landscape protection, such as the right to property (broadly interpreted to include customary rights or collective property) or the right to family and private life.[573] Importantly, the human rights approach to landscape therefore engages the relationships between people and landscape, not just with the physical space itself, and concerns rights of access to enjoy landscape as cultural heritage (since being deprived of such a right violates human dignity and freedom)[574] as well as the associated rights of customary rights or collective property.

3.2.4.2 International Human Rights Law in the Regional Courts: the European and Inter-American Human Rights systems

The European Court of Human Rights

The European Convention on Human Rights and Fundamental Freedoms (ECHR)[575] makes no reference to any right to the environment or cultural heritage in its text or protocols. Although environmental protection is not guaranteed under the ECHR, the case law has resulted in protection of the environment under certain circumstances, notably to facilitate effective enjoyment of other individual rights and freedoms, such as the right to family and private life and the right to property; and where those rights need to be restricted in the general interest of society, which could relate to environmental protection or safeguarding cultural heritage.[576] By contrast, there are explicit references to the environment in the American Convention on Human Rights. Article 11 of the Additional Protocol to the Convention (Protocol of San Salvador) refers to the right to live in a healthy environment, as well as to the protection, preservation and improvement of the environment.[577] Article 14 of the Protocol of San Salvador provides for the 'right to the benefits of culture', which is similar in normative content to the right to participate in cultural life.[578]

---

572 Strecker, *Landscape Protection in International Law* 129.
573 Ibid.
574 Francesco Francioni, 'Culture, Heritage and Human Rights: An Introduction', in Francesco Francioni, and Martin Scheinin, (eds), *Cultural Human Rights* (M. Nijhoff 2008) 7 and Ben Boer and Stefan Gruber, 'Heritage Discourses', in Kim Rubenstein and Brad Jessup (eds), *Environmental Discourses in International and Public Law* (Cambridge University Press 2012).
575 Council of Europe, European Convention for the Protection of Human Rights and Fundamental Freedoms, as amended by Protocols Nos. 11 and 14, 4 November 1950, ETS 5.
576 Strecker *Landscape Protection in International Law* 155.
577 Art 11. OAS Treaty Series No. 69 (1988) in Basic Documents pertaining to Human Rights in the Inter-American System OEA/Ser L V/II.82 Doc 6 Rev 1 at 67 (1992).
578 First enshrined in the Universal Declaration of Human Rights (art 27), followed by art 15(1)(a), International Covenant on Civil and Political Rights (16 December 1966, 999 UNTS 171. Entry into force: 23 March 1976) and art 27, International Covenant on Economic, Social and Cultural Rights (16 December 1966, 993 UNTS 3. Entry into force: 3 January 1976). See Strecker *Landscape Protection in International Law* 156.

Given the absence of landscape or cultural heritage in both these regional human rights treaties, Strecker has outlined the 'substantive' rights involved in cases dealing with landscape in human rights courts. Rights to landscape may include rights of access (for example to rights of way on public or private lands), usufruct rights (rights to fish, hunt or conduct other subsistence farming activities on public or private land); rights to enjoy sacred sites on public or private land, typified by cases involving indigenous communities and certain minorities; grazing rights on transhumance landscapes; rights to participate in planning decisions affecting the local landscape; and rights to a healthy environment. This latter right implies the right not to have landscape damaged to the extent that it will harm human health or well-being.[579]

Rights to landscape (envisaged as either the right to use or access a landscape, or as 'landscape protection') can therefore be indirectly achieved through the ECHR in a number of ways. First, the protection of other rights guaranteed in the ECHR (for example the right to life) might require the safeguarding of an environment of quality. This represents an indirect form of landscape rights. Second, the right to property might entail more than mere private ownership and include other usufructuary or customary rights, such as in the case of indigenous peoples. Third, the 'general interest in a democratic society' permits restrictions on the exercise of some rights and freedoms, such as the private right to property or those contained in Articles 8, 9, 10 and 11 of the ECHR[580] in favour of upholding the rights of others to access or enjoy landscapes of value.

The Court has held that conservation of European cultural heritage is in the general interest and can justify restriction of private property rights in certain cases.[581] By extension, rights to landscape (framed as rights to the protection of environmental and cultural spaces) could thus supersede individual rights and freedoms.[582] However, where ethnic minorities have brought claims concerning access to landscapes for dwelling purposes, the Court applies a restrictive approach.[583] Where landscape protection is the object of an applicant's claim, often involving indigenous peoples' claims concerning the right to use certain lands or protect them from destructive development, rather than to acquire title in the lands in question, the stance of the Court is even more conservative.[584] Traditional use of the landscape has not been accepted as sufficiently demonstrating the exercise of property rights, and in fact has been found to have no basis in law.[585] Notably, this caselaw postdates developments in indigenous rights in international law, such as the 2007 UN Declaration on the Rights of Indigenous Peoples.[586] This stands in contrast to the progressive approach of the Inter-American Court and Commission, which have recognised indigenous customary rights to lands despite lack of title (to be discussed below).

---

579 Strecker *Landscape Protection in International Law* 157.
580 Ibid.
581 *Kozacioglu v Turkey*, Grand Chamber Decision 19/02/09. Application No 2234/03; *Depalle v France*, Grand Chamber judgment 29/3/2010. Application No 34044/02.
582 Strecker, *Landscape Protection in International Law* 159.
583 *Chapman v the United Kingdom*. Grand Chamber judgment 18/01/2001. Application no 27238/95.
584 *G and E v Norway*, Application No. 9278/81 & 9415/81 (joined). Decision of 03/10/1983.
585 *Handölsdalen Sami Village and Others v Sweden*, Application No 39013/14. Judgment of 30 March 2010.
586 13 September 2007, A/RES/61/295.

There is thus a restrictive pattern in the European Court of Human Rights's approach with regard to rights to landscape, except when those rights entail landscape protection or preservation in the 'general interest of society'. Strecker makes two observations: while landscape protection is significant enough to warrant derogation from other rights and freedoms in certain scenarios, this is incidental to the aim of the applicants. Secondly, non-traditional forms of property rights, such as rights of use or access, are not seriously considered by the Court, neither in the case of minorities nor indigenous peoples. The Court relies on an interpretation of landscape in its visual sense, as a pastoral, pristine tableau, as well as a narrow conceptualisation of property, in keeping with the scope of ECHR, since that treaty makes no reference to cultural rights, and the definition of property, which is limited to individual enjoyment of one's possessions.[587] This is somewhat different from the approach of the Inter-American Court in cases concerning the landscape of indigenous peoples.

The Inter-American Court of Human Rights

The context of the Americas is quite different from Europe, as the region is home to much larger populations of indigenous peoples than Europe, and their resource rich traditional lands attract large-scale logging, mining and hydroelectric projects approved by the state.[588] As a result, the Inter-American Court of Human Rights receives a high number of cases concerning rights to access or use of traditional lands and has had numerous opportunities to develop this area of law.

Many cases concerning rights to landscape in the Inter-American system concern legal challenges to the granting of logging or mining concessions on communal or ancestral lands, where a community has traditionally occupied the area but lacks proper title, and whose way of life would be drastically altered by these agro-forestry projects. The Inter-American Court first held in 2001 that the international human right to property, particularly as affirmed in the American Convention on Human Rights, includes the right of indigenous peoples to the protection of their customary land and resource tenure.[589] This was the first legally binding decision by an international tribunal to uphold the collective land rights of indigenous peoples in the face of the state's failure to do so.[590]

Similarly the Inter-American Commission has clarified that indigenous peoples' right to property is based in international law and does not depend on domestic recognition of property interests, being 'grounded in indigenous custom and tradition' and further stated that 'the distinct nature of the right to property as it applies to indigenous people whereby the land traditionally used and occupied by these communities plays a central role in their physical, cultural and spiritual vitality'.[591] Cases that indirectly require the safeguarding of the landscape, such as the right to life, have

---

587 With the exception of some hunting and fishing rights – see Strecker, *Landscape Protection in International Law* 167.
588 Strecker, *Landscape Protection in International Law* 167.
589 *The Mayagna (Sumo) Awas Tingni Community v Nicaragua*, Judgment of 31/08/ 2001, Inter-Am. Ct. H.R., (Ser. C) No. 79 (2001).
590 Strecker, *Landscape Protection in International Law* 169 citing James Anaya and Claudio Grossman, 'The Case of Awas Tingni v Nicaragua: A New Step in International Law of Indigenous People.' *AJICL* 19(1) (2002): 1-15.
591 *Maya Indigenous Communities of Toledo District v Belize*, Case 12.053, IACtHR Report 40/04 (2004) at 155.

also been adjudicated in the Inter-American system.[592] The Commission has explicitly made the link between environmental quality and the right to life in upholding these rights, and placed special emphasis on indigenous people's special relationship with the land, recognising it as the source of their identity and repository for their heritage, and affirming that ancestral ownership is not undermined by lack of formal title.[593] This has been affirmed in subsequent cases concerning landscape preservation and use.[594]

As Strecker has remarked, this is groundbreaking, as the Court recognises that the diversity of the concept of property includes indigenous landscape rights. This aligns more closely with the right to landscape as discussed in Chapter Two, before private property gained ascendance, restricting the concept to abstract title or ownership of the property rather than the identification of the individual with the property through custom.[595] While this progressive approach to property restores landscape in substance, the Court does not extend this interpretation to protect the rights of non-indigenous applicants.[596] In the former cases, the Court and Commission viewed the right to property as inclusive of the customary right of indigenous communities to access and use the lands they had occupied but without title.

Thus the two main human rights courts have divergent approaches to protecting landscape rights. The European Court does not recognise non-traditional property rights such as rights of use or access. The Inter-American court adopts a much broader understanding of property that is defined by collective, customary and intangible aspects linked to a way of life, and transcends landscape preservation. This is partly due to the existence of a right to culture in the American Convention (Article 14, Additional Protocol) as well as right to healthy environment (Article 11, Additional Protocol).[597] But as Strecker notes, this collective approach has only been applied in relation to indigenous and tribal people. When it involves a case dealing with a nature reserve or public space, the Inter-American approach dovetails with the European system, and defines rights narrowly.[598]

Strecker highlights that the implication is that indigenous landscape is to be protected because of its use and dependency value in supporting indigenous culture, while non-indigenous or 'Western' landscape is framed in terms of aesthetic or environmental values.[599] This mirrors the approach to landscape in the European context, where the narrow conceptualisation of rights and the required level of standing preclude the admission of public interest proceedings, even if the area is protected by law and is of significance for the citizens of the state.[600] Strecker points out that this may be a false

---

592 *Moiwana Community v Suriname* (IACrtHR) Judgment of 15 June 2005, Series C No. 124.
593 Strecker, *Landscape Protection in International Law* 170.
594 Case of Xákmok Kásek Indigenous Community v. Paraguay, IACtHR Series C No. 214.
595 On property, see Graham *Lawscape* 26.
596 *Metropolitan Nature Reserve v Panama*, Case 11.533, Report no 88/03, IACtHR, OEA/SerL/V/II.118 Doc 70 Rev 2 at 524 (2003).
597 Amy Strecker, 'The Law is at Fault? Landscape and Agency in International Law,' in Tim Waterman and Ed Wall (eds), *Landscape and Agency* (Ashgate 2017) 60.
598 Strecker *Landscape Protection in International Law* 172.
599 Ibid, 173-174.
600 Ibid, 172.

dichotomy, as beyond the use and dependency value, both indigenous and non-indigenous cultures may share customary relationships with the land.[601]

International law has the capacity, as Strecker and O'Keefe have indicated, to engage human rights in a collective context where landscape is concerned.[602] Strecker enumerates the following factors in support: first, landscape is a cultural entity, which means that applying objective or universal criteria is inappropriate and impractical. Second, landscape, as a web of relationships representing community interaction with the land, is necessarily linked to the creation of group identity – whether regional or national.[603] Third, landscape can be interpreted as a collective good closely associated with cultural identity and common values, a 'heritage community'.[604] Fourth, participation in public decision-making is defined in terms of group, not individual rights. Finally, where there is landscape damage or destruction, damage is to the community as a whole, making quantification and the identification of individual victims difficult. Landscape, unlike property, has a collective dimension, so its destruction or degradation affects physical and mental well-being which cannot be measured in terms of personal injury, damage to property or monetary loss.[605] None of these aspects is exclusive to indigenous communities.

It has been argued by human rights scholars that the individualistic approach of human rights based on the principles of equality and non-discrimination no longer meets the current global issues relating to development and the environment, and the needs of communities.[606] Current debates over individuals' roles in society no longer dissociate the latter from the groups in which they live, and instead explore how an individual's presence within a group shapes their personality, aspirations, and ultimately rights formation. A nuanced view of individual human rights nowadays will necessarily take group-derived dimensions of an individual into consideration, referring to a 'socially-located individual', rather than merely an individual.[607] This by extension implicates space and spatial justice considerations.

While indigenous communities have a use and dependency value with landscape, this relationship is similar to Olwig's 'substantive nature of landscape,'[608] and many similar conceptions, understandings and relationships with landscape can be found outside the context of indigenous peoples.[609] Lastly, in the absence of an international environmental court, human rights courts offer one of the few potential avenues for ci-

---

601 Ibid, 174.
602 Strecker, *Landscape Protection in International Law* 142; Roger O' Keefe, 'The Right to Take Part in Cultural Life under Article 15 of the ICESCR.' *International Comparative Law Quarterly* 47(4) (1998): 904-923, 917. See also 'World Heritage Centre, Cultural Landscapes: the Challenges of Conservation, World Heritage 2002, Shared Legacy, Common Responsibility'; Associated Workshops, 11-12 November 2002 (Ferrara), *World Heritage Papers* 7, 59.
603 Simon Schama, *Landscape and Memory* (Knopf 1995).
604 A 'heritage community', as defined by Article 3(b) Framework Convention on the Value of Cultural Heritage for Society, 'consists of people who value specific aspects of cultural heritage which they wish, within the framework of public action, to sustain and transmit to future generations.'
605 Strecker, *Landscape Protection in International Law* 143.
606 Yvonne Donders, *Towards a Right to Cultural Identity* (Intersentia 2002) 94 in Strecker, *Landscape Protection in International Law* 175.
607 Lixinski 150.
608 See Chapter Two.
609 Strecker, *Landscape Protection in International Law* 143.

tizens to challenge governmental decisions and attempt to curtail state abuse of power. The approach by the Inter-American court demonstrates creative judicial activism in action, and could be an example for other systems where similar conditions exist. In addition, some Lesser Antillean states are parties to the ACHR, and are subject to the jurisdiction of the Inter-American Court (discussed later in this chapter). Strecker advocates for a broader interpretation of the content of property rights to include custom, use and access that would be adaptable to other communities and groups in relation to landscape rights.[610]

Centering communities in landscape protection has received even more attention in international law than ever before with the entry into force of the European Landscape Convention[611] (ELC, now the Council of Europe Landscape Convention), the first international instrument solely dedicated to landscape, albeit at regional level.

3.3 Regional Developments and Landscape Law

3.3.1 The European Landscape Convention and Beyond: Landscape as Public Space

While landscapes have secured their place in international law as a result of the evolution of cultural heritage law and the inclusion of 'cultural landscapes' within the scope of the WHC in 1992, the focus on 'outstanding universal value' placed undue emphasis on those landscapes that embody that 'ideal' balance of human-environment relations, which misconstrues the dynamic role of communities in landscape formation and misses the mark as far as landscape protection is concerned. The adoption of the European Landscape Convention sheds this hierarchical framing of heritage and 'democratises' landscape, leading to a paradigm shift in the understanding of landscapes as public spaces.[612]

Prior to the ELC, landscape was implicated in a number of treaties adopted under the auspices of the Council of Europe,[613] namely, the Berne Convention on the Conservation of European Wildlife and Natural Habitats (1979),[614] the European Convention on the Protection of the Architectural Heritage and the European Convention on the Protection of the Archaeological Heritage, also known as the Valletta Convention (Valletta, 16 January 1992).[615] In addition, a number of Council of Europe recommendations deal directly (and indirectly) with the issue of landscape

---

610 Strecker, 'The Law is at fault' 63.
611 Florence, 20 October 2000, 20/10/2000, ETS No.176.
612 Strecker, 'Landscape as Cultural Heritage' 287; Graham Fairclough, 'New Heritage Frontiers', in *Launching Colloquy of Heritage and Beyond: A Publication on the Contribution of the Council of Europe Framework Convention on the Value of Cultural Heritage for Society*, Lisbon, 20 November 2009, 31, available at: <http://www.coe.int/t/dg4/culutreheritage/heritage/identities/SpeechesLisbon/> accessed 6 October 2019.
613 Strecker, 'Landscape as Cultural Heritage' 276.
614 Council of Europe, Convention on the Conservation of the European Wildlife and Habitats (opened for signature 19/9/1979, entered into force 1/6/1982) ETS No. 104.
615 Council of Europe, European Convention on the Protection of the Archaeological Heritage (opened for signature 16/1/1992, entered into force 25/5/1995) ETS No. 143.

protection.⁶¹⁶ The most significant of these predecessor instruments of the ELC was Recommendation No. R(95)9 of 11 September 1995 on the integrated conservation of cultural landscape areas as part of landscape policies.⁶¹⁷ The Recommendation conceives of landscape broadly and proposes strategies for conservation, including sites that represent historic uses of land and distinctive activities, skills or traditions, or the artistic or literary representations inspired by them, or the significance of places for the historical events that took place there.⁶¹⁸ This would significantly influence the ELC's structure, scope and aims.

A number of proposals advocated for legal protection of Europe's landscapes, namely the IUCN's 'Parks for Life: Actions for Protected Areas in Europe' in 1994.⁶¹⁹ The driving force behind these proposals was the recognition that the implementation of EU directives had not been effective at the local level, where communities were absent in the decision-making process about local landscapes.⁶²⁰ Landscape was now seen as the critical element in the collective well-being of these communities. The preamble to the ELC therefore states that the protection, management and planning of landscape entail 'rights and responsibilities for everyone', and Strecker and others have noted that the language embeds spatial justice, human rights and democracy in this concept of landscape.⁶²¹

The ELC defines landscape as 'an area as perceived by people whose character is the result of the action and interaction of natural and/or human factors'.⁶²² Notably, there is no reference to aesthetic beauty or any visual feature to give the landscape its value. The ELC, contrary to the WHC, recognises landscape as a basic component of the European natural and cultural heritage and makes no reference to maintaining a certain interaction between these resources according to set criteria. It is the first legal text to explicitly recognise the dualism inherent in landscapes: the physical environment as well as the associative values as perceived by people. As the explanatory report on the ELC points out, '[i]t is not confined to either the cultural, man-made or natural components of the landscape: it is concerned with all of these and how they

---

616 Recommendation No. R(95)9 of 11 September 1995 of the Committee of Ministers on the integrated conservation of cultural landscape areas as part of landscape policies; Recommendation 79 (9) of the Committee of Ministers concerning the identification and evaluation for the protection of natural landscapes; Recommendation No. R(89)6 of the Committee of Ministers of 13 April 1989 relating to the protection and enhancement of rural architectural heritage; and Recommendation No. R (80) 16 on the specialised training of architects, town planners, civil engineers and landscape designers.
617 Adopted by the Committee of Ministers, 11 September 1995 at the 543rd meeting of the Ministers' Deputies.
618 Art 1.
619 IUCN Commission on National Parks and Protected Areas (CNPPA), *Parks for Life, Action for Protected Areas in Europe* (IUCN, 1994), at: <https://portals.iucn.org/library/sites/library/files/documents/1994-023.pdf> accessed 10 September 2019.
620 Report on the Preliminary Draft European Landscape Convention. Strasbourg, 5 May 1997, CG (4) 6 Part II.
621 Shelley Egoz et al (eds), *The Right to Landscape: Contesting Landscape and Human Rights* (Ashgate, 2011), and Strecker *Landscape Protection in International Law* 27.
622 ELC art 1.

interconnect.'[623] The ELC recognises that 'our environment has a cultural dimension, which cannot be separated from nature'.[624]

Landscape is a people's landscape in the ELC and therefore provides for the active participation of the public in the formulation of plans and polices.[625] It not only focuses on outstanding places, but also on the everyday and degraded landscapes where most people live and work. The ELC states that it includes 'natural, rural, urban and peri-urban areas. It includes land, inland water and marine areas. It concerns landscapes that might be considered outstanding as well as every day or degraded landscapes'.[626] This appears to return landscape to its earliest origins as described by Olwig, in which landscape reflected the interaction between people and the land, and this has a number of implications for human rights and democracy.[627] Here landscape transitions to public space, not just heritage,[628] and the ELC recognises processes of landscape change as intrinsic to their existence. In this case, protection from a purely conservationist angle could disrupt the rhythms of landscape essential to its functioning, and encompassing degraded as well as outstanding landscapes promotes a holistic approach to landscape management and protection.

In this regard, the ELC acknowledges the 'cultural, ecological, environmental and social' dimensions of landscape and obliges each State party: 'to recognise landscapes in law as an essential component of peoples' surroundings, as an expression of the diversity of their shared cultural and natural heritage, and as a foundation of their identity';[629] and to establish and implement landscape policies aimed at landscape protection, management and planning through the adoption of the specific measures.[630] To ensure that people are centred in the landscapes to which they belong, article 5(c) of the ELC underscores that 'each party undertakes to establish procedures for the participation of the general public, local and regional authorities, and other parties with an interest in the definition and implementation of landscape policies'. Landscape-quality objectives are defined after public consultation in accordance with article 5(c).[631] Reference is made to the Aarhus Convention in this regard.

While the ELC has been ambitious, transformative and innovative, its provisions are difficult to enforce. Its strengths lie in integrating landscape considerations within landscape quality objectives, national spatial strategies and planning processes, and ensuring public participation at each of these critical stages. But as Strecker has noted, its broad definition, which could be interpreted as 'environment', 'cultural heritage' or indeed 'economic development' by decision-makers), and lack of any criteria or list

---

623 Council of Europe 'European Landscape Convention: Explanatory Report', para 26, <http://conventions.coe.int/Treaty/EN/Reports?Html/176.htm> accessed 13 December 2017
624 Kate Clark, 'From Regulation to Participation: Cultural Heritage, Sustainable Development and Citizenship', in Council of Europe, *Forward Planning: the Function of Cultural Heritage in a Changing Europe* (Council of Europe, 2000) 106, as cited by Last, 'Article 1 – Cultural Landscapes' in the *WHC: A Commentary* 61.
625 Art 5(c).
626 Art 2.
627 Strecker, 'Landscape as Cultural Heritage' 272.
628 Ibid.
629 Art 5 (a).
630 Art 5(b).
631 Art 6(d).

means that it is legally very difficult to prove a breach of the ELC's obligations, as it is presumed that local populations will actively engage in the formulation of policies and that this will work in favour of landscape protection and avoidance of disputes in the long term.[632]

In addition, Strecker notes that since public participation is restricted to participation in plans and policies, it does not address other procedural rights, such as access to justice or judicial review, despite reference to the Aarhus Convention.[633] This limits the capacity of the ELC to resolve disputes, which may arise at later stages in the planning process when the aforementioned obligations have not been sufficiently provided for. This is critical as communities may not be aware of a project or its impact on the landscape until this later stage, nor does it account for situations in which stakeholders may be 'invisible and only materialize at this stage in the planning process.'[634]

Nevertheless, the ELC has had an enormous influence on raising awareness of the landscape, as well as on trans-frontier cooperation. Examples include joint projects for ecotourism, landscape conservation, restoration and development through protected areas or parks, protection against floods, sustainable forest and land management and tackling the cross-border impact of pollution, as well as pilot activities for improving the integrity of transboundary watersheds and ecosystems.[635] Because of its impact on landscape law, the ELC has transcended its regional influence. In 2016, a protocol was introduced to amend the European Landscape Convention.[636] Article 1 of the Protocol amends the title of the Convention to 'Council of Europe Landscape Convention', so as not to restrict the Convention's scope to 'European landscape'. A new paragraph in Article 2 of the Protocol to the text of the ELC states that the Protocol is 'to enable the application of the values and principles formulated in the Convention to non-European States who so desire.'[637]

The success of the ELC has inspired other initiatives,[638] and spurred calls for a global instrument on landscape protection. In 2011, the International Federation of Landscape Architects requested that UNESCO consider the feasibility of a global landscape convention.[639] While the experts at the meeting affirmed that such an instrument was needed, IFLA's resolution for a Global Landscape Convention was not

---

632 Strecker, 'Landscape as Cultural Heritage' 291.
633 Ibid.
634 Ibid.
635 Committee on Social Affairs, Health and Sustainable Development, Draft Protocol Amending the European Landscape Convention, B. Explanatory memorandum by Mr Schennach, Rapporteur, Report, Doc. 13989, 18 February 2016, para 6.
636 Protocol Amending the European Landscape Convention, ETS. No 219. <https://www.coe.int/en/web/conventions/full-list/-/conventions/treaty/219> accessed 18 September 2018.
637 New paragraph 13.
638 See the Latin American Landscape Initiative (LALI), a transdisciplinary partnership formed to implement the activities described in the LALI Declaration signed by the partners on the 19th October, 2012 in Medellín. LALI is a declaration of guiding principles to promote the recognition, valuation, protection, management, and sustainable planning of Latin American landscapes by means of binding and soft law agreements that recognise local, regional, and national diversity and values, as well as principles and processes to safeguard it. LALI explicitly references the ELC as a source of inspiration, as well as developments promoting a global landscape convention: The LALI Initiative, at p 6, <http://lali-iniciativa.org/> accessed 9 October 2019.
639 Expert meeting on 'The International Protection of Landscapes', Paris, UNESCO Headquarters, Room IV, 18 April 2011, Agenda.

adopted by UNESCO's Executive Board. Stakeholders were encouraged to integrate best practices regarding conservation and planning into wider goals for the urban environment.[640] Nevertheless, this forum stimulated further debate on the issue.

In the ensuing years, dialogue has continued on how best to address landscape issues at regional and international scales. At the UNESCO conference 'The International Protection of Landscapes: A Global Assessment', held in Florence in 2012, partners were sought to help build a strategy for its development and implementation. The Global Assessment highlighted core values in the WHC's approach to landscape, demonstrating its evolution: to commons and people, not heritage; dynamism, rather than preservation in stasis; everyday life not outstanding value; and protecting landscapes to promote communities.[641] This culminated in the Florence Declaration, affirming respect for communities and promoting participatory approaches, as well as calling for the creation in 2013 of an International Forum for the safeguarding of landscapes as a tool for sustainable development, with the aim of advancing proposals for the reflection on the Post-2015 International Development Agenda and 'to initiate the process for the creation of relevant international mechanisms.'[642]

Nevertheless, as Strecker has observed, in order for a new global instrument to be effective, it must protect landscape as a process, and offer robust mechanisms for addressing the ongoing degradation of landscapes beyond designating them as models of human activity and interaction with the environment.[643] The success of the ELC stems in part from regional commonalities, which facilitate the design of strategies that coordinate the many issues influencing landscape such as land use and food security, which are becoming more important in the face of climate change and impacts from globalisation. Landscape has come to represent all those diverse interests in land not accommodated by property, and the involvement of people in heritage and environmental policies.[644] Bearing in mind these challenges, how this may be adapted in the context of the Lesser Antilles is discussed in the next section.

3.3.2 The Lesser Antilles and Regional Developments: The OECS and the Escazú Agreement

The Revised Treaty of Basseterre, the constituting treaty of the Organisation of Eastern Caribbean States (OECS) contains principles addressing the protection of the cultural and natural heritage.[645] This treaty applies to the Lesser Antillean states with the exception of Barbados and Trinidad and Tobago. Article 23 of the treaty, on 'human and social development', addresses the promotion of sustainable, social and cultural development that would ensure societies are stable, safe and just and are based on the

---

640 The aforementioned 2011 Recommendation on the Historic Urban Landscape was promulgated in this regard.
641 UNESCO, 'The International Protection of Landscapes: A Global Assessment on the occasion of the 40th Anniversary of the World Heritage Convention and To Promote the UNESCO International Traditional Knowledge Institute (ITKI)', Florence, Italy, September 19-21, 2012 at 7.
642 The Florence Declaration on Landscape, September 19-21, 2012 on the occasion of the 40th Anniversary of the World Heritage Convention.
643 Strecker, 'Landscape as Cultural Heritage' 294.
644 Strecker, *Landscape Protection in International Law* 185.
645 *Revised Treaty of Basseterre Establishing the Organisation of Eastern Caribbean States Economic Union*, signed 18th June, 2010.

promotion and protection of human rights, non-discrimination, respect for diversity, equality of opportunity, solidarity, security, and participation of all people. Member states agree to promote respect for cultural expression (material and non-material), cultural rights and diversity and recognise the significance of such for development; the rights of indigenous peoples and the cultivation of shared values to facilitate overall development are also addressed.

Article 24 of the treaty concerns environmental sustainability and calls on Member States to implement the St. George's Declaration of Principles for Environmental Sustainability (SGD), in order to minimise environmental vulnerability, improve environmental management and protect the region's natural (including historical and cultural) resource base so that social and economic benefits for Member States may be optimised.[646] The SGD is originally a soft law document, outlining a regional framework for sustainable environmental management, with 21 principles grouped under four main goals. Each Member State is expected to implement the SGD via its national environmental management strategies (NEMS).

The preamble of the SGD acknowledges that the marine and terrestrial ecosystems of small islands states constitute a single unit, and that the impact of human intervention requires an integrated approach. The SGD also recognises 'the value and importance of the deeply embedded social connections between the region's culture and history and the ways in which its people perceive and make use of their environment'[647] and makes reference to multilateral environmental agreements, the Rio Declaration and other soft law documents on sustainable development, as well as international conventions addressing the protection of sites of cultural, historic and ecological significance.'[648]

Goal 3 concerns the protection and sustained productivity of the region's natural resource base, and Goal 4 addresses the contribution of natural resources to economic, social and cultural development. The corresponding principles are Principle 12, which specifically addresses the protection of the cultural and natural heritage, and Principle 17, which exhorts states to engage the international community to negotiate and implement multilateral environmental agreements. Each goal is accompanied by targets, indicators and supportive actions. There is one supportive action specifically for cultural sites. This requires 'the implementation of legal and other measures to document, protect, and where necessary rehabilitate, sites and areas of natural, cultural, and historic value, and avoidance of measures or acts that may harm them.'[649] There is therefore recognition of the relationship between communities and their environment,

---

646 Signed April 2001. At the OECS Environment Policy Committee (EPC) in September 1999, OECS Ministers of the Environment requested that the OECS Secretariat prepare an 'OECS Charter for Environmental Management' setting out a regional strategy and framework for environmental management. In accordance with the Ministers' request, the OECS Natural Resources Management Unit (now the Environment and Sustainable Development Unit, ESDU) developed the St. George's Declaration of Principles for Environmental Sustainability in the OECS. The Declaration sets out the broad framework to be pursued for environmental management in the OECS region. See the St George's Declaration, at <https://www.oecs.org/en/lsu-resources/st-george-s-declaration> accessed 16 September 2018.
647 Preamble, SGD.
648 Preamble, SGD.
649 SGD, Goal 3, at 17.

and the contribution to the cultural heritage, but no mechanisms for participation of these communities in processes to meet the goals outlined. This is not unexpected of soft law.

In recent developments, the adoption of the text of the Escazú Agreement[650] heralds the potential for a shift in environmental decision-making that could support the goals of the SGD and indirectly buttress the protection of landscapes. In June 1992, the United Nations Conference on Environment and Development adopted a declaration to strengthen the concept of countries' rights and responsibilities in the environment and development field. Principle 10 of the Rio Declaration on Environment and Development,[651] adopted in 1992, clearly emphasises the importance of public participation, access to information and access to justice for addressing environmental issues.

Initiated twenty years later at the United Nations Conference on Sustainable Development (Rio+20) in 2012, the Regional Agreement on Access to Information, Public Participation and Justice in Environmental Matters in Latin America and the Caribbean was adopted in Escazú (Costa Rica) on 4 March 2018 after two years of preparatory meetings and four years of negotiations, which involved significant public participation. This is the only binding agreement to emerge from Rio+20 and the first environmental agreement adopted by the Latin America and Caribbean region.[652] Based on the principle of sustainable development, the agreement underlines the interdependence between human rights and the environment, and represents a significant regional variation of Rio Principle 10.[653]

In 2012, The Declaration on the Application of Principle 10 of the Rio Declaration on Environment and Development provided the rationale for such an agreement:

> *Twenty years after the Earth Summit, we reiterate that, as recognized in Principle 10 of the Rio Declaration, environmental issues are best handled with the participation of all concerned citizens. To this end, each individual should have appropriate access to information, the opportunity to participate in decision-making processes and effective access to judicial and administrative proceedings. We thus affirm that to comply with this Principle, States should facilitate and promote education, awareness-raising and public participation by making information widely available and providing effective access to the proceedings outlined above.*[654]

The objective of the present Agreement is to guarantee the full and effective implementation in Latin America and the Caribbean of the rights of access to environmental

---

650 See <https://repositorio.cepal.org/bitstream/handle/11362/43583/1/S1800428_en.pdf> accessed 9 October 2019.
651 Rio Declaration on Environment and Development, Rio de Janeiro, 14 June 1992, UN Doc.A/CONF.151/26.
652 Declaration on the Application of Principle 10 of the Rio Declaration on Environment and Development 27 June 2012 <https://www.cepal.org/rio20/noticias/paginas/8/48588/Declaracion-eng-N1244043.pdf> accessed 9 October 2019.
653 Stephen Stec and Jerzy Jendroska, 'The Escazú Agreement and the Regional Approach to Rio Principle 10: Process, Innovation, and Shortcomings.' 2019 *Journal of Environmental Law* 31 (2019): 533-545, 536.
654 Declaration on the Application of Principle 10 of the Rio Declaration on Environment and Development 27 June 2012.

information, public participation in the environmental decision-making process and access to justice in environmental matters, and the creation and strengthening of capacities and cooperation, contributing to the protection of the right of every person of present and future generations to live in a healthy environment and to sustainable development. The adoption of the text reflects a willingness of the countries in the region to facilitate greater environmental protection.

Among its main provisions, the Escazú Agreement recognises the right of every person to live in a healthy environment, and the obligation to ensure that the rights defined in the Agreement are freely exercised. Article 4(1) states:

> *Each Party shall guarantee the right of every person to live in a healthy environment and any other universally-recognized human right related to the present Agreement. It provides for the adoption of legislative, regulatory, administrative and other measures to ensure the implementation of the Agreement, the provision of information to the public to facilitate the acquisition of knowledge on access rights, and the duty to provide guidance and assistance to the public, especially to vulnerable people and groups.*

Stephen Stec and Jerzy Jendroska point out the significance of this language. The guarantee of the right to a healthy environment is independent of the relationship between the right to a healthy environment and the access rights under Principle 10. In addition, the Parties include within this the obligation to guarantee 'any other universally-recognized human right related to the present Agreement.' This provides evidence that the right to a healthy environment is 'universally-recognized',[655] concerning the human rights dimension of landscape as discussed earlier.[656] In addition, Strecker has argued that the near universal ratification of the World Heritage Convention and caselaw invoking its provisions point to a general opinio juris on the binding character of the principles prohibiting the deliberate destruction of landscapes of significant importance for humanity.[657] This potentially establishes an obligation between Escazú parties and landscape protection as one of the universally recognised principles according to article 4(1).

Eleven guiding principles are recited in Article 3, many of which are well known, such as the precautionary principle and preventive principle, while others are not established norms of international environmental law.[658] Of note are the 'principle of non-regression and principle of progressive realization.'[659] They are not defined, but Stec and Jendroska highlight their similarity to the 'antibacksliding' provision in Article 4(7) of the Aarhus Convention, which is meant to establish Aarhus as a floor, and not a ceiling,

---

655 Strec and Jendroska 538. The authors also note that almost simultaneous to the adoption of the Escazu' Agreement, the Inter-American Court of Human Rights issued an advisory opinion on the environment and human rights confirming that a right to a healthy environment exists under the American Convention on Human Rights. See Advisory Opinion OC-23/17, Inter-Am Ct HR (ser A) No 23 (15 November 2017).
656 Strecker, *Landscape Protection in International Law* 129.
657 Ibid, 85.
658 Stec and Jendroska 538.
659 Escazú Agreement, art 3(c).

for progressive development of the law.[660] This may bode well for landscape protection in the future as communities continue to strengthen their participation in environmental matters, and place pressure on governments to avoid rollback of progressive language in legislation, which has occurred in the Lesser Antilles (to be discussed in later chapters).

Article 2 does not restrict the meaning of 'public' to minorities or indigenous communities, encompassing one or more persons, so potentially any group or community, and provides for vulnerable members of the public:

> *(d) "Public" means one or more natural or legal persons and the associations, organizations or groups established by those persons, that are nationals or that are subject to the national jurisdiction of the State Party;*
>
> *(e) "Persons or groups in vulnerable situations" means those persons or groups that face particular difficulties in fully exercising the access rights recognized in the present Agreement, because of circumstances or conditions identified within each Party's national context and in accordance with its international obligations.*

Environment is not defined, but in requiring each state to prepare an environmental information system, the sources of information reference only natural resources.[661] However, in publishing a national report on the state of the environment, each Party's report may contain information on collaboration agreements among public, social and private actors, and ensure that such reports are prepared 'in different formats and disseminated through appropriate means, taking into account cultural realities',[662] which suggests an understanding of the dimensions of community life, even if it is not an outright endorsement of landscapes.

Where the right of access to information is concerned, each Party is expected to promote access to information contained in concessions, contracts, agreements or authorisations granted, which involves the use of public goods, services or resources, in accordance with domestic legislation.[663] This has implications for the use and protection of landscape, as a public space.

In addressing the right to participation in decision-making, Escazú goes beyond the European Landscape Convention (although the ELC is not the treaty dealing with procedural rights) when it ensures participation throughout the decision-making process:

> *Each Party shall guarantee mechanisms for the participation of the public in decision-making processes, revisions, reexaminations or updates with respect to projects and activities, and in other processes for granting environmental permits that have or may have a significant impact on the environment, including when they may affect health.*[664]

---

660 Stec and Jendroska 539.
661 Escazú Agreement, art 6(3).
662 Art 6(7).
663 Art 6(9).
664 Art 7(2).

The information to be provided to the public concerns 'environmental matters of public interest' such as land-use planning, policies, strategies, plans, programmes, rules and regulations, which have or may have a significant impact on the environment.[665] Public participation cannot merely be an attempt to appease the public; each party is expected to establish conditions that are favourable to public participation in environmental decision-making processes and that are appropriate given the social, economic, cultural, geographical and gender characteristics of the public.[666] There is therefore scope here for considering the needs of specific local communities, reaffirming that the public is not understood as a homogenous entity in the text.

Throughout the text of the Escazú Agreement, environmental rights are rooted in the protection of human rights. The preamble contains several references to international human rights law.[667] In fact, Belén Olmos Giupponi notes that the right to public participation as prescribed in the Escazú Agreement is markedly influenced by the work of the OAS on the freedom of expression, as well as the 2010 Inter-American Model Law on Access to Public Information.[668] This has practical implications, since the Escazú Agreement provisions on procedural environmental rights could be invoked and enforced through the human rights protection system of the OAS, which aims to defend and promote fundamental rights and individual freedoms in the Americas. This is noteworthy given the case law referred to earlier in this chapter concerning indigenous and local communities and landscape rights, the judicial activism of the Inter-American Court, and that some Lesser Antillean States are States parties to the ACHR.[669]

Sustainable Development Goals (SDGs) are also considered in the preamble, Goal eleven of which concerns sustainable cities and communities, and target 11.3 concerns enhancing the capacity for participatory, integrated and sustainable settlement planning and management. Target 11.4 aims at strengthening efforts to protect and safeguard the world's cultural and natural heritage, and target 11.7 addresses providing universal access to safe, inclusive and accessible, green and public spaces, while target 11.A supports positive economic, social and environmental links between urban, peri-urban and rural areas by strengthening national and regional development plan-

---

665 Art 7(3).
666 Art (10).
667 Recital Five of the Preamble, Escazú Agreement: Reaffirming the importance of the Universal Declaration of Human Rights and recalling other international human rights instruments that underscore that all States have the responsibility to respect, protect and promote human rights and fundamental freedoms for all, without distinction of any kind, including those related to race, colour, sex, language, religion, political or other opinion, national or social origin, property, birth or other status...
668 Belén Olmos Giupponi, 'Fostering environmental democracy in Latin America and the Caribbean: An analysis of the Regional Agreement on Environmental Access Rights.' *RECIEL* 28(2019):136-151, 143, and see Edison Lanza, 'The Right to Access to Public Information in the Americas: Specialized Supervisory and Enforcement Bodies. Thematic Report included in the 2014 Annual Report of the Office of the Special Rapporteur for Freedom of Expression of the Inter-American Commission on Human Rights' (March 2015) <http://www.oas.org/en/iachr/expression/docs/reports/access/thematic%20report%20access%20to%20public%20information%202014.pdf>. OAS, 'AG/RES. 2607 (XL-O/10) Model Inter-American Law on Access to Public Information' (2010) <https://www.oas.org/dil/AG-RES_2607-2010_eng.pdf> accessed 9 October 2019.
669 Barbados, Dominica, Grenada, and Trinidad and Tobago. See <https://www.oas.org/dil/treaties_B-32_American_Convention_on_Human_Rights_sign.htm> accessed 28 October 2019.

ning by 2030.[670] Nevertheless, while the preamble acknowledges the cultural dimension of environmental rights when it references the multiculturalism of Latin America and the Caribbean and their peoples, Olmos Giupponi observes that this was a missed opportunity to incorporate more direct references to land rights, cultural rights and even the jurisprudence of the IACtHR on indigenous rights.[671]

The Escazú Agreement was opened for signature on 27th September 2018. It was signed by 16 countries in the following days and weeks, and Guyana became the first ratifying state in April 2019. St Vincent and the Grenadines signed it in July 2019. During a high-level ceremony on the sidelines of the general debate of the 74th UN General Assembly (UNGA), on 26 September 2019, in New York, US, two additional countries signed the Agreement (Grenada and Jamaica) and five countries ratified it (Bolivia, Jamaica, St Kitts and Nevis, St Vincent and the Grenadines, and Uruguay). The next day, it was also signed by Nicaragua and Saint Lucia. Of the Lesser Antillean states, Barbados, Dominica and Trinidad and Tobago are not signatories. Currently, the Escazú Agreement has acquired 21 signatory countries and six ratifications. Eleven ratifications are required for entry into force by September 2020.[672]

While the Escazú Agreement is not a landscape treaty, and does not use that term anywhere in its text, it is the first regional binding agreement on the environment to delineate a framework for enhancing local governance and achieving full implementation of procedural environmental rights. This lays the preconditions for landscape protection by strengthening the mechanisms through which local communities can engage state authorities on issues affecting the natural resources that they rely on for their way of life, and provides a route to environmental justice as it aligns with the practices and legislative and judicial developments of the Inter-American system. Because public is expansively defined, including the most vulnerable populations, and information concerning land use and development must be culturally, socially, geographically appropriate, the nuances of the landscape are accounted for in the Escazú Agreement, even if it is not referred to by name. The potential effect of Escazú is that while it is not intended to substantively protect the landscape, it implicitly contributes to landscape protection by strengthening procedural environmental rights for communities while explicitly requiring States parties to uphold all related universally recognised human rights, which would include by extension the human rights and cultural rights dimensions to landscape. This should make landscape protection a key consideration in the future, as these states grapple with environmental and climate change induced events that threaten local livelihoods and landscapes.

As Arif Bulkan has noted, the influence of international law is likely to be substantial – not immediately or dramatically, but incrementally over time.[673] These trea-

---

670 <https://www.un.org/sustainabledevelopment/cities/> accessed 9 October 2019.
671 Olmos Giupponi, 141 referring to Recital Ten of the Preamble, Escazú Agreement.
672 Leila Mead, 'Escazú Agreement on Rio Principle 10 Gains Signatures, Ratifications <http://sdg.iisd.org/news/escazu-agreement-on-rio-principle-10-gains-signatures-ratifications/> accessed 9 October 2019; 'In Key Week for Sustainable Development at the UN, Latin American and Caribbean Authorities Sign and Ratify the Escazú Agreement', ECLAC Press release, 26 September 2019.
673 Arif Bulkan, 'From Instrument of Empire to Vehicle for Change: The Potential of Emerging International Standards for Indigenous Peoples of the Commonwealth Caribbean.' *Commw L Bull* 37(3) (2011): 463-489, 477.

ties and their resulting jurisprudence have contributed to common global standards, which have been invoked and applied by a variety of international bodies, such as the OAS. The proliferation of international bodies applying these various treaties provides fora for indigenous and local communities to exchange ideas and strategies, which in turn has heightened consciousness and reinvigorated their struggles for recognition of rights in both domestic and international forums.[674] The Escazú Agreement potentially provides another pathway for institutional actors, communities and individuals to engage in this regard.

3.4 Conclusion

This chapter has shown that advancements in international law have catapulted landscape from its soft law origins in cultural heritage law to a discrete subject of an emerging area of law, international landscape law. The recognition and inclusion of landscape is a reflection of the evolution of international cultural heritage law, which no longer approaches heritage as artefact-centred and alienated from communities, but embedded in a dynamic process that is community-driven, enriched by the diverse customs, relations and lived-in experiences embodied in the landscape that generates it. The protection of landscape is therefore critical to the protection of heritage as a living, dynamic resource.

The category of cultural landscapes within the World Heritage Convention first recognised the importance of people in the management of World Heritage sites and proved influential in the developments leading to a more people-centred approach to landscape protection. Cultural landscapes were included within the scope of the WHC to give recognition to the intangible dimension to landscapes, including sacred sites, customary land use practices, and communities living in harmony with their environments. A significant aspect of landscapes that challenges World Heritage classification as well as State discourses on heritage is that there can be a multiplicity of uses competing and in contention with one another. In addition, the World Heritage system relies on States parties to implement its provisions, which often undercut any real participation of communities, even if their heritage was now recognised.

It is the European Landscape Convention that truly 'democratises' landscape, by distinguishing landscape not for its aesthetic qualities but rather its significance in the daily life of its inhabitants.[675] The ELC situates people at the heart of landscape, regardless of that landscape's features, without distinguishing its cultural dimensions from the natural. The 'landscape approach' is now synonymous with involving people in heritage and environmental policies.[676] By highlighting spatial justice, human rights and democracy, the ELC has raised the profile of landscape and stimulated efforts to create a global convention. While there are challenges with this concept, regional initiatives such as LALI in Latin America have developed regional principles to guide both soft law and binding instruments in the protection of landscape.

---

674 Ibid.
675 Strecker, *Landscape Protection in International Law* 100.
676 Ibid, 185.

Focusing on people and their communities shows that international law has become more attuned to human rights issues, even bypassing the State where necessary to protect local communities in the face of State inaction or abuse. Human rights courts appear to be the fora of necessity for indigenous communities in lieu of appropriate mechanisms to address their needs, while local communities continue to face hurdles where landscape protection is concerned. While the European Court of Human Rights has assumed a more conservative stance, the Inter-American Court of Human Rights continues to demonstrate the capacity to be innovative in protecting rights beyond private property, though this has been so far confined to indigenous communities. Nevertheless, this is relevant for the Lesser Antilles as post-colonial states in the Americas and OAS member states. For the Lesser Antillean states that are WHC parties, WHC implementation is addressed through capacity building for local institutions to nominate landscapes. While landscape protection is not yet a distinct priority, UNESCO's Caribbean Capacity Building Programme and regional action plans have tailored strategies to the small island context for enhancing domestic heritage frameworks, which does call for recognition of landscapes.

Looking to the future, the Escazú Agreement, the first regional environmental treaty for Latin America and the Caribbean, holds much promise for landscape protection though this is not obvious at first. It builds on OAS legislative developments, enhancing local institutions to strengthen local governance capacity, and providing for procedural environmental rights such as access to environmental information, participation in environmental decision-making and access to environmental justice. There is awareness of landscape in Escazú even if it is not identified as such. Having regard to the geographic, social and cultural circumstances of communities indicates a realisation that private property has occluded understanding of the relationships communities have with land, and cannot provide information on practices with local resources that may be crucial to the formation of sustainable development strategies for the future. In this regard, the Escazú Agreement, should it enter into force, equips the region with the mechanisms and tools to effect participatory governance of natural resources, which involves landscape protection indirectly.

Having examined landscape protection in international law, we now turn to a discussion of the domestic legislative framework for heritage protection in the Lesser Antilles. The following chapter examines the current laws for antiquities protection, museums and National Trusts, and subsequent chapters address planning law and finally parks and protected areas legislation.

4

Antiquities and Heritage Legislation

4.1 Introduction

Physical evidence of the past has been legislated by governments for centuries.[677] Archaeological heritage was first regulated in the West through the application of the law of treasure trove; while this was viewed as the common patrimony in Europe, England required individual property rights to be respected through the payment of compensation upon government retrieval of such objects.[678] This intertwining of property rights and heritage protection is rooted in a particular understanding of the land in England, rather than landscape. British land law and rights to property have influenced the management of land resources in former British colonies throughout the world, and therefore underpinned the protection of heritage.[679] Domestic heritage legislation in the Lesser Antilles thus crystallised in unique spatial circumstances as described in Chapter Two, influenced by a particular geographical location, and an understanding of land as denial of place. This has important implications for the conceptualisation and administration of heritage.

A further challenge is accommodating post-colonial and progressive notions of heritage, which have arisen since the Cultural Turn.[680] As discussed in Chapter Three, this influenced the World Heritage Convention's pivot away from the restrictive concept of heritage as property, from objects and monuments viewed in isolation from a culture, to emphasising heritage as inheritance and promoting landscapes as the setting of communities who are the creators of that heritage. Considering the implications of these developments for the Lesser Antilles requires a review of existing relevant laws within those nations.

---

677 O'Keefe and Prott, *Law and the Cultural Heritage* 32; John Carman, *Valuing Ancient Things: Archaeology and Law,* (Leicester University Press 1996) 34-35. See also Ben Boer and Graeme Wiffen, *Heritage Law in Australia* (Oxford University Press 2006).

678 See Tim Bonyhady, *The Law of the Countryside: the Rights of the Public* (Professional Books 1987) 268-285 for a general discussion of the law of treasure trove in England. For its effects on other common law jurisdictions, see K Wiltshire *Heritage, Federalism and the Environment* (R L Matthews 1985) 47-63, 48 for discussion of the Australian example.

679 See Peter C James, 'Anglo-Australian Law and the Aboriginal Cultural Heritage.' *Historic Environment* 11(2, 3) (1995): 52-56, 53.

680 Strecker *Landscape Protection in International Law* 122.

In this chapter, the core domestic legislation concerning protection of the archaeological heritage in the Lesser Antilles is analysed. These laws include antiquities and heritage protection legislation. Laws establishing institutions for the protection of this heritage, such as museums and National Trusts, provide the administrative apparatus of the heritage protection framework in this region. The analysis makes a distinction between laws developed during the colonial era and later consolidated as part of the laws of newly independent nations (Grenada, St Vincent and the Grenadines, and Barbados are compared in this regard); and post-independence heritage protection legislation, developed recently in the states of Antigua and Barbuda and St Kitts and Nevis. This area of law is very much in flux (laws were repealed during the writing of this chapter), so proposed laws not yet in force have also been examined for insight into the evolving understanding of the regulation of heritage resources.

4.2 The Role of Heritage Legislation in the Caribbean and the Modern Concept of Heritage

Early forays into cultural policymaking in the Caribbean ignored the role of cultural heritage. Suzanne Burke has remarked that culture has never been considered an autonomous area of policy, usually requiring a relationship with other policy domains, such as tourism, education, community development, industry and trade, to justify its protection.[681] Indeed, developing countries with rich heritage resources tend to be focused on economic development, and poverty drives looting as a form of alternative income. Protecting heritage sites is often deemed a peripheral consideration when governments are confronted with the immediate needs of the population, such as jobs, health care and education.[682] Nevertheless, at the state level, the preamble of the Constitution of Grenada acknowledges that cultural rights play a central role in achieving the ideal standard of living required for individuals in a free society.[683] This is in keeping with international conventional law,[684] and signals an understanding that culture is relevant to quality of life. But where does cultural heritage repose in this relationship?

Heritage resources have been defined, classified, excluded and reincorporated over time due to what Janet Blake calls the uncertainty 'over the exact nature of its subject matter'.[685] International cultural heritage law has recommended that a traditional heritage law regime should include State control over and grant approval for excavations, oblige any person finding archaeological remains to declare them, define the legal status of the archaeological subsoil, classify historical monuments and supervise restora-

---

681 Suzanne Burke, 'The Evolution of the Cultural Policy Regime in the Anglophone Caribbean.' *International Journal of Cultural Policy* 13(2) (2007): 169-184, 170. I would also add that cultural policymaking in the region continues to ignore sustainability and environmental considerations in favour of cultural festivals, which produce immediate monetary benefits, and which can be linked to the cultural industries and economic development, as Barbados has done most recently with its Cultural Industries Development Authority Act (not discussed in this research).
682 O'Keefe and Prott 18.
683 The Grenada Constitution 1974, s 2(e).
684 ICESCR, art 15 – the right to participation in cultural life. Grenada became party to this treaty in 1991.
685 Janet Blake, 'On Defining the Cultural Heritage.' *ICLQ* 49 (2000): 61-85.

tion, approve the removal of monuments, create and maintain reserves and parks in zoned areas, promote education of the public, and facilitate access to the sites.[686] As the previous chapter has shown, the definition of heritage is not fixed, having evolved from a focus on objects and sites to now encompass dynamic relationships with those objects and sites, from universality of heritage to the local communities who generate and give value to these heritage resources.[687] The intangible heritage central to cultural relationships, responsible for generating 'a sense of place', is critical to social identity, diversity and sustainability.[688]

The traditional conservation associated with colonialism and the new concept of heritage as expressed in the preceding chapters on landscape and international cultural heritage law are therefore recurring underlying themes in this analysis of heritage law of the Lesser Antilles. As a result of the Cultural Turn, heritage protection has moved away from its elitist colonial roots and antiquarian traditions. This is of particular significance to post-colonial states such as the Lesser Antilles, because it affords these countries the opportunity to deconstruct the inherited regulatory framework for heritage protection. This will be addressed in the following sections on heritage law, as applicable.

4.3 Antiquities Legislation

The oldest antiquities legislation in the Lesser Antilles is the Preservation of Historic Buildings and Antiquities Act 1976 from St Vincent and the Grenadines. The Minister responsible for the implementation of the legislation is the Minister for Tourism, linking the management of heritage resources to tourism assets.[689] 'Antiquity' is defined as any object, other than a historic building, the preservation of which is desirable because of 'traditional, archaeological, palaeontological or historic interest'.[690] The inclusion of traditional value as one of the criteria for assessing heritage raises the question as to whether this is progressive and would allow for heritage valued by the community to be protected, or conservative in the sense of the colonial tradition.

Listing is a duty of the Minister.[691] The Minister can do all that is necessary to restore a building where the owner does not comply.[692] Acquisition of a historic building or antiquity is an option, but must be for a public purpose as outlined in the Land Acquisition Act.[693] However, the Antiquities Act has since been amended by the

---

686 Originally laid down in various soft law documents such as the New Delhi Recommendation on International Principles Applicable to Archaeological Excavations, adopted on 5 December 1956, the Recommendation concerning the Safeguarding of the Beauty and Character of Landscapes and Sites, adopted on 11 December 1962, and the Recommendation concerning the Preservation of Cultural Property Endangered by Public or Private Works, adopted on 19 November 1968, to name a few.
687 Blake, *International Cultural Heritage Law* 9.
688 Simon Molesworth, 'Managing Heritage Cities in Asia and Europe: The Role of Public-Private Partnerships'. Delivered at the Public Forum and Experts' Meeting – *International National Trusts Organisation's Network Experiences in Public Private Partnership Approaches towards Management of Heritage Cities*, 12-14 July 2012, Yogyakarta, Indonesia.
689 St Vincent and the Grenadines Preservation of Historic Buildings and Antiquities Act 1976, s 2.
690 SVG Preservation of Historic Buildings and Antiquities Act 1976, s 2.
691 Ibid, s 4.
692 Ibid, s 4(3) and 4(8).
693 Ibid, s 3.

Planning Act, which empowers the Minister for Planning to make this list. The implications of conflicting mandates are addressed in this chapter, and the potential incapacitation of these laws is discussed in the subsequent chapter on planning legislation.

The St Kitts National Trust Act was drafted to work in tandem with the St Kitts and Nevis National Conservation and Environmental Protection Act (NCEPA),[694] and contemplates the possibility of concurrent jurisdiction.[695] This is because Part IX of the NCEPA concerns Antiquities and Historic Buildings. This is the only other antiquities legislation in force in the Lesser Antilles. Section 47 of NCEPA defines antiquities to include:

(a) any ancient monument which dates or may reasonably be believed to date from a period prior to 1900;

(b) any statues, engravings, carvings, inscriptions, paintings, writings, metallurgic art, coins, gems, seals, jewels, arms, tools, ornaments and all other objects of art which date or may reasonably be believed to date' from a period prior to 1900;

(c) any abandoned wreck and all objects of archaeological association which have remained unclaimed for fifty years in the territorial waters of Saint Christopher and Nevis.

Unlike the Vincentian legislation, there is a minimum age required to qualify as an antiquity. A licence must be obtained in order to excavate antiquities, and the licence will only be granted by the Minister after consultation with the Conservation Commission, once it has been determined that the potential licensee is competent and possesses sufficient funds for the excavation.[696] Conditions may be attached to such a licence. The Minister must be furnished with all proposed excavation plans and a list of all antiquities excavated, and he must personally inspect those excavated antiquities.[697] Nevertheless, antiquities excavated may be divided and delivered to the licensee, and the law of salvage applied, once the Minister in consultation with the Conservation Commission, determines whether any of those antiquities should be retained as cultural property or are required for educational, scientific, archaeologic or historic purposes of the Nation.[698] The commercial value of antiquities therefore appears to be weighed against their archaeological value. Where antiquities are accidentally discovered, they must be reported to the Minister and are prohibited from export unless licensed.[699]

---

694 St Kitts and Nevis is a federation, and its Constitution empowers Nevis to make its own laws in a number of specific areas – s 106 Constitution of Saint Christopher and Nevis 1983. These areas however do not override Parliament's lawmaking powers – s 37. Where the title of a law does not refer to Nevis, it applies to the island of St Kitts only.
695 St Kitts National Trust Act 2009, s 4(2).
696 St Kitts NCEPA, s 48(2).
697 SKN NCEPA, s 48 (3).
698 Ibid, s 49.
699 Ibid, ss 50-51.

NCEPA is the only law in the region to outline the form and content of a list as originally devised in the common law.[700] A building can only be listed where it has been recommended by the Conservation Commission, although owners of listed buildings must also be notified and have a right of appeal.[701] Private property rights are therefore given consideration, but the implication is that all persons with a legal interest in the land must consent to protection of the heritage.[702] The effect of listing is that alterations cannot be made to such buildings without the permission of the Building Board, in consultation with the Conservation Commission.[703] Where such acts are committed, a fine is to be paid, but no remedies concerning restoration are proffered and no development rights for such buildings are withdrawn, confirming Richard Harwood's assertion that listed buildings, in contrast to monuments, are intended to remain in 'an active, commercially viable use'.[704] Indeed, the legislation underscores this by stating that the Building Board 'shall give special consideration to the public interest in preserving the features for which the building is listed, and *shall endeavour to use all means reasonably available* to preserve those features.'[705] For conservation legislation, such protection is not very robust at all.

The Act does provide tax incentives to restore historic buildings. These include exemption from land and house tax, exemption from custom duties and consumption tax, professional advice from public officers without charge, and use of plant and equipment from the Public Works Department. In exchange for this support, owners are expected to make such buildings open for public visits.[706] This is a much stronger and practical framework than what is contained in planning legislation in some countries in the Lesser Antilles, as will be discussed in the next chapter. However, these incentives have not been extended to archaeological sites.

The Act makes provision for implementation via regulations, which may include the regulation and use of protected areas; the prevention of deterioration of historic sites; and prescribing terms for salvage as they apply to antiquities and wrecks.[707] Offences are also addressed. It is an offence to dig or remove an artefact, and an offence to deface, damage, or destroy historic buildings.[708] The Kittitian legislation therefore integrates cultural heritage within its conservation legislation, outlines a permitting system for antiquities and establishes relatively progressive mechanisms for the protection of built heritage.

With the repeal of Grenada's heritage protection legislation to accommodate new museum legislation (discussed later in this chapter), there are few examples of antiquities legislation in the remaining Lesser Antilles. Nevertheless, St Kitts' antiquities legislation may be compared to the Barbados Preservation of Antiquities and Relics Bill 2012 (Antiquities bill) and Antigua's Cultural Heritage Protection Bill 2016 (Cultural Heritage bill).

---

700 On listing, see Richard Harwood, *Historic Environment Law: Planning, Listed Buildings, Monuments, Conservation Areas and Objects* (Institute of Art and Law 2012) 53.
701 SKN NCEPA, s 52.
702 Also at issue in Australia, see Lesley-Anne Petrie, 'An Inherently Exclusionary Regime: Heritage Law – The South Australian Experience.' *Macquarie Law Journal* 5(2005): 177-199, 192.
703 SKN NCEPA, s 53.
704 Harwood 13.
705 SKN NCEPA, s 53(1) (emphasis added).
706 Ibid, s 54.
707 Ibid, s 56.
708 Ibid, s 57.

The Preservation of Antiquities and Relics bill, if passed, would represent the first piece of formal heritage legislation to be prepared by Barbados. The purpose of the bill is the preservation of places, structures and relics or other objects of archaeological, historical and cultural interest, by providing for export control of protected heritage, and licenses for archaeological excavation, to be administered and enforced by a board.

Of note is the interpretation section. Antiquities and relics have been given legal definitions. 'Relics' are objects exceeding one hundred years old 'which in the majority opinion of the Board is considered to be of such overarching value to Barbados that the Board is empowered to establish control or acquire the said object in the interest of preserving the patrimony of the nation'.[709] This is interesting as patrimony is not a term found within the common law. Antiquity is also defined to include sites.[710] It is nevertheless curious that 'relic' is used. For one, it is a synonym for antiquity, and outdated at that. Its wider meaning in contemporary society points to objects that are outmoded, obsolete, or fragmented.[711] A relic is an object or custom whose original culture has disappeared, having historical value, but no modern use. And while technically accurate, it brings to mind Raymond Goy's 'dead musea',[712] and whether this conceptualisation would promote heritage as relevant for a dynamic national identity and contemporary Barbadian society, stimulate public participation, and support cultural enrichment as a public good outcome.

The bill however introduces new mechanisms to protect Barbados' heritage. A control list identifying categories of relics subject to export control is to be maintained, and illicit trade in cultural objects is deemed an offence with prescribed penalties.[713] Export of antiquities is illegal unless an export certificate has been granted by the Minister.[714] While there are no criteria given for this assessment, objects on the control list may not be exported and doing so will result in a fine or imprisonment.[715] A licensing system is outlined in Part 2 of the bill. Licenses are required for excavation, and must be recorded in a register.[716] Persons applying for licenses must have sufficient training and experience to undertake excavations, but these qualifications are not elaborated in any regulations. Conditions may also be imposed when granting the license.[717]

A cultural heritage statutory board is created, although cultural heritage is not defined.[718] The Board's composition is not specified, except to say that members must

---

709 Barbados Preservation of Antiquities Bill, s 2.
710 Barbados Preservation of Antiquities Bill, s 2 defined 'antiquity' as any (a) place or site; (b) monument or structure together with their settings and fixtures erected, formed or built by human agency that is affixed to the land or under the land; including: (i) works of monumental sculpture and painting; (ii) elements or structures of an archaeological nature; (iii) inscriptions; (iv) cave dwellings; and (v) combinations of above features (c) monument or structure erected, formed or built by human agency that is located under water or on the seabed that is of historical, cultural or archaeological interest or is believed to be of historical or archaeological interest.
711 'Relic'. The Oxford English Dictionary, Oxford <http://www.oxforddictionaries.com/definition/english/relic> accessed 20 July 2016 and cf 'relic', the Merriam Webster Dictionary, Merriam Webster <http://www.merriam-webster.com/dictionary/relic> accessed 20 July 2016.
712 Goy 117.
713 Barbados Preservation of Antiquities Bill, ss 4 and 8.
714 Ibid, ss 5 and 6.
715 Ibid, ss 4 and 7.
716 Ibid, ss 9 ad 15.
717 Ibid, s 11.
718 Ibid, s 20.

have experience relevant to cultural heritage.[719] The functions of the board are to advise the government on matters pertaining to the classification of relics, and to manage the control list as well as administer licenses and export certificates.[720] Compensation is to be paid where an antiquity is acquired by the State.[721] Where an antiquity is damaged, penalties are prescribed, which may be a fine or imprisonment or both.[722] The language pertaining to export control, licensing and acquisition is similar to the Kittitian legislation, discussed above.

In many ways, the bill appears to be an extension of the town planning legislation to manage the cultural heritage. The bill relies on the planning authorities through the use of preservation orders – section 19 states that preservation orders pursuant to section 28 of the Barbados Town Planning Act are to be issued where an antiquity needs protection or may be damaged or destroyed. Reference is also made to listed buildings and the use of enforcement notices in the town planning legislation. The bill introduces stronger mechanisms for protection of heritage, such as the use of definitions, export control, permitting and protection through ownership via compulsory acquisition, but ultimately, these types of measures tend to be weak and acquisition and ownership can be difficult to enforce and monitor.[723] The proposed framework protects property rights through limited controls on listed buildings, and the system introduced for protecting heritage is based on its economic value. Even if the property is identified as being of heritage significance, a non-consenting owner can put a stop to any protection being provided, because of the highest protection accorded to private property rights.[724]

The incremental development of Barbados' regulatory framework for heritage seems to reflect the growth and acceptance of the archaeological discipline in that country. There is an increased use of technical terminology in the Antiquities bill. Nevertheless, the traditional definition of heritage in which ancient objects are protected yet detached from the wider environmental and social context prevails.

In contrast, Antigua has chosen to draft implementing legislation for the Underwater Heritage Convention and incorporate general principles of heritage law. The long title of Antigua's bill makes clear that the scope of this law is comprehensive, as it is 'for the protection of cultural heritage, encompassing land-based as well as submerged immovable heritage as well as movable objects, in Antigua and Barbuda'. 'Cultural heritage' is thus broadly defined to include underwater heritage, undiscovered heritage, and any trace of human existence that is older than 50 years.[725]

Section 3 states that the competent national authority (CNA) is the National Parks Authority, which would integrate cultural heritage legislation with the natural heritage, and update Antigua's parks legislation (discussed in chapter 6). The role of the CNA is both substantive and administrative. The CNA is responsible for 'issuing permissions' to ensure the effective control, protection, conservation, presentation and manage-

---

719 Ibid, s 22.
720 Ibid, s 21.
721 Ibid, s 17.
722 Barbados Preservation of Antiquities Bill, s 16.
723 Andrew North MacLaren 'Protecting the Past for the Public Good: Archaeology and Australian Heritage Law.' PhD diss., University of Sydney, 2006, 135.
724 Petrie 192.
725 Antigua Underwater Cultural Heritage Bill, s 2.

ment of cultural heritage. The CNA's functions also include the promotion of research, public awareness, appreciation and education in cultural heritage, supporting NGO establishment and cooperation, and fostering the establishment of museums, as well as establishing and updating an inventory.[726] Here we see similarities to the functions of the National Trust, particularly in the Grenada National Trust Act, which has similar museum-making powers (discussed in Section 4.5). The inventory will include a list of important public and private cultural heritage whose export would constitute an 'appreciable impoverishment of the national cultural heritage', which is more precise and focused than the Barbados bill's reference to ensuring the patrimony of Barbados; a list of underwater cultural heritage that is located within the limits of national jurisdiction; and a list of underwater cultural heritage, located beyond the limits of national jurisdiction if that underwater cultural heritage has a verifiable link with the State. The inventory will also be open to limited public access, to ensure that no information that would endanger the heritage is disclosed, which is the most modern feature of such legislation in the region.

Part III of the bill addresses the discovery, report and displacement of cultural heritage. A permit is needed for the exploration and displacement of the cultural heritage.[727] This is the only law that explicitly states that safety and environment procedures must be in place in order to be granted a permit.[728] Part VI of the bill concerns 'activities incidentally affecting heritage'. Developers are required to report their proposed activities to the CNA 60 days in advance of such activity, if those activities take place in an area containing cultural heritage or there is a reasonable expectation that it may do so.[729] Such heritage may include sites, battlefields, ports or trade routes, on land or sea. An impact assessment must be undertaken and the costs are to be borne by the developer where the development involves industrial activity.[730] Nevertheless, criteria are provided for the contents of the heritage impact assessment, which must include:

> *(a) the assessment of the project area and the identification of cultural heritage therein;*
>
> *(b) the prevention, to the extent possible, of impact to cultural heritage caused by the project in the project area and its surrounding environment;*
>
> *(c) the mitigation of negative effects caused by the project in the project area and its surrounding environment;*
>
> *(d) the conservation of the affected cultural heritage; and the promotion of affected cultural heritage and the dissemination of knowledge about it.*[731]

---

726 Ibid, s 5.
727 Ibid, s 6.
728 Ibid, s 7(7)(b).
729 Ibid, s 15.
730 Ibid, s 15(2) and (4).
731 Ibid, s 15(4).

It is mandatory to consult the CNA, not just the planning authorities, before development permission can be granted.[732] This section would therefore modify the planning permission process and would be the only legislation in the Lesser Antilles making explicit provision for heritage impact assessments. In addition, the bill vests cultural heritage of an archaeological character in the State, abolishes the law of finds, and limits the application of the law of salvage.[733] The Government of Antigua and Barbuda may also acquire any cultural heritage for the benefit of the nation.[734]

Annex 2 of the Schedule to the Antigua bill addresses 'rules concerning activities directed at cultural heritage of an archaeological character, including underwater cultural heritage'. The Schedule states that any activity directed at cultural heritage must be authorised in a manner consistent with their protection and for the purpose of making a significant contribution to their protection and enhancement or to gain knowledge about them. In situ preservation of the cultural heritage of an archaeological character is considered the first option before engaging in any activity, including recovery or displacement. Commercial exploitation or sale is prohibited, but responsible public access, museum exhibition, exchange between museums and scientific research are exceptions to this rule. This addresses for the first time the value of heritage beyond excavation, although the language does not go so far as to reference community relationships with such sites.[735]

Commercial exploitation is also addressed in more detail, which is stated as fundamentally incompatible with the protection of the cultural heritage, while enumerating the following as exceptions to the general rule: professional archaeological services in conformity with the law and authorised by the CNA, and authorised research projects that do not compromise the scientific or cultural interest or integrity of the material.[736] Any adverse effects on the cultural heritage must be mitigated. Non-destructive techniques and surveys are preferred to excavation and recovery.[737] Also addressed is the treatment of human remains as well as the need for international cooperation to ensure exchange of historical, technical and scientific knowledge, professional exchange and access to effective protective measures.[738]

There are rules governing archaeological research, specifically the content of project proposals, which must include a site maintenance policy, safety policy, environmental policy, a plan for documentation and archiving recovered cultural heritage and a publication programme.[739] The methodology and techniques must be as non-intrusive as possible.[740] Preliminary assessment of the site is required, including background studies of the archaeological and environmental characteristics of the site, as well as the consequences for the long-term stability of the cultural heritage of the site.[741] All team members must be qualified and have demonstrated competence appropriate to

---

732 Ibid, s 15(3).
733 Ibid, s 16(1) and (2).
734 Ibid, s 17.
735 Antigua Underwater Cultural Heritage Bill, schedule, rule 1.
736 Ibid, rule 2.
737 Ibid, rule 3.
738 Ibid, rules 4 and 5.
739 Ibid, rule 6.
740 Ibid, rule 9.
741 Ibid, rule 10.

their roles in the project.⁷⁴² A conservation programme must be put in place, in close cooperation with the competent authorities and in keeping with professional state of the art standards.⁷⁴³ There is, however, no mention of community consultation.

A site management programme must be developed in close cooperation with the competent authorities to provide for in situ protection and management of the cultural heritage in the course of and upon termination of fieldwork.⁷⁴⁴ It must include public information, reasonable provision for site stabilisation, monitoring, and protection against interference but once more, no community element. Activities must be documented in accordance with current professional standards of archaeological documentation.⁷⁴⁵ A safety policy and an environmental policy are required.⁷⁴⁶ Reporting obligations, including archiving of such reports are addressed.⁷⁴⁷ Public archaeology initiatives are expected where appropriate. This includes access to a synthesis of the final report, barring the inclusion of any information that is confidential or sensitive in nature; and making the report available in relevant public records.⁷⁴⁸

Were it enacted, the Antigua Cultural Heritage bill would advance heritage law in the region with its approach to the law of finds, integration of environmental principles, and modern conservation mechanisms such as the use of impact assessments and access to information, as well as communicating best practices for archaeological excavations for the benefit of the people of Antigua and Barbuda.

4.4 Museum Legislation

The framework for antiquities management in the Lesser Antilles also includes museums. As repositories for the tangible remains of the past and present, and centres for educational and technical advancement, museums can be public or private institutions. Legal incorporation facilitates ownership of property and grants perpetual existence.⁷⁴⁹ This section focuses on state museums. Alissandra Cummins notes that museums in the English-speaking Caribbean evolve out of the natural resource collections that flourished during the height of the British Empire, especially the Great Exhibitions, which showcased resources, valuables, and even peoples from the colonies as a means of civilising unruly nature in these imperial outposts.⁷⁵⁰ These origins thus made museums places of 'order and surveillance'.⁷⁵¹ This establishes a relationship between the museum and the imperial landscape. The museum as an instrument of civilisation and edification was later linked to social reform through education, with

---

742 Ibid, rule 13.
743 Ibid, rule 14.
744 Ibid, rule 15.
745 Ibid, rule 16.
746 Ibid, rules 17 and 18.
747 Ibid, rules 19 and 20.
748 Ibid, rule 21.
749 Patty Gerstenblith, 'Museum Practice: Legal Issues' in Sharon Macdonald (ed), *A Companion to Museum Studies* (Wiley-Blackwell 2011) 442-456, 442.
750 Alissandra Cummins, 'Natural History = National History: Early Origins and Organizing Principles of Museums in the English-speaking Caribbean.' In Cummins, Farmer and Russell (eds) *Plantation to Nation* 11-46, 28.
751 Ariese 14.

the earliest colonial legislation establishing public libraries featuring museum displays throughout the British West Indies.[752]

Originally, conservative museums considered collection the 'sole reason for the museum, with exhibition, education, culture, and the social good ... rationalizations and window dressing used to justify the basic collecting passion.'[753] While other heritage and cultural institutions are concerned with the advancement of knowledge, it is this collection and interpretation function-through objects, spoken written and visual transmission-that originally distinguished the museum.[754] Collections contained in a museum represent this generation's legacy to the next.[755] Ideally, museums protect and share heritage, enhance our understanding of these resources, and so contribute to the public good. Collections have to be registered and studied, otherwise they have no interpretive value. They must be catalogued and researched. Without scholarly research, thoughtful study and documentation, the interpretive educational function of the museum is shallow, offering little understanding and appreciation for the collective heritage.[756]

The new museum discourse has transformed this perception. This shift specifically occurred in the 1980s as part of the Cultural Turn, during which questions about representation, how meanings come to be inscribed, and by whom, were recognised as political.[757] What was researched and why, was just as important as what was ignored, or taken for granted, meaning that museology can continue to exclude and uphold certain regimes of power, especially the status quo.[758] Museums are now a space in which the heritage making process is conducted, where heritage is performed, constructed, promoted and transformed, and to apply the logic of legal geography, this means who is afforded space and who is not has implications for spatial justice. Heritage now relies less on artefacts and more on meanings and the intangible.[759] Displays are no longer treated as 'chronological visual storage' and the incorporation of vernacular architecture into the displays is intended to attract a more general rather than specialist public.[760] The old museology was concerned with methods for administration, conservation and education, and not the purpose of the museum. The three main departures from old museology concerned a) museum objects, now understood as situated and contextual rather than having inherent meaning; b) expanding museological functions

---

752 Alissandra Cummins, 'Caribbean Museums and National Identity.' *History Workshop Journal* 58 (2004): 224-245, 229.
753 Edward Alexander, *Museums in Motion: An Introduction to the History and Function of Museums* (Nashville 1979) 9.
754 John Whiting, *Museum-focussed heritage in the English-speaking Caribbean* (UNESCO 1983) 2.
755 Whiting 2.
756 Ibid.
757 Ariese 24.
758 Sharon Macdonald, 'Expanding Museum Studies: An Introduction' in Sharon Macdonald (ed), *A Companion to Museum Studies* (Wiley-Blackwell 2011) 1-12, 2.
759 Ariese 31. See also Laurajane Smith, 'Theorizing Museum and Heritage Visiting' in Andrea Witcomb and Kylie Message (eds), *The International Handbooks of Museum Studies: Museum Theory* (John Wiley & Sons, 2015) 459-484 and Emma Waterton, Laurajane Smith and Gary Campbell, 'The Utility of Discourse Analysis to Heritage Studies: The Burra Charter and Social Inclusion.' *International Journal of Heritage Studies* 12(4) (2006): 339-355.
760 Alexander 10.

to commercialism and entertainment; and c) the public perception of the museum and its exhibitions.[761]

For the Caribbean, this requires decolonisation of the museum, because museums play a role in the way that the history and culture of communities are represented and defined.[762] Decolonising the museum has been crucial for the empowerment of marginalised peoples who have been dispossessed and misrepresented, and strengthening identity via truth-telling, knowledge-making, education and the restoration of memory.[763] These museums have moved away from being 'temples of elitism' to 'forums for community engagement'[764], supporting public spaces and becoming public spaces themselves. Csilla Ariese's work on the Social Museum in the Caribbean wrestles with these post-colonial themes of challenging the Authorized Heritage Discourse (AHD) to reclaim space and deconstruct colonial power dynamics by being more participatory and community-centered.[765] One post-colonial mechanism envisions the museum as contact zone[766] in this regard, in which it critically engages with the Western analytical perspective, and arguably with the imposed spatial definitions it upholds.[767]

Today, the three traditional museum objectives – collection, conservation and research – are integrated in the institutional mandate, and through exhibition, education and interpretation can bring understanding and appreciation to contemporary life, and contribute to the social welfare of these communities.[768] This requires collaboration with source communities, which is considered a best practice, in order to challenge 'objectifying traditions that uphold colonial power relations and perpetuate colonizer serving images and models'.[769] Decolonisation can benefit from a robust regulatory framework, as museums interact with the law in a variety of ways. Legislation can support the protection of the collective heritage, and implement international cultural heritage law principles. Museums also play an important role in the fulfilment of cultural rights: for the full realisation of the right to take part in cultural life, the

---

761 Macdonald, 'Expanding Museum Studies: An Introduction' 20.
762 See Kevin Farmer, 'New Museums on the Block: Creation of Identity in the Post-Independence Caribbean' in Cummins, Farmer and Russell (eds), *Plantation to Nation* 169-177.
763 Amy Lonetree, *Decolonizing Museums* (University of North Carolina Press, 2012) 1, 4-5, 9.
764 Lonetree 6.
765 Ariese 31: The characteristics of the AHD are as follows: heritage was seen as intrinsic (that is, inherently known and unchanging such as sites, monuments and objects that physically exist in the environment) and experts were in charge of defining what was or was not deemed to be heritage. Special attention was paid to heritage that was considered to be significant for all of humanity (so-called 'universal heritage').
766 Originally introduced by linguist Mary Louise Pratt, the contact zone refers to 'social spaces where cultures meet, clash, and grapple with each other, often in contexts of highly asymmetrical relations of power, such as colonialism, slavery, or their aftermaths as they are lived out in many parts of the world today'. See Ariese 30. The concept has also been used by museologists in a more optimistic sense, as a dialogical space of equal reciprocity. But Robin Boast has argued that the contact zone can also entrench power imbalances – and so can be considered neo-colonialist in orientation. See Robin Boast, 'Neocolonial collaboration: Museum as Contact Zone Revisited' (2011) *Museum Anthropology* 34(1): 56-70, 64.
767 Ariese 31.
768 Alexander 15.
769 Lonetree 16-17, 171.

availability of and access to cultural goods and services (via libraries, museums, theatres and cultural events) is necessary, and states must guarantee such access.[770]

Nevertheless, not all museums in the Lesser Antilles have enabling legislation – Trinidad and Tobago, Barbados, and Grenada are the exception. As will be discussed later in the chapter, the National Trust often performed museum functions and in the case of Grenada, was empowered to set up museums, so there is an entangled relationship. It would seem that Antigua's Antiquities bill would introduce such functions for its CNA. Distinguishing these roles and responsibilities has been an incremental process following independence.

Trinidad and Tobago's National Museum and Art Gallery Act establishes a national museum with responsibility for a national collection.[771] The Museum board is composed of members with technical and scholarly expertise relevant to the collection and interpretation of historical and cultural material; public law; natural history; the visual arts; and management of museums and analogous institutions.[772] The Board's functions include the establishment of a National Collections Policy and all other policies required for the facilitation of the operations of the TT National Museum; research in historical and cultural material relevant to the national collection; dissemination of information relating to the national collection, and to the museum and its functions in Trinidad and Tobago and abroad; and exhibiting historical and cultural material, both in Trinidad and Tobago and abroad.[773]

The Board is empowered to receive historical material on loan or as a gift, loaning such material from the collection, and disposal of historical and cultural material. Copyright law applies to the reproduction of material for sale. The Board is also charged with maintaining the museum property. It is also established that the museum acts on behalf of the Government of the Republic of Trinidad and Tobago in the administration of a trust relating to historical and cultural material. Importantly, it is stated that the museum collects revenues by way of fees for the viewing of the national collection, and may operate any other business which may further the purposes of the TT National Museum.[774] The TT National Museum is therefore empowered to function as a modern body, through its diverse functions and array of mechanisms, such as this capacity to establish related businesses.[775]

Nevertheless, the legislation reflects the traditional character of a museum, since the remaining provisions are devoted to administrative matters, such as the transfer and disposal of material, use of technical guidance, the role of the Director as general and technical director, funding, staff remuneration and capacity strengthening.[776] There is no explicit relationship between international cultural heritage law and museum management, as the museum appears to be dedicated to managing the national collection.

---

770 Blake, *International Cultural Heritage Law* 300, 302.
771 Trinidad and Tobago National Museum and Art Gallery Act 2000, ss 2 and 3.
772 Ibid, s 4(2).
773 Ibid, s 12.
774 Ibid, s 13.
775 This is similar to the UK Museum and Galleries Act 1992, s 3, which empowers its Board to form companies.
776 Trinidad and Tobago National Museum and Art Gallery Act, ss 14-18, and ss 25-26.

Unlike Trinidad and Tobago, the Barbados Museum and Historical Society Act predates independence and consists of one page. The Barbados Museum and Historical Society is in fact a historical society that functions as a museum, and not a national museum, an impression cemented by the fact that the entity throughout the act is referred to by its abbreviated name, 'the Society'. Much of the content of the Act concerns liability for debts, powers of the Society including the preparation of by-laws, the recovery of fines, dispute resolution and saving rights of the Crown.[777] The Barbados Museum nevertheless functions as a de facto national museum and is very active, sitting on the Barbados World Heritage Committee and advising Town and Country Planning authorities on the mapping of heritage resources such as archaeological sites for input in the national development plan and vetting development applications where consulted.[778]

Given the sparseness of this legislation, it is remarkable that the Barbados Museum is among the best-run in the Lesser Antilles. One reason for this is the fact that the institutional arrangements for heritage protection, which involve major stakeholders such as Planning and the National Trust, are centralised within the planning system, and these stakeholders enjoy a positive relationship.[779] Barbados is one of the most politically stable countries in the English-speaking Caribbean, with a fairly homogenous polity, and established heritage practices have been in place in Barbados prior to independence. The Barbados World Heritage Committee, which counts the National Trust, Museum and Planning Authority among its members, has seen the successful inscription of Historic Bridgetown and its Garrison on the World Heritage List.[780]

The highest level of policy decision-making for Historic Bridgetown and its Garrison is public sector-led through the Cabinet of the Government of Barbados, which holds ultimate responsibility for the management of the property but has delegated authority to the Barbados World Heritage Committee, which in turn shares it amongst the respective responsible government agencies and also collaborates with several non-governmental organisations and civil society, including a number of property owners.[781] This means that there is community representation and participatory governance in the administration of the property, through advisory functions on conservation policies and programmes for the property, as well as evaluation and monitoring of the property and implementation of international conventional law for heritage.[782] The museum is a stakeholder in managing this important site.

This is in stark contrast to Grenada, which has recently enacted comprehensive legislation to establish a national museum, broadly defining its objectives and establishing a governance structure. This new legislation combines museum governance with antiquities protection. The museum property is state-owned, but previously its

---

777 Trinidad and Tobago National Museum and Art Gallery Act, ss 3-7.
778 Interview with Mr Kevin Farmer, Deputy Director, the Barbados Museum (Bridgetown, Barbados, 9 March 2016)
779 Ibid.
780 Interview with Dr Donna Greene, Senior Cultural Policy Officer, and Sheron Johnson, Cultural Policy Officer and UNESCO focal point, The Ministry of Community Development and Culture, Government of Barbados (Bridgetown, Barbados, 9 March 2016).
781 UNESCO website for Historic Bridgetown and its Garrison <http://whc.unesco.org/en/list/1376> accessed 27 March 2016.
782 Ibid.

management had been undertaken by a privately incorporated company. The Grenada National Museum Act was gazetted on 21st July, 2017. The GNM is established as a statutory body with a Board to manage and preserve the national collection of objects, records and other historical and cultural material that provide evidence of the history of the people of Grenada, Carriacou and Petite Martinique.[783] Its drafting has been influenced by the Trinidadian legislation, particularly in its scope, functions and powers.

The national collection is defined as the national collection of objects, records and other historical and cultural material providing evidence of the history of the people of Grenada, Carriacou and Petite Martinique, and is in the sole ownership of the National Museum. Also defined are 'antiquity' and 'artefact'. An antiquity may be an artefact or a place, building, site or structure which is at least fifty years old. An artefact is defined as a movable object or fossil remains or impressions.[784] 'Monument' means a place, building, site or structure, which the Minister considers to be of public interest by reason of its historical, anthropological, archaeological or palaeontological significance, but this definition does not go so far as to say that these heritage resources attract any distinctive legal protection, as with the UK Monuments Act, wherein monuments are scheduled and development is forbidden.[785] However, as with that Act, places and sites are included within the legal definition of monument. Similar to Trinidad and Tobago's legislation, 'historical and cultural material' is defined to mean any material that pertains to the 'historical, geological, biological, cultural or artistic heritage' of Grenada, which would include natural heritage.[786]

The National Museum is responsible for the establishment, operation and administration of museums in Grenada (originally a responsibility of the National Trust); the preservation and display specimens, artefacts, and other materials that illustrate the natural or human history of Grenada; maintaining and providing access to the national collection in accordance with the national collections policy; research and communication of the knowledge of the natural and human history of Grenada by exhibits, publications and other means; and serving as an educational organisation.[787]

As with Trinidad and Tobago's law, the Board is responsible for shaping policy, the establishment of the national collection, museum operations, research and excavation, public records, exhibiting material and museum finances.[788] The powers of the Board are laid out in language that mirrors the analogous provision in Trinidad and Tobago's legislation. The Board may set up specialised committees to assist the Museum in its work and also form one or more bodies corporate to further the purposes of the National Museum.[789] Board members must have technical or scholarly expertise relevant to the collection and interpretation of historical, natural and cultural material; public law, company law or intellectual property law; qualifications or adequate knowledge in history, the natural sciences, pedagogy or heritage management; technical knowledge in the field of the visual and performing arts; qualifications in

---

783 Grenada National Museum Act 2017, s 3.
784 Ibid, s 2.
785 Harwood 14-15. UK Monuments and Archaeological Areas Act 1979 s 2.
786 Grenada National Museum Act 2017, ss 2 and 4.
787 Ibid, s 4.
788 Ibid, ss 6-7.
789 Ibid, s 8.

accounting or marketing and fundraising experience; or qualifications or experience relating to the functions, operations and management of museums, archives and analogous institutions.[790] These areas of expertise reflect a new direction in museum management and policy, particularly in valuing marketing, fundraising, and intellectual property expertise. In addition, the Schedule to the Act concerns the constitution and procedure of the Board, and requires representation from the National Cultural Foundation and the National Trust, ensuring linkages between tangible and intangible heritage for a harmonised approach to heritage protection.[791]

The Grenada National Museum can apply for grants in addition to any funding committed by Parliament.[792] Funds are to be applied in a manner similar to Trinidad and Tobago's legislation, for the maintenance of the National Collection, museum property, for staff salaries and also for enhancing technical capacity of museum staff.[793] All artefacts found in Grenada are vested in the Government, and the Minister may request in writing the return of any artefact, save those discovered prior to the passage of the Act, and where ownership and rights have been waived and extinguished. Failure to surrender a requested artefact is an offence.[794] Where antiquities have been discovered, or there is knowledge of a discovery, this is to be reported to the Museum Director or adequate person.[795] All reasonable measures must be taken to protect the find. It is an offence to excavate, search or remove any antiquity other than for the purpose of protection. Nevertheless, it is within the government's discretion to pay a reward.[796]

To operationalise the law, regulations may be made inter alia, for the conduct of excavations, preservation, restoration, analysis, documentation and presentation of antiquities, management and control of antiquities and monuments, access to excavations, payment of fees, operation and administration of the National Museum, and reproduction and sale of artifacts.[797] Such regulations do not prohibit or restrict the access of lawful owners, occupiers, and persons beneficially interested to monuments, or such persons authorised by same, thereby ensuring recognition and protection of the rights of private landowners.[798] Notably, the GNM Act repeals the National Heritage Protection Act, which was ineffective, but had provided legal protection for sites of Amerindian significance via scheduling and a permitting system facilitated by the National Trust.[799] No alternative method of protection for these sites was provided in the new Act, or mechanisms for involving communities that interact with these resources.

While Grenada has a cultural policy that addresses the enhancement of the museum and protection of archaeological sites,[800] there are challenges facing museum law implementation even when new institutional arrangements are put in place. Archaeological

---

790 Ibid, s 11.
791 Grenada National Museum Act 2017, schedule, para 2.
792 Grenada National Museum Act 2017, s 12.
793 Ibid, s 14.
794 Ibid, s 21.
795 Ibid, s 22.
796 Ibid, s 22(3) and (4).
797 Ibid, s 23.
798 Ibid, s 23(2).
799 Grenada National Museum Act 2017, s 24.
800 The Government of Grenada. Grenada National Cultural Policy 2012, Positions 2.4 (Museum) and 2.5 (Historical and Archaeological Sites) respectively.

objects and sites are but components of the landscape, which develop new meanings as places are used and reinterpreted by communities. Failure to understand this impairs the functioning of museums in their role as guardian and interpreter of heritage, when these objects are singled out for protection but communities who interact with them are excluded from strategies for such protection.

A 1983 study commissioned by UNESCO examined the development plans of museums in the Caribbean to determine whether these institutions adequately met the needs of their communities, both in terms of the preservation of the historical and cultural heritage and the education of people in these matters.[801] Its author, Whiting, made a number of recommendations that appear to hold true today, almost forty years later.[802] He observed that the isolation of museums from other elements of a nation's heritage community does not allow material support or synergy in progressing with plans. Museums are outliers in the institutional framework for heritage protection, competing for sparse resources, instead of appearing to contribute to and support the nation.[803] The observation on institutional fragmentation seems to affirm Burke's thesis that culture is not perceived as an independent policy area worthy of focused funding.[804]

Although Whiting's study does not reference landscape, his recommendations concern the integration of cultural and natural heritage, which he believed would remedy the lack of control over export of archaeological material, and lack of control of excavation sites, which a museum that coupled national park functions or an eco-museum could address; in fact he notes that a small island may be considered analogous to a US national park.[805] The museum's evolving remit today includes the environment, as the new ICOM definition has moved from the 1960 definition of collection including only material objects, to the more general ICOM emphasis on 'the tangible and intangible heritage of humanity and its environment'.[806] Overall, Whiting concludes that a clear heritage policy is needed with the role of the museum clearly defined.[807]

The most successful museum assessed in this chapter, is in fact a historical society. The Barbados Museum and Historical Society has managed to develop local practices with very little legislative support. It engages with the Barbados National Trust and the Town and Country Planning Office, and other local stakeholders, and publishes a journal on Barbadian history, as there is active research on local history. In Trinidad and Tobago's legislation there is no indication of such institutional linkages between the local National Trust and other heritage stakeholders. With Grenada's new legislation, implementation arrangements are not yet in place, making any analysis premature. There is representation from the Ministry of Culture, the National Trust

---

801 Whiting 1.
802 Ibid, 6.
803 Ibid, 12.
804 Burke 170.
805 Whiting 13.
806 Patrick O'Keefe, 'Preliminary Study on the advisability of preparing an International Instrument for the protection and promotion of Museums and Collections (legal and technical aspects)' (UNESCO, n.d.) 15. And International Council of Museums Statutes, Adopted by the Eleventh General Assembly of ICOM: Section IIF Definitions: Article 3 (Copenhagen, Denmark, June 14, 1974). In *Development of the Museum Definition According to ICOM Statutes* (1946-2001). Paris: International Council of Museums, 2009. Electronic document, <http://archives.icom.museum/hist_def_eng.html> accessed May 25, 2018.
807 Whiting 13.

and National Cultural Foundation on its Board. The Grenadian legislation also gives the National Museum a role in the preservation of antiquities, as they are recognised as important to the national interest. However, the legislation does not locate antiquities within their wider communities, and given that the museum's track record of institutional coordination is poor, there is danger that the legislation may not support the needs of communities unless there is true institutional transformation that addresses institutional and enforcement weaknesses.

In all three states, the government dominates the institutional arrangements. The need to localise the museum is in keeping with the needs of heritage protection in the Lesser Antilles. Museums as legislated are instruments of empire, institutions that reordered the colonised world by objectifying and representing cultures, communities and land according to the spatial dictates of the paternalistic imperialism that characterised the nineteenth and early twentieth centuries. The new museology sees museums as postcolonial, able to reconstitute themselves following the dissolution of the colonies in the later twentieth century, a museology that promotes 'education over research, engagement over doctrine, and multivocality over connoisseurship.'[808] But at their core, museums retain collecting and exhibiting functions, which are colonial in origin.

This tension is expressed in the museum as contact zone, which Boast argues continues to be used instrumentally as a means of 'masking far more fundamental asymmetries, appropriations, and biases', in spite of the new museology transforming the museum from a site of determined edification to one of educational engagement in the 21st century.[809] This masking is a function of the imperial landscape and confronting the museum's role in spatial injustice is necessary. As Ariese has stated, museums in the Caribbean can become more resilient as they diversify, embrace the dynamism inherent in heritage, and act more purposefully as subjective actors in their societies through community engagement processes.[810]

4.5 National Trust Legislation

4.5.1 Background: the National Trust for England, Wales and Northern Ireland

Institutions thus have played a significant role in the preservation of heritage, and no institution exemplifies this better than the National Trust. Britain's consciousness of a national heritage manifested in an interest in preserving landscape and historic buildings, and can be traced to the nineteenth century with the establishment of voluntary organisations such as the National Trust, for which legislation was passed in 1895, the first heritage law of its kind.[811] When documenting the emergence of national

---

808 Boast 64.
809 Ibid, 67.
810 Ariese 226.
811 Other organisations include the Commons Footpaths and Open Spaces Preservation Society (1865) and the Society for the Protection of Ancient Buildings (1877). John Anthony Floy, 'Sustainable Heritage Tourism, Climate Change and the National Trust.' PhD diss., University of Birmingham, 2015, 14 and at 15-16.

heritage law, the Trust's role in both landscape protection and heritage conservation is therefore central.

Since the mid-nineteenth century onwards, interest in the preservation of open spaces and common land had been slowly building. With the passage of the Statute of Merton in 1235, Lords of the Manor had been given the right to enclose their common lands, gradually leading over the centuries to increased private ownership of land across Britain.[812] Preservation of the ancient heritage of England was influenced by the Picturesque movement in the eighteenth century, which aestheticised wilderness, inspired nostalgia for 'olden-time' England, and begat the institutionalisation of visual landscape.[813] With enclosure came displacement of the rural poor, emparkment of the countryside and urban migration. Enclosure thus fostered a specific notion of heritage as a counterpoint to mass industrialisation, a constructed pastoral idyll that never existed. The National Trust was founded in the late nineteenth century to protect this type of heritage, as a response to these social and physical impacts of industrialisation on people and the environment, as well as the growing movement towards social welfare reform.[814]

The Trust's founders were active campaigners for the preservation of open spaces, but open spaces for whom? It has been argued that while the Trust established itself as an organisation for effecting social change, it was in fact represented by a circle of educated, privileged and influential people, with a specific and exclusive vision of society, and remains centralised and paternalistic to this day.[815] Octavia Hill, one of the founders, was a social housing reformer interested in protecting the countryside from the evils of urban sprawl and building development.[816] The Duke of Westminster, who was influential in the Trust's early years through his wealth and political connections, was well known for his patronage of projects associated with public parks and slum clearance.[817] However, the Trust's dual role of preserving landscape with places of historic interest aligned the preservation of the commons movement with the late nineteenth century Fine Art tradition, which normalised a bourgeois interpretation of history and society.[818] This is in keeping with the entrenchment of landscape as visual space, rather than shaped by community custom, and the spatial cleansing practices that so often require the expulsion of local communities in order to regulate access to public space.

The conferment of the principle of 'inalienability' on Trust holdings established by the 1907 National Trust Act effectively legitimised the perception of protecting private property in the national interest, and as Floy notes, reinforced this image of the Trust as a substantial private landowner who may not necessarily have had everyone's interests in mind.[819] Throughout the twentieth century, the organisation evolved in response to changing political, economic and social conditions. By the

---

812 Floy 15.
813 Ibid, 18.
814 Ibid, 16.
815 Ibid, 18.
816 Ibid, 15-16.
817 Ibid, 121.
818 Ibid, 15-16.
819 Patrick Wright, *On Living in an Old Country* (Verso 1985) 52 as cited in Floy 18.

1930s, the Trust, a charity since the National Trust Act of 1919, was operated largely on a voluntary basis through local committees across the country overseen by land agents, with direction from a central office in London. The Trust was governed by a Council and an Executive Committee whose expertise lay in matters of finance, land management and heritage. The National Trust Acts of 1937 and 1939 were introduced at a time when the safeguarding of English country houses was seen as important for retaining part of the national heritage and culture. The Acts enabled an owner to donate their estate to the National Trust with an endowment, in return for exemption from death duties and the right to remain at the premises rent-free. These properties were acquired as part of the Trust's statutory purpose to preserve buildings of historic interest.[820] Following the era of country house expansion in the 1950s, the Trust began to turn its attention to protecting the natural environment in the 1960s.[821]

The original mission of the Trust concerned the preservation of open spaces and countryside from urbanisation, but protecting the landowners who enclosed much of these spaces for their personal exclusive use and deprived communities of common land belies a fundamental contradiction that was intentionally replicated in the British colonies, where the heritage movement was championed by the National Trust.[822] Stately homes and colonial mansions represent the heritage of the upper socio-economic classes who are the arbiters of culture. While preserving these buildings is undoubtedly of great regional and/or national importance, they do not reflect the whole history and heritage of the general population. By cementing the position of the dominant actors in society while devaluing subordinate identities, the Trust reinforced the colonial power dynamic, and ensured the colony's continued existence.[823] Trusts are therefore designed to maintain and promote unjust uses of space in the plantationscape.

By failing to recognise the importance of vernacular, everyday heritage to the communities for whom it is significant, there is also a failing to afford associated protection. A lack of protection can result in the loss of such heritage, which can ultimately result in the fragmentation of these social communities. When communities have no cultural heritage with which they can identify, there is a lack of a sense of well-being through exclusion, and a prevailing feeling of disengagement and displacement from mainstream society; the result being no sense of meaning, significance or place.[824] As the concept of heritage value shifts, so the vernacular and everyday heritage has been recognised as possessing value for communities and enhancing cultural diversity for the nation as a whole.[825] Trusts therefore have the potential to play a significant role in the recognition and protection of the heritage of all communities.[826]

---

820 Floy 122.
821 Ibid.
822 Petrie 178.
823 Petrie 177-178.
824 Ibid, 180.
825 Ibid, 182.
826 Ibid, 179.

4.5.2 National Trusts in the Lesser Antilles

The National Trust figures most prominently as the main institutional actor responsible for heritage in the Lesser Antilles, which is unsurprising as they are former British colonies. They are modelled on the English Trust, although a number of islands have adapted the Trust to suit their needs. While the National Trust for England, Wales and Northern Ireland is a registered charity describing itself as independent from government,[827] this is in contrast to Trust organisations in the Lesser Antilles, which are parastatal bodies having a measure of political independence but charged with government advisory functions. The following analysis begins with the most traditional of these institutions, and then proceeds to examine the more recent iterations of the Trust.

The Barbados National Trust Act of 1961 appears to be the basis for the Grenada National Trust Act 1967, as both laws share similarities in format and structure. For both countries, the legislation primarily focuses on the powers and administration of the trust as an organisation. Both laws establish the Trust as a membership organisation in the preamble, identify the founding members and the objectives of the Trust, create a Council to carry out the executive functions of the Trust, and address aspects of company law, such as its tax-exempt status.[828] They have public education functions, can acquire property, manage funds for the benefit of protecting heritage, and are charged with pursuing 'a policy of preservation, and acting in an advisory capacity.'[829] There are however, distinctions.

In terms of scope of the organisation, the Barbados National Trust (BNT) is empowered to list buildings and monuments of historic and architectural interest, while the Grenada legislation also includes objects of prehistoric value within its list, as well as the power to establish museums.[830] This latter power has never been exercised, and is even unlikelier a prospect with the enactment of new museum legislation in Grenada. Grenada's legislation states that certain Trust property 'shall' be inalienable, which is a reminder that the Trust can be a landowner representing private interests.[831] On the other hand, such a provision could secure the interests of the more general populace, since it includes not just architectural heritage, but a diversity of resources valued by local communities, such as marine and submarine areas, lakes and rivers.

The Barbados National Trust is very active in that country, working in tandem with the Barbados Museum and sitting on the Barbados World Heritage Committee. Legislation for the BNT has provisions that are identical to the law establishing the Grenada National Trust (GNT), and in some ways is even more limiting. Yet the BNT was effectively functioning prior to independence and continues to have a good working relationship with the Town and Country Planning authorities.[832] The

---

827 Floy 8.
828 The Barbados National Trust Act 1961, s 2 (incorporation), s 3 (funds), and s 4(rules of the Trust); and the Grenada National Trust 1967 s 2(incorporation), s 3 (liability) and s 4(establishment of the Council) are virtually identical.
829 The Barbados National Trust Act 1961, preamble; the Grenada National Trust Act 1967, preamble.
830 The Barbados National Trust Act 1961, preamble; preamble of the Grenada National Trust Act 1967.
831 Grenada National Trust Act 1967, s 5.
832 Interview with Dr Karl Watson, President, Barbados National Trust (Bridgetown, Barbados 16 March, 2016).

GNT does not enjoy a similarly consistent relationship with the Government of Grenada and coordination is sporadic. It is rarely active in the listing and protection of sites, although it sits on a number of advisory heritage committees. It has never acquired or managed property.[833]

The St Vincent and the Grenadines National Trust Act of 1969 is similarly rudimentary, but provides clear, detailed objectives that demonstrate an incremental progression in the understanding of the role of the Trust as a heritage institution charged with the protection of heritage resources. The Trust is charged with the responsibility to locate, restore and conserve areas of beauty, including marine areas, and conserve the natural life therein, making it the first Trust in the Lesser Antilles to include wildlife conservation within its remit.[834] Another innovation is the responsibility to make and keep inventories, which are to include natural heritage resources.[835] No other Trust in the post-Independence period contains this explicit reference. The St Vincent National Trust is also responsible for cooperating with persons and associations having similar objects, which indicates that the St Vincent Act envisages the involvement of other heritage partners and recognises the value of participatory governance to heritage protection.[836] The St Vincent Act also contemplates the allocation of funds to specifically execute these projects, which is more forward thinking than the National Trust laws of Barbados and Grenada.[837] However, the Vincentian legislation does not specify these funding sources, such as the grants, donations and bequests to be applied to such protection, as is stated in the Barbados and Grenada trust legislation.

The progressive development of Trust law continues with the Saint Lucia National Trust Act, passed in 1975. As with the Grenadian legislation, the Saint Lucia Trust can establish museums, and as with its Vincentian counterpart, list both natural and cultural resources as heritage.[838] However, the Saint Lucian legislation varies the preservation criteria to include resources of 'traditional interest', although this term is not defined in the legislation, so it is not clear if this is in the colonial tradition, or traditional to the community.[839] The legislation establishes a council, the composition of which includes two members of the Saint Lucia Archaeological and Historical Society.[840] Inviting representation from fellow stakeholders ensures cooperation between the two main heritage institutions in that state. Unlike the aforementioned laws, the Saint Lucian legislation addresses matters of membership in subsidiary legislation.[841] The law also contains language concerning inalienability of Trust property.[842] Notably, this is the first National Trust law to address enforcement in detail, making it an offence to deface

---

833 Interview with Mr Michael Jessamy, Heritage Officer, Ministry of Tourism, Civil Aviation and Culture (St George's, Grenada 1 April, 2016).
834 Saint Vincent and the Grenadines National Trust Act, s 4(a).
835 Ibid, s 4(e); s 4(d) states 'to list the flora and fauna in areas of natural beauty for the purpose of conservation.'
836 Ibid, s 4(h).
837 Ibid, s 4(i).
838 Saint Lucia National Trust Act, s 4(a), (b) and (c), and section 4(d).
839 Ibid, s 4(d).
840 Ibid, s 6.
841 See the Saint Lucia National Trust Rules 1984, which are prepared by the Council pursuant to s 9 of the SLNT Act.
842 Saint Lucia National Trust Act, s 10.

historic buildings, authorising officers to arrest offenders, and also making it an offence to obstruct such officers.[843]

Trinidad and Tobago's National Trust Act was established in 1991 and postdates that state's independence. This legislation has the most developed criteria for listing.[844] Key terms include 'listing', which means the identification, cataloguing and recording of any property of interest; 'Minister' means the Minister to whom responsibility for culture is assigned; 'monument' means any building, structure or other work of man or nature, whether above or below the surface of the land or the floor of the sea, of national architectural, aesthetic or historic interest; and 'property of interest' means any monument and any fossil, place or site of natural beauty or national, historic, scientific or archeological interest.[845] Interestingly, the legislation was later amended so that the definition of 'The Minister' is now the 'Minister to whom responsibility for the Trust is assigned.'[846] This indicates that the Trust is no longer permanently subsumed by the Ministry of Culture.

The functions of the Trinidad and Tobago National Trust (TNTT) include listing and acquiring property of interest as the TNTT considers appropriate, and advising the Government on the conservation and preservation of properties of interest,[847] amongst the usual conservation functions. The Trust 'may with the approval of the Minister'[848] prepare lists. This includes the ability to revise or revoke listings.[849] The Minister must maintain a Register of all lists prepared in accordance with this section and make such lists available to the public.[850] Damaging or destroying listed property is an offence, and orders for the protection of listed property can be executed.[851] However, a landowner can also appeal against listing.[852]

A number of sections address the institutional arrangements of the Trust, which have been somewhat modernised. The Minister appoints 6 of the 11 members of the Council.[853] The Trust should consult with other government and non-government entities performing functions pertaining to preservation.[854] Mechanisms for coordination such as memoranda of understanding are to be used to facilitate implementation of integrated programmes for the preservation of monuments or the protection and management of the environment. Tiers of membership are prescribed in the first schedule to the Act, including family members, junior members, visiting members and corporate members, and this is the only Trust in the Lesser Antilles to recognise and address the diversity of the public.

The National Trust regulations are contained in the Second Schedule and outline the listing process in detail. The criteria for assessing whether a property should be

---

843 Ibid, ss 16(e) and 16(o), 17-18.
844 National Trust Act of Trinidad and Tobago Act, s 2.
845 Ibid.
846 The National Trust of Trinidad and Tobago (Amendment) Act, 2015, s 2.
847 National Trust Act of Trinidad and Tobago Act, s 5(a) and (h).
848 Ibid, s 8.
849 Ibid, s 8(1)(c).
850 Ibid, s 8(4).
851 National Trust Act of Trinidad and Tobago Act, ss 27 and 26.
852 Ibid, s 9.
853 Ibid, s 12.
854 Ibid, s 15B(1).

listed appear to be heavily influenced by the World Heritage Convention, such as natural or outstanding beauty, ecological balance, uniqueness, artistic excellence, or aesthetics.[855] This would seem to justify protection of heritage on a hierarchical basis, and brings to mind the traditional, exclusionary philosophy of colonial heritage.[856] An optimistic interpretation would suggest that the criteria may be evidence of the Trust in transition. While the process employs thorough and robust standards, and the listing criteria focus on natural or outstanding beauty, aesthetics, rarity, uniqueness, and artistic excellence, reference is nevertheless made to provenance, Caribbean patrimony, and indigenousness to Trinidad and Tobago.[857] In regulation 4, which pertains to listing buildings, mention is made of sociological interest and association with well-known characters or events.[858]

The Trust with the most modern legislation is located in St Kitts. The Saint Christopher National Trust Act was passed in 2009 and its focused language reflects the experience of developing a functioning legislative framework for the protection of heritage. The long title states that the Trust is to 'provide for the establishment of a National Trust for the purpose of administering and preserving sites, buildings and objects of historical, archaeological, architectural, environmental and artistic importance to the Island of Saint Christopher'. The Act establishes a new organisational structure, as it transfers the assets of the Saint Christopher Heritage Society to this new reconstituted trust. Notably, the objects of the Trust are to be applied in a manner consistent with St Kitts' planning and environment and conservation legislation.[859] This recalls St Vincent's Historic Building and Antiquities Act discussed earlier in Section 4.3, which was amended to empower the Minister for Planning to identify heritage resources for listing, essentially subjecting heritage preservation to planning prerogatives.

The influence of the World Heritage Convention is seen, not in the listing criteria as with the Trinidad and Tobago Trust Act, but in the delineation of the cultural and natural heritage categories; the Saint Christopher Trust is responsible for the protection, preservation, restoration and interpretation of buildings, objects and monuments of archaeological, historical, architectural or artistic interest,[860] as well as the protection, conservation, interpretation and enhancement of the natural environment, including its animal and plant life, its submarine and subterranean areas and other places or natural and historical interest and beauty.[861] The Trust is also responsible for assisting in the preservation of traditional arts, craft, dance, song, language and other forms of expression, and documentary heritage, such as manuscripts and photographic records, books and works of art for the benefit and enjoyment 'of the people of the

---

855 National Trust of Trinidad and Tobago Act, second schedule, reg 2.
856 Petrie 178.
857 National Trust of Trinidad and Tobago Act, second schedule, reg 2(i), (j) and (m).
858 Ibid, reg 4(c) and (e).
859 Saint Christopher National Trust Act s4(2)(a): The objects of the Trust as set out in subsection (1) paragraphs (a) and (b) are not intended to derogate from or to supercede the provisions of the (a) National Conservation and Environment Protection Act; or (b) Development Control and Planning Act, 2000 and in the event that there is any conflict between the Acts referred to in subparagraphs (a) and (b) and this Act, the provisions of those Acts would prevail to the extent of the inconsistency.
860 Saint Christopher National Trust Act 2009, s 4(1)(a).
861 Ibid, s 4(1)(b).

community'.⁸⁶² Here, traditional and community aspects of heritage appear to lean towards the general population and not the exclusive colonial heritage. The Trust is expected to promote Kittitian heritage through modern means, such as through the production of written, audio-visual, electronic or other appropriate material, and to present and interpret the cultural heritage of St Kitts by means of museum displays and exhibitions and other relevant productions, which implies a working relationship with local museums, or a blending of Trust and museum functions as with Grenada's National Trust legislation.⁸⁶³

The remaining functions are similar to those of the other National Trusts reviewed, concerning the attraction of funding and the vesting of property, as well as acting as a clearinghouse for knowledge and ideas.⁸⁶⁴ But St Kitts' legislation also specifies that the Trust is to act in an advisory and lobbying capacity on:

> *(a) matters concerned with the objects of the Trust that may be affected by public policy;*
>
> *(b) areas that have been designated or are to be designated as Trust property and the policy to be pursued for the preservation of the property and the means of enforcing that policy; and*
>
> *(c) matters that the Trust is desirous of promoting or supporting.*⁸⁶⁵

The Trust is responsible for the management of the properties or sites specified in the Schedule, which lists an Amerindian petroglyph site, St Kitts' World Heritage site (Brimstone Hill Park), a number of estates, and a catch-all provision for 'other monuments, buildings and sites which may from time to time be donated to, vested in or acquired by the Trust.'⁸⁶⁶ Any immoveable property vested in the Trust will be determined to be inalienable only by the Cabinet in consultation with the board. If any lands, properties or areas should be determined to be inalienable, then the Cabinet must make an order so designating the land, property or area in question.⁸⁶⁷ St Kitts' National Trust has therefore progressed the most in terms of overcoming the traditional features of the National Trust by recognising vernacular and community interests; nevertheless it is constrained by planning and environmental concerns.

4.6 Conclusion

Managing diverse cultural resources can be challenging for small island developing states in the postcolonial era. The colonial influence still denies the public a greater role in the definition and protection of heritage, and national decisions about land use reflect that property rights remain the cornerstone of the common law, while cultural heritage

---

862 Ibid, s 4(1)(c) and 4(1)(d).
863 Saint Christopher National Trust Act 2009, s 4(1)(e) and 4(1)(i).
864 Ibid, s 4(1)(f)- (k).
865 Ibid, s 6.
866 Ibid, s 7 and schedule.
867 Ibid, s 13.

remains undefined and placeless. The laws appear fragmented, precisely because of this placelessness, and the museums, historical societies and National Trusts existing throughout the Lesser Antilles only seem to be effectively coordinated where they are integrated within the institutional framework for planning, as in Barbados. Nevertheless, the Barbados scenario calls for caution, as it is meant to support planning objectives which are not always compatible with heritage protection, a theme addressed in more detail in Chapter Five.

While the main purpose of antiquities laws is to promote and protect archaeological objects, the current approach offers a view of heritage that is disembodied, without meaning for communities. When heritage institutions fail to consider place-based implications of collections, such as their wider meaning in community and environmental contexts, and instead assign arbitrary numbers to determine their significance, they are likely to be unsuccessful. Museums remain underdeveloped, underused in terms of their ability to protect the cultural and natural heritage and protect cultural rights. These institutions must be embedded in the communities they serve to be effective.

The same may be said for the National Trust, which originally relied on an exclusive interpretation of heritage in order to maintain open spaces for the elite and protect their estates formed through enclosure. When tasked with the stewardship of heritage in the Lesser Antilles, these institutions reflect the spatial cleansing prerogatives of their colonial ancestor; their legislation is conservative and fails to interrogate their role in the preservation of colonial spaces. As a result, National Trusts lack strong language for protection of the vernacular heritage in their legislation.

There have been attempts to challenge this framework, and the National Trust's evolution makes it a barometer for the effectiveness of the heritage protection framework. Both Trinidad and Tobago and St Kitts and Nevis have been influenced by the WHC in drafting modern laws for the National Trust, seen in Trinidad's assessment criteria and in St Kitts' definition of heritage categories. Yet St Kitts appears to be the only state to truly modernise its trust by engaging in institutional consolidation and promoting heritage protection valued by its communities. Nevertheless, there has been no opportunity to address its effectiveness to date. Where other National Trusts remain active and effective, they must be aligned to traditional planning legal principles (Barbados), or suffer the consequences (discussed in Chapter 7). National Trusts therefore have an important role to play in landscape protection and spatial justice, if they can evolve to meet the needs of post-colonial Caribbean societies. Most Trusts appear not to have maximised their potential, and this is in keeping with the role and state of heritage in the region.

Ultimately, an understanding of landscape is critical when drafting robust effective heritage legislation, because it ensures recognition of the relevance of community relationships with land to heritage and embeds sustainability in its protective mechanisms. Without this approach, heritage possesses purely economic value in the form of tourist attractions, rather than any significance in the daily life of a citizen. When contextualised as part of an individual's environs, a range of historical, social and scientific meanings become apparent, and it becomes possible to protect heritage as living custom. Legislation should therefore refocus its definitions and its protective mechanisms away from object- or site-based controls towards a broader landscape concept that reflects the spatial and temporal relationships that give life to communities. The current state of legislation reveals the deficiencies that arise from the object-based approach.

While Antigua's Antiquities bill attempts to move beyond the law of finds, it nevertheless finds itself in the same dilemma as Barbados and Grenada. These countries have restrictively drafted legislation, by focusing on a system of heritage exploitation, rather than protection, and prioritise arbitrary distinctions such as date range for valuing heritage objects, rather than engaging with what makes a place (and its features which might include such objects) significant. The heritage laws of St Kitts and Nevis, St Vincent and the Grenadines and Trinidad and Tobago in turn, are curtailed in effectiveness by planning prerogatives. An examination of planning law's relationship with heritage protection is the subject of the next chapter.

5

Planning Legislation

5.1 Introduction

Land is the connective tissue linking planning, heritage and environmental law. The development of planning law principles parallels the diminishing of landscape and heritage, and the emergence of spatial justice issues in the history of Britain and its colonies. In fact, Nicole Graham observes that enclosure is an early form of planning, and responsible for the fabrication of landscape as scenery.[868] This practice upheld land's conversion to property law, defining land by its ability to be exclusively possessed.

Planning law regulates the development of land, and tangible, terrestrial natural and heritage resources are protected by virtue of their connection to the land.[869] This concept of land, as private property, depends on the legal concept of land as abstract space.[870] Space could be surveyed, mapped and regulated unlike landscape, which is formed by local conditions and local relationships. The idea of space folds land within the realm of human knowledge and control. Standardised, universal and measurable space could be grafted over place so that physicality and particularity of places become irrelevant.[871]

It is thus no accident that planning, environmental and heritage law began to crystallise as distinct bodies of law following the consolidation and creation of landed estates in Britain. The loss of common land stimulated emigration from rural areas, and led to increased urbanisation during Britain's early industrial period. The environmental health consequences of overpopulation were exacerbated by inadequate city planning, and this compelled public authorities to develop new planning laws to reconcile incompatible land use. Planning and environmental law therefore share a close relationship.[872] At the same time, the rapid urbanisation of settlements stimulated a wave of nostalgia for a purer time, when nature was pristine and man had closer ties to the land and his history. The heritage movement was launched to protect monuments

---

868 Graham 63.
869 James 53.
870 Ibid.
871 Graham 66.
872 Winston Anderson notes that because of this common origin 'planning and environmental law' can still be found as a taught course in many universities; see Anderson, *Principles of Caribbean Environmental Law* 171.

and sites, some of which were endangered by demolition to make way for new urban infrastructure.[873] This chapter explores the role of planning law in the destruction of place, and by extension the implications for heritage in the Lesser Antilles today.

5.2 The Industrial and Post-war Foundations of Planning Law in the Lesser Antilles

Planning law in Britain today concerns itself with reconciling conflicting interests in land in order to achieve sustainable development,[874] but this was not the system's raison d'etre. Planning emerged as a response to the environmental consequences of economic growth following the rapid urbanisation of Britain's population in the eighteenth century. Migration of workers to settlements developing around increasingly mechanised industrial centres led to new public health crises as a result of overcrowding and haphazard expansion of towns.[875] The need for public health and housing policies to address the resulting economic costs created a new government role via town and country planning. Local authorities could control development of new housing areas, and were empowered to make and enforce building bylaws for controlling street widths, and the height, structure and layout of buildings; eventually these laws were consolidated in the 1909 Housing, Town Planning Act.[876]

As the previous chapters have shown, the effect of industrialisation was landscape's 'ideological transformation into private property';[877] a national development agenda that abhorred 'waste' in favour of improving the land through cultivation (pastoralism and agriculture) using the processes of enclosure and emparkment;[878] and the arrival of a heritage movement that now ascribed value to a constructed pastoral ancient England that appeared to be rapidly disappearing, relying on heritage institutions such as the National Trust to uphold this imagined past, protect public spaces and prevent the growth of slums. Indeed, the interwar years saw rapid suburbanisation and urban congestion due to developments in transportation, challenges that the existing administrative machinery was ill-equipped to face. A central authority was needed, one that would be responsible for formulating a plan for dispersal from congested urban areas.[879] The fillip for undertaking such comprehensive planning on a national scale was provided by the Second World War following the destruction of parts of Britain.[880] The Attlee Labour government introduced the Town and Country Planning Act 1947 as a means of controlling the rebuilding process. Highly centralised, the law had two main features: local authorities had to produce their own local plans, which detailed land-use policies and proposals for certain developments; and planning

---

873 Dennis Rodwell, *Conservation and Sustainability in Historic Cities* (Wiley-Blackwell 2007) 25.
874 Barry Cullingworth and Vincent Nadin, *Town and Country Planning in the UK* (Routledge 2006) 1-2.
875 Ben Christman, 'A Brief History of Environmental Law in the UK.' *Environmental Scientist* (November 2013): 4-8, 4.
876 Cullingworth and Nadin 15 and 16.
877 Olwig, 'Recovering the Substantive Nature of Landscape' 638.
878 Graham 35 and 100.
879 Cullingworth and Nadin 20.
880 Ibid, 21.

permission was required from local authorities for developments to ensure that they adhered to local plans.[881]

The result was an unprecedented shift in the state's control over the use of private property, by nationalising the development value of land. The development of planning controls combined the promotion of public health and pleasant urban development, with the restriction of private interests, although a bias in favour of development remained.[882] Each phase of planning has thus been shaped by historical developments in the UK. Containing urban sprawl and maintaining open spaces is related to early industrialisation. Town and country planning was not about meeting social and economic goals, but rather was largely administrative in character.[883] Planning tended to be procedural, with very little content; there was no guidance on the information to be contained in plans, which could change from time to time,[884] and so plans did not have the force of law.[885] While modern planning has diverged from its post-war roots, it is these early influences and signature features that shape postcolonial planning systems. It is therefore unsurprising that when transposed to the colonial outposts of the Caribbean, the planning system by design could only serve imperial objectives.

Because land's placelessness or 'atopia' now elevated possession as its defining characteristic,[886] land all over the globe could be acquired and cultivated for the benefit of the nation state. With the removal of native populations and the importation of enslaved West Africans, land in the British Caribbean colonies was cultivated based on these 'scientific' principles, which, as proof of their superiority, were universal in application, with no reference to local or native knowledge, customs or practices, since these 'primitive' cultures had allowed land to lie fallow and untapped.[887] Rather than adapt an appropriate economy to the new or local ecology and then adapt the law to suit, colonial property law was imposed with the old or foreign economy regardless of its property. Colonial land law was inappropriate, literally 'out of place', but land law was expected to adapt to the law.[888]

The colonial era therefore established a pattern of planning practice at odds with the local conditions, relationships and needs of modern democratic states, [889] because the very notion of planning was an extension of colonial hegemony. Colonial planning superimposed the accomplishments and reforms in public health from London over the colonies; early planning was simply an instrument to serve the interests of the colonial administration and business interests.[890] Notions of the public good and public discourse had little meaning. There were no attempts to inform or involve the population, let alone any conception of the 'public interest' as local community and

---

881 Christman 4.
882 Ibid, 5.
883 Cullingworth and Nadin 10.
884 Ibid, 11.
885 Ibid, 3.
886 Graham 91.
887 Olwig, *Landscape, Nature and the Body Politic* 114 and 157-158.
888 Graham 88.
889 Jon Talbot and Ronnie Buddley, 'Postcolonial Town Planning in Commonwealth Nations: A Case Study of the Solomon Islands – An Agenda for Change.' *The Round Table* 96(390) (June 2007): 319-329, 323.
890 Talbot and Buddley 322.

custom could be erased from the land, and environmental determinism underpinned land use. The complete reduction of ecosystems in slave colonies as a result of planning diktats therefore had important ramifications for land use and cultural memory in these islands, since planning upholds exclusive use of privately owned property by the landowner, regardless of community interests in the land.[891] But the ownership model of property that avers that 'property can be assigned unproblematically and clearly to a single individual or corporate owner works more as ideology than fact'.[892]

Herzfeld notes that in the postcolonial era, planning relied on these globally dominant images of 'the West' to reinforce the process of the social and cultural evacuation of space, now for the purpose of nationalist or culturally fundamentalist projects.[893] Spatial cleansing by municipal and state authorities in the planning sense often manifests as 'a persistent streak of nouveau-riche abhorrence of anything that looks dilapidated'.[894] Planning is not viewed as destructive, but rather an expedited pathway to civilised living, where spatial boundaries are simplified and former inhabitants are viewed as intruders or squatters.[895] Heritage and planning law continue to be at cross purposes, because urban development is often seen as an obstacle to heritage protection and vice versa. The perception of heritage as purely pastoral and idyllic has led to the rejection of urbanisation in favour of this idealised conception of the past.[896] At the same time, planning law has supported the conservation of the architectural heritage, since this is the aspect of heritage that lends itself most readily to managed change and complements the aesthetic and morphological features of the landscape.[897] Today, property rights continue to be held as sacrosanct, despite their potential for inefficiency and development viewed as forward-thinking modernisation while heritage conservation is expensive and outmoded.

5.3 Heritage in the Planning Process in the Lesser Antilles

The eight independent Lesser Antillean states as former subjects of the British Empire have legal systems that bear the imprint of colonialism. Much of statutory law is modelled on British legislation, and planning law is no different, reflecting the earliest developments of the planning system.[898]

As in Britain, colonial town planning was linked to housing issues. Town planning legislation based on the 1932 English legislation was introduced in Trinidad and Tobago in response to local political pressure for better living conditions, at a time when the British Empire needed to ensure loyalty of the colonies as the Second World War loomed.[899] Notably, the response to this conflict between local needs and impe-

---

891 Anderson 126.
892 Mitchell, 'Go Slow' 124.
893 Herzfeld 132.
894 Ibid, 142.
895 Ibid, 143 and at 142.
896 Rodwell 26.
897 Ibid, 55.
898 Desmond Heap, 'New Developments in British Land Planning Law – 1954 and After.' *Law and Contemporary Problems* 20 (Summer 1955): 493-516: 493-516.
899 Robert Home, 'Transferring British Planning Law to the Colonies: The Case of the 1938 Trinidad Town and Planning Regional Ordinance.' *Third World Planning Review* 15(4) (1993): 397-410, 408.

rial policy was not to consider local needs at all. Subsequently in the post-war world order, 'town planning played a part in the British attempt to delay nationalist pressure for decolonisation and constitutional change through promises of better living conditions within the overall programme of colonial development and welfare.'[900] It was inevitable that town planning was incapable of providing real change, as the relationship of physical planning to wider issues of development planning or social issues was non-existent. The 1938 legislation in Trinidad and Tobago marked the beginning of a new government role in land management and land use regulation responding to the demands of population growth.[901] Trinidad's legislation was deemed suitable for West Indian conditions, and was adopted in Saint Lucia in 1945, St Vincent, Dominica, and Grenada in 1946, and St Kitts and Antigua in 1948.[902]

This law was subsequently updated with the introduction of the Physical Planning and Development Control Act (PPDCA), a modern planning law that supplanted the town and country planning legislation of the colonial era. This model physical planning legislation was drafted by the OECS for its member states and has been enacted by all with the exception of St Vincent and the Grenadines.[903] St Vincent, and the non-OECS states Barbados and Trinidad and Tobago, have retained their town and country planning laws. Nevertheless, the model legislation has roots in that earlier law, echoing traditional ideas of maintaining a balance between urban and rural areas that reflect British historical developments rather than Caribbean ones. The relationship between planning and heritage is one such retention, and has a profound impact on heritage resources, their regulation and existence in the region.

5.3.1 Town and Country Planning Legislation

Barbados' Town and Country Planning Act (TCPA), replicates many standard UK provisions in planning law, starting with the long title:

> *An Act to make provision for the orderly and progressive development of land in both urban and rural areas and to preserve and improve the amenities thereof, for the grant of permission to develop land and for other powers of control over the use of land, to confer additional powers in respect of the acquisition and development of land for planning, and for purposes connected with the matters aforesaid.*

Such a 'scene-setting statement' is meant to convey the overall policy or principles guiding the planning process and establishes the essential character of the planning system.[904] It makes clear that the planning process concerns land use, the focus of which in this case is the development (not conservation) of land and enhancing its desirability via the preservation of associated amenities. There is a Town and Country Advisory Committee, which is empowered to advise the Minister on any relevant matters, inclu-

---

900 Home 408.
901 Ibid.
902 Ibid, 403.
903 Jonathan Pugh and Janet Henshall Momsen (eds), *Environmental Planning in the Caribbean* (Ashgate Publishing 2005).
904 Cullingworth and Nadin 2.

ding the preparation of development plans.[905] The preparation of the plan falls to the Chief Town Planner, who can include nature reserves and open spaces in this plan.[906]

Heritage is associated with the architectural heritage, specifically historic buildings.[907] Protection of such heritage is provided via the use of a Building Preservation Order (BPO), where deemed expedient by the Minister to protect any building of 'special historical or architectural interest'. The test for a BPO is that the works proposed would 'seriously affect the character of the building',[908] though this standard is not explained. No criteria are provided for determining 'special architectural or historic interest' and in fact none of these terms, inclusive of heritage, is defined in the legislation. Section 29 states that a 'List of Buildings of special architectural or historic interest' can be made by the Minister, or any pre-existing list, compiled by the Barbados National Trust may be approved by same. In terms of the listing process, the Minister must decide that it is 'expedient' to list such a building, but he is required to engage in consultation with experts before compiling, modifying or approving the list.[909] Nevertheless, consultation does not require the Minister to accept the contributions of the authorities consulted as it is a procedural step; in effect the list, whether pre-existing or a current compilation, can be amended without any input.

While contravention of a BPO results in a fine[910] section 30 also confirms the lack of appropriate safeguards for built heritage. The chief difference between a listed and a non-listed building is that once a building is listed, a contractor must contact the Chief Town Planner for permission at least two months before the works (which can run the gamut from alteration to demolition) are scheduled to take place. This permission may be granted should the Chief Town Planner deem it acceptable to do so, regardless of the special architectural or historic interest that secured the building's listed status in the first place. Unlawful alteration or demolition may trigger requirements for reinstatement or restoration, but these remedies involve enforcement notices that give the offender twenty-eight days to undertake the restorative works, which can be further delayed if an appeal is sought. Subsequent monitoring would be necessary to determine whether the reinstatement meets an acceptable standard, for which there appear to be no guidelines.[911]

In spirit, Barbados' Town and Country Planning Act faithfully upholds planning law's relationship with the historic environment. Heritage is referred to in the Second Schedule to the Barbados TCPA, entitled 'matters for which provisions in development plans may be made'. In Part IV, which concerns 'amenities', heritage preservation is a discretionary form of land use, particularly as 'preservation of buildings, caves, sites and objects of artistic, architectural, archaeological or historical interest.' The ordinary dictionary meaning of amenity relates to a function or visual appeal; this puts the emphasis on the aesthetic value of terrestrial heritage resources, which is a legacy of British land law and essential to maintaining the concept of landscape as scenery. Notably,

---

905 Barbados Town and Country Planning Act, s 4.
906 Ibid, s 5 and s 6.
907 Ibid, s 28.
908 Ibid, s 28(2).
909 Ibid, s 28(4).
910 Ibid, s 28(6).
911 Barbados Town and Country Planning Act, ss 40(4), 45 and 46.

Barbados has no separate legal regime for the protection of heritage resources, akin to Britain's monuments legislation. Britain's monuments law distinguishes between monuments and listed buildings, with the former to be preserved in its current condition, minimal works being permissible to preserve the structure or allow public access, while the latter are usually intended to remain in an economically viable state and significant works may be allowed to meet modern living standards or transition to a viable use.[912] There is no such distinction in Barbados' legislation, because there were no local rural communities following the enclosure process to drive a similar process to protect heritage as the heritage movement did in Britain.

St Vincent and the Grenadines' Town and Country Planning Act of 1992 also retains structural similarities to early planning legislation. Section 3 establishes a Physical Planning and Development Board, which does not specify any representation from any heritage organisation in St Vincent, although the legislation does not explicitly exclude such a presence. The Board is required to prepare a national development plan, regional and local plans.[913] Factors to be considered in the preparation of these plans include economic and social development trends, prevailing physical and environmental conditions, and the need for national parks, public open spaces and forestry reserves.[914] However, no cultural or community concerns are explicitly required to be taken into account in the planning process.

BPOs are provided for and reflect the language contained within the Barbados TCPA.[915] The Minister, where he finds it expedient based on the Board's recommendation, may make such an order if the building is of 'special architectural or historical interest', a term not defined in the Act. This standard is qualified by other considerations: to be found objectionable, the works proposed must seriously alter the character of the building, or affect public health and safety, which brings to mind the public health origins of planning law.[916] A fine is to be paid on contravention of this order.[917] In terms of listing, sections 24 and 25 repeat sections 29 and 30 of the Barbados TCPA, although in this case the Minister does not compile lists but is obliged to approve, with or without modification, pre-existing lists of buildings of architectural or historic interest, where prepared by the St Vincent National Trust or similar body. This was discussed in Chapter Four. As with Barbados, consultation (but not participation) is mandatory in the decision to amend such lists. Upon gazettal of the list, the listed building's status is similar to its counterpart in the Barbados TCPA. Heritage is therefore subject to the prerogatives of Planning.

Structurally, Trinidad and Tobago's Town and Country Planning Act mirrors Barbados' TCPA. There is no mention of managing heritage resources in its planning law. This is due in part to the fact that the National Trust of Trinidad and Tobago is empowered to compile a register of listed buildings, to monitor their status, and to enforce orders for listed property where damaged or destroyed.[918] Co-operation

---

912 Harwood 13.
913 St Vincent and the Grenadines TCPA 1992, s 7.
914 Ibid, s 8(2) and (3).
915 Ibid, s 23.
916 Ibid, s 23(2) and (4).
917 Ibid, s 23(5).
918 National Trust of Trinidad and Tobago Act, ss 8, 26 and 27, as discussed in detail in Chapter Four.

between the Trust and relevant government departments such as the planning authorities is relegated to ad hoc arrangements via the use of memoranda of understanding and other un-named mechanisms to effect 'integrated programmes for preservation of monuments or the protection and management of the environment'.[919] Both Trinidad and Tobago and St Vincent and the Grenadines may be contrasted in terms of the application of planning law to heritage.

5.3.2 Physical Planning Legislation

The most striking feature of the new model physical planning legislation that was drafted for the OECS member states to replace town and country planning laws is that it enumerates broader social, economic and environmental objectives than originally envisaged in town and country planning legislation.

By way of illustration, two objectives of the Antigua Physical Planning Act 2003 (APPA) are to 'protect and conserve the cultural heritage of Antigua and Barbuda as it finds expression in the natural and the built environment' and 'to foster awareness that all persons and organisations owning, occupying and developing land have a duty to use that land with due regard for the wider interests, both present and future, of society'.[920] This is the first time that planning legislation in the Lesser Antilles explicitly mentions preservation of cultural heritage as a goal of planning, taking into account cultural heritage's relationship with the environment, the sustainable use of land by alluding to future generations, or intergenerational equity, as well as the wider general interests of society in the environment, which implies the need to transcend private interests in land where necessary. The APPA establishes a Development Control Authority, of which the Town and Country Planner serves as the Chief Executive Officer.[921] In preparing development plans, the Town and Country Planner must be inclusive and develop strategies for obtaining representations from the public.[922]

Publicity and a duty to consult have also been introduced for environmentally vulnerable projects.[923] Environmental impact assessments (EIAs) are required only for a specific class of projects listed in the Third Schedule of the APPA. Projects impacting cultural heritage are not explicitly referred to but may be captured in the catch-all provision of 'any other matter'.[924] In addition, development permits may attract conditions such as the preservation of any buildings or sites of importance to the cultural heritage of the country[925] but the law does not oblige the Development Control Authority to do so and no listing criteria or listed buildings are identified in the APPA.

The 'preservation of buildings, sites and other features for architectural, cultural or historical reasons' is a factor that 'may' be considered by the Town and Country Planner in the preparation of development plans.[926] Part VI of the Act addresses environmental protection, and integrates cultural heritage with natural resources requiring protec-

---

919 National Trust of Trinidad and Tobago Act, s 15B.
920 APPA, s 3(f) and (g).
921 Ibid, ss 5 and 6(2).
922 Ibid, s 9(2).
923 Ibid, ss 20 and 22.
924 Ibid, s 23(2)(f).
925 Ibid, s 27(1)(a)(viii).
926 Ibid, s 10(4)(c).

tion. However, this seems to be restricted to the traditional definition of built heritage, and omits archaeological sites. The Town and Country Planner is responsible for compiling a list of such buildings, in consultation with local heritage bodies and which must be finally approved by the Minister.[927] The BPO is reintroduced, now an interim preservation order that lapses after 90 days unless renewed by the Minister.[928] The presumption therefore is that development is the default legitimate land use unless active intervention is approved for heritage protection. The Authority 'shall have regard to' a number of factors in considering whether to preserve the building: whether it is desirable having regard to the importance of preserving the landscape, architectural, cultural or historical heritage and whether the economic activity in the building would facilitate its preservation and the quality of architectural design.[929]

The Town and Country Planner is not required to consult with technical expertise on matters concerning preservation of the historic environment, and in keeping with this trend, Part IV of the Second Schedule concerning amenities retains language identical to that of the Barbados TCPA in the preparation of development plans. In addition, the First Schedule, which addresses the composition of the Development Authority, makes no explicit provision for any cultural or archaeological heritage representation, although environmental expertise is required.

The APPA echoes much of the language contained in Dominica's Physical Planning Act (DPPA), which was passed a year earlier. BPOs are addressed in similar language,[930] as are environment protection areas.[931] In addition to a survey of the area and representations from the public, heritage-pertinent criteria that can be considered in designating an environment protection area include:

(iii) any outstanding geological, physiographical, ecological, or architectural, cultural or historical features of the area which it is desirable to preserve and enhance;

(iv) any special scientific interest in the area;

(v) any special natural hazards to which the area is or may be subject; and

(vi) the characteristics, circumstances and interests of the people living and working in the area.[932]

This language suggests that environment protection areas can potentially protect landscapes, which distinguishes such areas from traditionally regulated protected areas and national parks. However, the Authority is required to submit a report to the Minister, who will make an environment protection order if he believes it is desirable to do so.

---

927 Ibid, s 43.
928 Ibid, s 44.
929 Ibid, s 44(6).
930 DPPA, s 47.
931 DPPA, s 56 and APPA s 52(3)(c).
932 DPPA, s 56(3)(c) (emphasis added).

In addition, while development is limited, it is not withdrawn entirely.[933] An environment protection area management plan may be produced to support its maintenance.[934] Part IV of the First Schedule also includes the language on heritage as an amenity value that may be considered in development plans.

The Saint Lucia Physical Planning and Development Act 2005 (SLPPDA) states that one of its objects is to 'protect and conserve the natural and cultural heritage of Saint Lucia'.[935] This act, as well as Antigua and Dominica's planning legislation, calls for a purposive and liberal interpretation to facilitate attainment of the objectives of the act.[936] Physical plans may allocate land for conservation,[937] and zoned areas may be reserved for 'specific purposes'.[938] The Head of the Physical Planning and Development Division cannot approve any application for the development of land in that area that is inconsistent with the purposes for which the area is reserved,[939] which could conceivably include landscapes. The Head of the Physical Planning and Development Division is required to compile lists of buildings, monuments and sites of special prehistoric, historic or architectural interest, which may be approved lists from other sources such as the Saint Lucia National Trust.[940] This law is the first to include preservation orders for sites; nevertheless, the regime for protection, in terms of the standard to be met, the factors to be considered, enforcement and remedies, is mostly unaltered from traditional provisions. There is also the matter of whether it is appropriate to list both monuments and sites, given the distinct legal effect each category attracts in the common law, discussed later in this chapter. The First Schedule addresses composition of the Physical Planning and Development Appeals Tribunal, which does not specify heritage management expertise. Part IV of the Second Schedule concerning heritage as an amenity value is reproduced verbatim.

The Development Control and Planning Act of St Kitts and Nevis is also modelled on the OECS physical planning legislation, and provides for similar objects under its Act,[941] introduces a procedure for the designation of environment protection areas that contemplates landscape as a protected resource (though not identified as such),[942] and can impose conditions on development permission.[943] Like Saint Lucia, preservation orders are extended to sites[944] and interim preservation orders may be made for any building or site not already listed under section 52 of the National Conservation and Environment Protection Act, for which there is a separate regime. It should be noted however that in cases of conflict, the Development Control Act prevails. As with St

---

933 Ibid, s 57. Conservation areas first appear in the UK Civic Amenities Act 1967. Because even minor alteration can severely affect a conservation area, development rights can be completely withdrawn in these areas. See Consuelo Sanz, *The Protection of Historic Properties: A Comparative Study of Administrative Policies* (WIT Press, 2009) 134 and 136.
934 DPPA, s 59.
935 SLPPDA, s 3(1)(e).
936 Ibid, s 3(2).
937 SLPPDA, s 11.
938 Ibid, s 32.
939 Ibid, s 32(2).
940 Ibid, s 33.
941 SKDCA, s 4.
942 Ibid, ss 12 and 54.
943 Ibid, s 31.
944 Ibid, s 49.

Vincent, development is prioritised over heritage preservation. The First Schedule addresses composition of the St Kitts Development and Planning Board; environment is represented and there is a catch-all provision for any other area of public interest that the Minister considers relevant to physical planning. Part IV of the Second Schedule preserves the language on heritage as an amenity value.

Finally, Grenada's Physical Planning and Development Control Act (GPPDCA) states that the Planning and Development Authority has the duty 'to contribute to the protection and conservation of the cultural heritage as it finds expression in the natural and built environment'.[945] Interestingly, the Act was passed in 2016 and replaced the 2002 Act, which had much stronger language on heritage preservation, making it an objective of planning in keeping with the model Act and stated that the Act should be given a liberal and purposive interpretation. The Physical Plan for Grenada prescribes land use, and 'may' allocate land for conservation.[946]

The GPPDCA devotes Part VI to the conservation of natural and cultural heritage. The Authority is designated as the national service for the identification, protection, conservation and rehabilitation of the natural and cultural heritage of Grenada, in accordance with the World Heritage Convention, to which Grenada is a party.[947] This is significant, because this is the only planning law in the Lesser Antilles that serves as implementing legislation for a State Party's commitments under international heritage law. The Authority coordinates with other departments via a cross-sectoral 'Natural and Cultural Heritage Advisory Committee' comprising officers from Ministries with portfolios for culture and tourism, as well as representatives from the National Trust, the Grenada Society of Architects, the Grenada Institute of Engineers, and members from civil society.[948]

On the advice of the Committee, the Authority 'may' compile a list of buildings, monuments, and sites, or 'may' adopt and amend lists already prepared by the National Trust.[949] Critically, there is no distinction between buildings and monuments, so all listed heritage resources are subject to potential development or demolition. This merges two separate and distinct regimes, where listed buildings were to be developed with an eye to their aesthetic and architectural character, while 'monuments that were scheduled were not in active use and not intended to evolve the way that buildings and structures usually do as uses and ways of living change. The emphasis in scheduling is to preserve the monument as it is, subject only to works designated to preserve it.'[950] With the exception of St Vincent, these islands have no legislation corresponding to the UK's monuments legislation, though the term seems to have been imported into the law along with the listed building regime. This merging of listed buildings and monuments also characterises the aforementioned physical planning legislation of Saint Lucia and St Kitts. Such a conceptual blurring appears to indicate a misunderstanding or lack of knowledge on the part of the authorities as to the significance of the distinction in law, as well as ignorance of the range and diversity of national heritage,

---

945 GPPDCA, s 3.
946 Ibid, s 11.
947 Ibid, s 38.
948 Ibid, s 39.
949 Ibid, s 39(1)(a).
950 Harwood 13.

which should direct the development of protective mechanisms appropriate to the various categories of heritage, rather than vice versa. The Town and Country Acts do not make reference to monuments and sites at all.

The Committee may also advise the Authority on applications for the altering or demolition of listed sites; declaring environmental protected areas as well as permitting development in such areas and incorporating the protection, conservation and rehabilitation of the natural and cultural heritage into the planning policy at the level of local, regional and national development plans; preparing plans for protecting buildings or groups of buildings of historic or architectural merit; designating Heritage Conservation Areas for such buildings, and permitting development in such Areas or near listed sites; and preparing abatement notices for the preservation of amenities.[951]

What is clear from the Advisory Committee's powers is that its primary function is to facilitate development as defined in section 2 of the legislation, 'the carrying out of building, engineering, mining or other operations in, on, over or under land, the making of any material change in the use of land or buildings or the subdivision of land'. This could potentially conflict with its responsibilities as the focal point of the World Heritage Convention. The Committee is not empowered to advise the Authority on the treatment of heritage resources valued by communities, nor is there provision for consultation with other bodies that may provide guidelines on such activities. As an advisory body, none of its findings or recommendations is binding.

There are several mechanisms offering protection to private landowners. Owners and occupiers of the listed building or property, as well as any other person are permitted to make objections or representations, which must be taken into consideration in determining whether to list the building, or site.[952] A notice that the building, monument or site has been listed is to be served on any owner or occupier, and the list is to be gazetted.[953] The language outlining the effect of listing replicates the corresponding provision in the Barbados Town and Country Planning Act, as well as the model legislation, requiring two months' notice of any proposed works to a listed building, which may be refused or granted, with or without conditions. Works are permitted where it can be proven that it was necessary in the interests of health and safety, again pitting public health against heritage conservation. Where consent has not been granted, this act constitutes an offence and is liable on summary conviction to a fine of eighty thousand dollars, or a term of five years' imprisonment, or both.[954] Significantly, no remedies involving restoration of the building, monument or site are included.

Interim preservation orders are available for protecting any unlisted building, monument or site from threat and development activity.[955] The effect is to treat the unlisted heritage resource as listed, but as discussed, this protection is minimal. Interestingly, where works are carried out in contravention of an interim preservation order, restoration of the affected building, monument or site to its former state at the expense of the owner or occupier of the building, monument or site is required.[956] This is not a

---

951   GPPDCA, s 39(2)(c) – (j).
952   Ibid, s 40(2)(b) and (c).
953   Ibid, s 40(3).
954   Ibid, s 41.
955   Ibid, s 39(2)(b) and s 42.
956   Ibid, s 42(7).

requirement for listed buildings where unlawful works have taken place. Nevertheless, this section creates a cumbersome process for unlisted heritage, rather than a streamlined approach in keeping with the capacity of a small island state.

General responsibility for conservation and rehabilitation of these buildings, monuments and sites is placed entirely on owners and occupiers of listed buildings.[957] The government may assist owners of listed heritage with the procurement of technical and financial assistance and issue notices where conservation or rehabilitation is necessary.[958] Where these notices have not been complied with, planning authorities may enter the premises, take steps to rehabilitate and recover the debt in court or compulsorily acquire the heritage resource.[959] This may be contrasted with the language in St Vincent's Preservation of Historic Buildings and Antiquities Act 1976, which charges the Planning Minister to do all that is necessary to restore a building where the owner does not comply.[960] Grenada's approach relies on punitive mechanisms, rather than the practical strategy of educational or technical support as in the St Kitts NCEPA. There are no national or harmonised standards for heritage protection, or plans for monitoring and reporting by these landowners, or mechanisms for exchange of information or collaboration with local communities, which are some of the components of international best practice laid down in UNESCO guidance.[961]

The Authority, on advice from the Advisory Committee, may by order published in the Gazette, designate any area containing a group of separate or connected buildings which, because of their history or architecture, their homogeneity or their place in the landscape, are of outstanding universal value, including such other land in the vicinity of that group of buildings as is necessary, to provide a peripheral protection belt or buffer zone, as a Heritage Conservation Area.[962] Outstanding universal value is a well-known criterion in designating heritage sites in accordance with the WHC -this does not appear to be appropriate for designating national heritage protection as it requires the heritage resource to be recognised globally before national authorities will designate it. Provision is made for representations from private landowners.[963] The Authority can publish proposals for Heritage Conservation Areas, including conditions for the use of buildings and land other than listed buildings, monuments and sites within the area, and such proposals must be incorporated into the physical plan for the part of Grenada in which the Heritage Conservation Area is located, if any.[964] While innovative for domestic cultural heritage law, HCAs have yet to be designated.

Lists of areas of natural beauty may be compiled, including submarine and subterranean areas and their flora and fauna. A new area, a natural area, that is explicitly defined as excluding reserves, parks and marine protected areas as designated under

---

957 Ibid, s 43.
958 Ibid, s 43(3).
959 Ibid, s 43(4).
960 SVG Preservation of Historic Buildings and Antiquities Act 1976, s 4(3) and 4(8), as discussed in Chapter Four.
961 UNESCO *Recommendation concerning the Protection, at National Level, of the Cultural and Natural Heritage* 16 November 1972, and see the WHC arts 4 and 5.
962 GPPDCA, s 44.
963 Ibid, s 44(2).
964 Ibid, s 44(3).

other legislation, is also introduced.[965] Where such an area deserves special protection, it may be declared an environmental protection area and gazetted.[966] Representations may be made by affected persons, and provision is made for the authorisation of works and the undertaking of EIAs to facilitate development in such areas, the restriction and prohibition of development and public access, as well as controlled uses for the purposes of agriculture, forestry and fisheries.[967] Such areas have also never been declared. Notably, the law maintains the division between the cultural and natural heritage, and between maintaining a rural pristine natural area versus a lived in landscape.

In addition to opportunities to make objections to the listing or designation of heritage in conservation areas, owners and occupiers of listed heritage may appeal any listing before the Physical Planning Appeal Tribunal established under section 58.[968] The Tribunal must consist of not less than three or more than five members appointed by the Minister, of whom the Chairperson must be a legal practitioner of not less than ten years standing, and the other members must have training or experience in environmental services, physical planning, engineering, architecture, land surveying or land development.[969] Notably, heritage-related disciplines are absent. An appeal may lie against inter alia, a development permit, conditions subject to which a permit is granted, revocation of a permit, refusal of a building permit, and a preservation order.[970] Where the Tribunal decides that a listed building, monument or site should be removed from a list, or that any building or other land should be excluded from a Heritage Conservation Area, the Authority amends the list or designation order accordingly.[971]

These appeal procedures, in addition to other mechanisms in the GPPDCA (the listing process, preservation orders, the Advisory Committee, and the creation of conservation areas) reinforce that heritage is subject to many of the same derogations that afflict the physical planning laws in other islands, which can result in the upholding of property law priorities such as requiring the Authority to take into account objections from landowners whose property may fall within a proposed heritage conservation area.[972] While this may enable landowners to assert their rights where outdated colonial law applies, it can also result in damage to heritage resources where common law rules uphold landowners' rights to exclude heritage users and even (mis) use resources as legal owners. In addition, protection for environment and culture is subject to development prerogatives, because applications may be submitted for development of these areas.[973] All proposed developments in the Third Schedule to the GPPDCA are subject to an EIA, 'unless the Authority for good cause otherwise determines'.[974] While projects concerning parks or sensitive areas are subject to an EIA, there is no such requirement for heritage resources. No standards are provided for the rehabilitation of listed

---

965 Ibid, s 45.
966 Ibid, s 45(2).
967 Ibid, ss 45(3) and (4).
968 Ibid, s 50.
969 Ibid, s 58(2).
970 Ibid, s 59(2).
971 Ibid, s 50(3).
972 Ibid, s 44(2).
973 Ibid, s 39(2)(e).
974 Ibid, s 22(2).

buildings, or the designation process, or the management of heritage conservation areas to enable implementation of the law. It is unclear whether two new categories for conservation areas, especially categories that isolate environment from heritage, are feasible or even desirable. In fact, the GPPDCA's Second Schedule describes heritage as an amenity value to be addressed in development plans 'as appropriate', virtually identical to the language in Barbados' TCPA.

What is noticeable about these laws, whether located within the traditional town and country planning cluster or the more modern physical planning cluster, is that they fail to reflect best practice when it comes to accommodating indigenous and local communities in the development process.[975] Participatory mechanisms are limited, and there are gaps in the criteria for environmental impact assessments where cultural heritage is concerned, such as designing protocols to guide interaction with local communities and benchmarks for assessing impacts on their livelihoods, use and access to resources, local practices involving land use, and social cohesion.[976] Examples of planning situations illuminating these shortcomings and the consequences for heritage protection are considered in depth in Chapter Seven.

5.4 Conclusion

Planning and heritage law rarely work in alignment. This is because planning law promotes development objectives, which can conflict with heritage protection. Planning law does not recognise the multiplicity of uses of public space, focusing on preserving aesthetically pleasing architectural buildings while paying little attention to the contexts in which communities may value those buildings. Because it cannot accommodate various spatial definitions, there is friction between heritage and planning law. Where it does recognise heritage, it is narrowly defined, as degraded heritage resources are associated with public health risks, in keeping with spatial cleansing narratives.

Planning law in the Lesser Antilles reflects the needs, norms and values of postwar Britain, not the islands themselves. Because that legal system is spatially located, these laws are regulating development somewhere else, regulating a different place in a different time, to the detriment of the present day communities they should be serving. This is the essence of spatial injustice, because failure to consider factors such as the geographic location, its features and significance to the local people, means that implementation or lack thereof will disadvantage community access to heritage, loosen critical bonds over time and ultimately lead to erasure.

Because community valuation of heritage is excluded, communities are not involved in heritage protection, except for the duty to consult in certain instances. Knowledge, both technical and local, is relegated to the advisory and procedural aspects of decision-making, rather than playing a substantive role in determining the significance of heritage. Mechanisms for public consultation do not equate to a community-led definition of heritage. In valuing 'placelessness' of property, land's specific features have no meaning, and the meanings attached as a result of community interaction

---

975 Akwé: Kon Voluntary Guidelines for the Conduct of Cultural, Environmental and Social Impact Assessment.
976 Akwé: Kon Voluntary Guidelines para 43.

are irrelevant. Cleaving land from community excludes people. Minimal consultation with stakeholders secures minimal interest in protecting these resources.

Private landowners with clear evidence of ownership are therefore afforded rights to make representation and appeal any planning decision that affects their private property. This is underscored in the recent amendments to Grenada's physical planning legislation. In its current iteration, property does not allow for the incorporation of the concept of a duty to preserve and protect (and is therefore unsustainable), because it implies control by the owner, expressed by his ability to alienate, exploit and exclude others from the object or site in question. This excludes any communal interest in heritage, and leaves unacknowledged other forms of land use. The aim of the planning framework should be to geographically situate its planning tools in the Caribbean islands so that spatial justice is realised.

Such an approach would ensure that the law reflects the needs of local communities and an understanding of local conditions. In such a framework, the relationships between people and their environment could be captured as a dynamic process. The present narrow concept of heritage vis à vis land use and protection of property rights is a legacy of colonialism that inhibits a sustainable approach to heritage protection, because heritage is secondary to property. Heritage bodies rarely have representation, safeguards for heritage resources are subject to a number of exceptions, and there are no technical guidelines for assessing development impacts on the variety of existing heritage resources. Given these challenges with planning law, the next chapter examines the success of protective mechanisms such as parks and protected areas in the sustainable protection of heritage resources.

6

National Parks and Protected Areas Legislation

6.1 Introduction

When national parks were first established to protect pristine natural environments, they were underpinned by imperial interests that manifested as environmental racism.[977] As Karen Fog Olwig and Kenneth Olwig write with respect to the English landscape garden parks discussed in Chapter Two, the natural park was originally the symbolic justification for the social and environmental changes that undermined the very landscape.[978] There was nothing natural about the English landscape park, as it was a pastoral illusion employed as a device to disguise the brutal economic realities of destruction of peasant village communities through enclosure.[979]

When transposed to the United States, the park ideal transcended the need to hold nature and society in balance, and now excluded society in the search for pure, untamed 'wilderness'. Fog Olwig notes that this was spurred by the loss of the American frontier as the country rapidly developed.[980] Yellowstone Park, the first American national park, was originally admired for its resemblance to the British landscape garden park, a factor in its eventual preservation in 1872.[981] Local land use was considered an obstacle to conservation by the authorities, and in the colonies, local populations were either expelled or had their access to landscape restricted to create parks and reserves.[982]

In slave colonies such as those in the Caribbean islands, colonial reserves dominated in order to maintain plantation agriculture, and also served as living laboratories that nurtured the embryonic disciplines of colonial botany and ecology. These proto-parks and their underlying philosophy have come to influence present day legislation in the region. This chapter considers the role of parks legislation in the protection of landscape today, and the implications for heritage protection. Specifically, parks and

---

[977] Dahlberg et al, 209.
[978] Fog Olwig and Olwig, 'Underdevelopment and the Development of 'Natural' Park Ideology' 17.
[979] Ibid.
[980] Fog Olwig, 'National Parks, Tourism and Local Development: A West Indian Case' 22.
[981] Fog Olwig and Olwig, 'Underdevelopment and the Development of "Natural" Park Ideology' 18.
[982] Dahlberg et al, 210. See also Chapter Two on landscapes and the eviction of commoners and later Native peoples, and Chapter Three on landscape's influence on the philosophical roots of the World Heritage Convention.

protected area laws in the Lesser Antilles are assessed in terms of their ability to protect the local heritage in the context of spatial justice.

6.2 The History of the English Commons

As explicated in Chapter Two, Olwig's framework for landscape shows that the commons symbolically epitomised shared abstract values as well as democracy. Historically, the commons represented an area in which citizens of a landscape territory would have use rights in the common land. These rights derive their power from the common, customary laws of the town or land, in contrast to the rights bestowed by statute and state bureaucracy.[983] Rights in the commons were central to the establishment of one's rights, membership and standing in the wider community, and guaranteed one's right to its protection and fellowship.[984]

Property rights and use rights are not synonymous: while 'property can be sold under legal statute and title, use rights are customary and rooted in an ever changing practice rather than title or deed, and cannot be sold as such. Customary rights are, in principle, unwritten and subject to constant revision in the light of current practice'.[985] Olwig emphasises that while the classic commons is nominally the property of the Lord of the Manor, the lord need not have use rights to the commons.[986] The present day park is largely inspired by the pastoral artistic tradition of the English landscape park ideal that flourished in the eighteenth century, masking the dissolution of communal land.[987] At the same time as many working English commons were being enclosed for intensive agriculture, many estate owners chose to allocate the lands surrounding the manor house to grassy parks.[988]

The commons today are simplified iterations of shared resource regimes characterised by participatory forms of governance rooted in ancient custom, because agriculture no longer dominates the landscape.[989] Olwig observes that this new expression of the commons is a recreative and symbolic commons, rather than an 'old' productive commons. The landscape of the commons might be insignificant in economic value, but socially and symbolically central in community life.[990] The contested character of the commons, Olwig argues, has less to do with friction between differing property institutions, than with a conflict at the abstract symbolic level of social ideals, between the institution of property itself and its symbolic opposite, the pastoral commons. They reproduce ancient tensions concerning 'the commons as a locus of community identity

---

[983] The commons predate the institutionalisation of the modern state, since such rights could not have been expressed, as now, by the statutes and bureaucratic institutions that certify citizenship and issue passports. Rights were rooted in the land – to lose one's rights in the land was tantamount losing one's citizenship. See Kenneth Olwig, 'Commons & Landscape'. *Landscape, Law & Justice: Proceedings from a Workshop on Old and New Commons,* Centre for Advanced Study, Oslo, 11-13 March 2003, 15.
[984] Olwig, 'Commons & Landscape' 19.
[985] Ibid, 20.
[986] Ibid, 17.
[987] Fog Olwig and Olwig, 'Underdevelopment and the Development of "Natural" Park Ideology' 18.
[988] Olwig, 'Commons & Landscape' 17.
[989] Ibid, 16.
[990] Ibid, 19.

and cultural capital within a changing and evolving historical relationship between the symbolic and economic dimensions of the commons'.[991]

Parks in the UK today thus evolve out of the restoration, albeit to a very limited extent, of the commons, which had been enclosed since the 1700s, resulting in the loss of public spaces. During the first decades of the twentieth century, the British labour movement demanded access to the countryside by invoking the ancient customary rights of commons,[992] and now the idea that cities and nations ought to have shared common landscapes, in which the larger citizenry have rights of access, has gained traction.[993] The UK National Parks and Access to the Countryside Act 1949[994] implemented the so-called 'right to roam' long sought by the Ramblers' Association and its predecessors on certain upland and uncultivated areas of England and Wales. The Act required the mapping of all local rights of way, the establishment of national parks and the delegation of power to local authorities to secure access to open country areas.[995] It made provision for the recording, creation, maintenance and improvement of public paths and for securing access to open country, and amended the law relating to rights of way. This element of the act was implemented in stages as definitive maps of different regions were produced.[996]

6.3 Challenges for Commons in Caribbean Parks Law: Exclusive Conservation and the Emergence of Colonial Reserves

There is no counterpart to the UK National Parks Act in the Lesser Antilles, because there was no such restoration of communal land practices in the former British slave colonies, where native populations had been displaced and local custom lost. The destruction of cultural life and identity had disastrous social and ecological consequences as a result of the transition from the living, dynamic social and legal force of customary practices to the oppressive imperial landscape. Enclosure often went hand in hand with the construction of reserves, which transformed working commons (shaped by practice and custom) into ideal pastoral landscape scenes[997] while literally alienating enslaved populations from the land.

As noted in Chapter Two, the earliest legal interventions in the Lesser Antilles relevant to heritage concerned the creation of colonial reserves. Prior to the 1760s, rare island species and more mundane though no less important sources of food, timber and fuel were regulated, but these laws were often fragmented. However, in the mid-1760s, responses to deforestation in particular suddenly changed. A suite of forest reserve legislation, responding to fears of deforestation-induced climate change slowly began to spread around the world, especially throughout the French, British, and Dutch

---

991 Ibid, 20.
992 Olwig, 'Representation and Alienation' 29.
993 Olwig, 'Commons & Landscape', 17.
994 Subsequently amended by the Wildlife and Countryside Act 1981 and the Countryside and Rights of Way Act 2000.
995 Dahlberg 217.
996 See Parts IV and V, National Parks and Access to the Countryside Act 1949.
997 Dillman 185.

empires.[998] The King's Hill Act established a botanic garden in St Vincent and the Grenadines in 1763 as part of a wider improvement ideology.[999] Alexander Gillespie notes that this is the first commonly recognised environmental sanctuary, as in one established by the State, and not by an individual.[1000]

Grove highlights that colonial conservation in the Eastern Caribbean was more about constructing a new landscape, through the displacement of 'primitive' peoples, since uncultivated forests represented wildness and lawlessness.[1001] Property law and environmental law were not rooted in the needs and capacities of these environments, and a lack of understanding of these ecosystems quickly led to their decline.[1002] Graham emphasises that this dismissal of space makes property law promote a lack of care for place.[1003] Therefore, conservation, especially in former colonial societies, is hardly ever neutral, even when grounded in science, and especially challenging when it comes to the natural environment and the historic relationship with communities. This is exclusive conservation, in which conservation is for the purpose of perpetuating colonialism, to the detriment of colonised environments and peoples.

6.4 National Parks Legislation in the Lesser Antilles

The islands with national parks legislation in place in the Eastern Caribbean are Antigua and Barbuda, Dominica, Grenada, St Kitts and Nevis, and St Vincent and the Grenadines.[1004]

Antigua and Barbuda's National Parks Act of 1984 makes no reference to protected areas. The long title of that act states that its purpose is to 'provide for the establishment of National Parks and a National Parks Authority; to make provision for the preservation, protection, management and development of the natural physical and ecological resources and the historical and cultural heritage of Antigua and Barbuda…' which indicates that both cultural and natural resources are contemplated as deserving of protection under national park status.

'Park' is defined very narrowly as a 'National Park established under and by virtue of section 20 and the Nelson's Dockyard National Park established under and virtue of section 24.'[1005] Nelson's Dockyard was recently designated a UNESCO World

---

998 Damodaran 133-134.
999 Grove, in *Nature and Society* 155.
1000 Alexander Gillespie, *Protected Areas in International Law* (Martinus Nijhoff 2007) 7.
1001 Grove, *Green Imperialism* 280.
1002 Beattie, Melillo and O'Gorman, 'Introduction' in Beattie, Melillo, and O'Gorman (eds), *Eco-Cultural Networks and the British Empire* 3-21, 15.
1003 Graham 205.
1004 Barbados and Saint Lucia do not have national parks legislation, although Saint Lucia has individual parks. The St Lucia Conservation Authority established under legislation allows for licences to conduct business in parks. Trinidad and Tobago has no national parks and protected areas legislation, although there have been plans to establish a national protected area system plan since the 1960s. Currently, protected areas have been declared under the Forest Act (Chap 6:01), Conservation of Wildlife Act (Chap 67:01), Environmental Management Act 2000 (Environmentally Sensitive Areas Rules), and the Marine Preservation and Enhancement Act (Chap 37:02). These areas formally designated total over 50 locations, and increased under an OAS project to 75 sites. A national protected areas policy was promulgated in 2011. See <https://www.protectedareastt.org.tt/> accessed 5 February, 2018.
1005 Antigua and Barbuda NPA 1984, s 2.

Heritage site and has always held specific historical significance for Antigua and the international community given Admiral Horatio Nelson's association with the site. The Minister may, on the request of the National Parks Authority, by Order published in the Gazette declare any area of land or water or both land and water described in the Order to be a National Park; and such Order is subject to affirmative resolution of the Legislature.[1006] The 'Minister' means the Minister to whom responsibility for Economic Development and Tourism has been assigned, which suggests that national parks are envisaged as primarily commercial assets to be marketed as tourism attractions, and not solely as mechanisms for the protection of heritage.[1007]

The NPA establishes the National Parks Authority, which is empowered to protect, preserve manage and develop the natural, physical and ecological resources and the historical and cultural heritage of Antigua and Barbuda. The Authority is a non-profit making organisation using any surplus funds it acquires for the enhancement of the natural, historical and cultural resources of Antigua and Barbuda in general and, in particular, of Parks. The Authority may carry out or permit to be carried out the repair, restoration and maintenance of any historic building in Parks.[1008]

Management plans are authorised for the management of parks. Specifically, the plan should -

> *(a) identify the Park and assess the present state of its development;*
>
> *(b) contain a statement of objectives and policies on matters relating to, but not limited to-*
>
> *(i) the development and use of all land in the Park;*
>
> *(ii) maintenance and protection of natural resources and sensitive environmental areas;*
>
> *(iii) protection and conservation of heritage resources and archeological sites (including buildings, structures and views);*
>
> *(iv) provision of infrastructure and transportation*[1009]

Provision is made for the protection of both natural and heritage resources, but there is no mention of an integrated approach to their protection, affirming the placement of parks within the remit of tourism; parks are to be developed, rather than exist as public spaces from which development rights have been withdrawn. Notably, the heritage resources to be protected include buildings, structures and views, which is a reminder of landscape as both site and sight, in which the extinguished commons creates a shift in the way landscape is perceived as scenic space.[1010] This legislation, however must now

---

1006 Antigua and Barbuda NPA 1984, s 20(1).
1007 Ibid, s 2.
1008 Ibid, s 4(a), (c) and (d)(i).
1009 Ibid, s 10.
1010 See Chapter Two.

be interpreted in conjunction with Antigua's recently passed environmental legislation, discussed later in this chapter.

Antigua's national parks legislation may be contrasted with Grenada's National Parks and Protected Areas Act 1991, which addresses the designation and maintenance of national parks and protected areas. The relevant minister is the minister responsible for the national parks system,[1011] which is vested in the Governor-General for the public uses of Grenada.[1012] The Minister is supported by clear organisational infrastructure in the form of a National Parks Authority,[1013] through which the Minister discharges his functions, the National Parks Council, which is an advisory body with representatives from government and civil society in the areas of tourism, environment and heritage, and the National Parks Fund, comprising admission fees, contributions and borrowed moneys, from which the park system is administered, and park staff is to be remunerated.[1014]

Interestingly, though parks and protected areas are not distinguished in the interpretation section, the Minister may establish parks by proclamation, which may include private land leased, purchased or donated.[1015] Protected areas may be established by Order for the purpose of preserving the natural beauty or flora and fauna of the area; creating a recreational area; commemorating an historical event of national importance; or preserving an historic landmark or place or object of historic, prehistoric, archaeological, cultural or scientific importance.[1016] It may therefore be inferred that protected areas attract legal protection for a specific stated purpose.

The objective of the National Parks Advisory Council is to ensure the land comprising the national parks system 'endures unimpaired' for the enjoyment of present and future generations.[1017] The legislation therefore appears to contemplate a sustainable development model, not the strict conservationist approach traditionally applied to protected areas. A high threshold is set for these resources to remain in an unimpaired state, which is the first reference to the concept of integrity. A regulatory framework has been created for parks and protected areas, but in both the Antiguan and Grenadian legislation there is an absence of mechanisms for engaging communities. Antigua's legislation explicitly states that the Minister responsible for the parks system is the Minister for Economic Development and Tourism. Grenada's legislation is vague, saying only that it is the Minister responsible for the time being for the park system – currently national parks are the responsibility of the Ministry of Tourism.[1018]

National parks and protected areas legislation in Dominica and St Vincent and the Grenadines evince a higher level of protection for these resources than Antigua and Grenada. Dominica's National Parks and Protected Areas Act 1975 explicitly states that the national parks system is dedicated to the people of Dominica.[1019] All

---

1011 Grenada NPPA 1991, s 2.
1012 Ibid, s 3.
1013 Ibid, s 7.
1014 Ibid, ss 8, 9 and 10.
1015 Ibid, s 4.
1016 Ibid, s 5.
1017 Ibid, s 3(3).
1018 Interview with Mr Michael Jessamy, Heritage Officer, Ministry of Tourism, Civil Aviation and Culture (St George's, Grenada 1 April, 2016).
1019 Dominica NPPA 1975 as amended, s 3.

lands in the parks and all lands set apart as protected areas constitute the national parks system, and are vested in the State and dedicated to the people of Dominica for their benefit, education and enjoyment. Lands within the national parks system are to be maintained and made use of so as to leave them unimpaired for the enjoyment of future generations,[1020] which is similar but stronger language than Grenada's legislation, which also calls for sustainable management of parks and protected areas. The provisions concerning the establishment of national parks and protected areas are similar to Grenada's.[1021] The organisational apparatus for park management takes the form of an advisory council but no provision is made for a fund or authority as with Grenada. Dominica's legislation establishes participatory mechanisms that are not found in Antiguan or Grenadian law. Notably, any proposed management plan for parks and protected areas must be published in the Gazette for inspection by the public and mechanisms for providing comments are provided.[1022]

St Vincent and the Grenadines' National Parks Act 2002 states that the act is for the establishment of an authority for national parks and for further preservation and protection, management and development of the natural, physical and ecological resources and the historical and cultural heritage, which is similar to the objectives of Antigua's national parks act. However, 'national park' is specifically defined as any park, reserve, river or beach declared a national park under this Act and any other site prescribed by Order.[1023] The Minister promotes national parks for the preservation and protection, management and development of the natural, physical and ecological resources and the historical and cultural heritage of St Vincent and the Grenadines.[1024]

The Vincentian legislation is the most far reaching in terms of innovation and protection. The National Parks, Rivers and Beaches Authority is the authority responsible for managing parks, and its functions include advocacy and the promotion of conservation, use of historic resources for promoting tourism, and establishing a system for prioritisation and classification of parks.[1025] It is noteworthy that the legislation contemplates a classification system and the need to identify areas for immediate protection, not mentioned by the other laws in the Lesser Antilles. The authority must also ensure that activities outside park boundaries do not negatively impact the parks, and mediate and resolve potential conflicts between users of the park, namely between fishermen and tourist interests – this is the only law to acknowledge potential conflicts in access to public space and the only law empowering the regulating authority to engage in conflict resolution.

Parks must have management plans, based on scientific data, and the Authority must maintain a list of natural resources, specifically rivers, streams, springs, swamps, waterfalls, water pools and beaches in the State. The Authority is also required to establish an effective interpretation programme, to establish public information and education programmes to create national conservation awareness, and to network with other agencies managing parks and conducting biological research. This is the only

---

1020 Ibid, s 3(1) and (2).
1021 Ibid, ss 4 and 5.
1022 Ibid, ss 11(4) and (5).
1023 SVG NPA 2002, s 2.
1024 Ibid, s 3.
1025 Ibid, s 4.

parks authority in the Lesser Antilles with such extensive roles allocated for community engagement, environmental monitoring and the collection of data for the sustainable management of parks.[1026]

The National Parks Board is empowered to set policy for the preservation, protection, management and monitoring of parks, as well as an advisory role to the Minister on the facilities necessary for use and enjoyment of the parks. This is the only law to make mention of a policy developed specifically for parks.[1027] Another mechanism addressed is the national park plan; this plan must include an inventory of the park's resources, policies concerning land use, maintenance and protection of natural environmental areas, and protection and conservation of heritage resources and historical and archaeological sites.[1028] However, the term 'heritage resources' is not defined, and not distinguished from 'historic resources', which is also used in the legislation.[1029] In preparation, review or amendment of a national park plan the Director must consult with members of the local community, local authorities and other persons or groups of persons affected by the national park plan.[1030] This is the most participatory of the provisions on community engagement, more extensive than Dominica's, and notably absent in Antigua and Grenada's legislation.

The Vincentian legislation is also more robust than its Lesser Antillean counterparts because it prohibits acts in national parks, including the removal of archaeological or cultural material, and performing any act or engage in any activity likely to destroy, endanger or disturb wildlife.[1031] This is the only park legislation that prohibits clandestine excavations, although it should be noted that in some of the islands referenced above, offences concerning heritage are addressed in heritage or antiquities legislation, as discussed in Chapter Four. Nevertheless, St Vincent's law is the most progressive, in terms of the degree to which natural and cultural heritage is integrated, the number of mechanisms created to support effective management, and the participatory approach taken to managing public conflicts and involving local communities in park management.

It is clear that many of the islands have aligned park protection with the tourism industry. In many cases, parks are considered the responsibility of the tourism sector, as in Antigua and Grenada. In recent years, some countries have attempted to integrate park management with environmental conservation. Antigua has enhanced park protection with its new environmental legislation, the Environmental Protection and Management Act 2014 (hereafter EPMA 2014), which defines archaeological sites as 'an area declared to be a site of historical significance under this or the National parks act or any other related Act', indicating that the new environmental legislation is intended to complement Antigua's National Parks Act.[1032] 'Cultural resource' is now defined as 'a historical, architectural, archaeological or cultural site or an artifact, and includes a place or object that enhances the knowledge or preservation of the environment and

---

1026 Ibid, s 7.
1027 Ibid, ss 8 and 9.
1028 Ibid, s 10(2)(b) and 10(2)(c).
1029 Cf SVG NPA 2002, ss 7(2)(c) and 10(2)(c)(iii).
1030 SVG NPA 2002, s 10 (3).
1031 Ibid, s 23(1)(g) and s 23(1)(i).
1032 Antigua EPMA 2014 s 2.

cultural heritage of people of Antigua and Barbuda', while 'protected area' is defined as an area of national significance based on the biological diversity located in the area and can be a wildlife or forest reserve'.[1033]

The EPMA is also ambitious in terms of environmental law, including amongst its objects the sustainable management of the country's resources.[1034] The 'polluter pays' and precautionary principles, central guiding principles in environmental law, are both enshrined in the law.[1035] In addition, the EPMA refers to the St George's Declaration of Principles of Environmental Sustainability 2001, concluded under the auspices of the OECS, and is the normative framework for the sustainable development of the Eastern Caribbean sub-region (discussed in Chapter Three).[1036] This reference to the sub-regional authority is unique amongst the park laws reviewed in this chapter. The law strengthens the national framework for environmental management as well as offers enhanced and focused protection for the cultural heritage.

The EPMA makes provision for protected areas in Part VII of the legislation. Protected areas, although defined, do not explicitly provide for heritage resources.[1037] Interestingly, they speak to the need to 'propagate, protect, conserve, study and manage any ecosystem, flora, fauna or *landscape.*'[1038] A category for multiple-use resource areas, which offers protection to ecosystems and resources while providing secondary social and economic benefits is also created.[1039] A natural resources inventory that includes cultural, archaeological and historic sites is required.[1040] These protection mechanisms demonstrate attempts to manage the cultural and natural resource endowment in an integrated fashion, and contemplate a version of the commons though not expressed as such.

St Kitts and Nevis introduced the National Conservation and Environment Protection Act (NCEPA) in 1987. The purpose of the legislation is to provide for improved management and development of the natural and historic resources of Saint Christopher and Nevis for purposes of conservation; the establishment of national parks, historic and archaeological sites and other protected areas of natural or cultural importance including the Brimstone Hill Fortress National Park (a World Heritage site); and the establishment of a Conservation Commission. Of the laws reviewed here, the Kittitian legislation is most explicit in its protection of natural and historic resources and sets their protection on equal footing.

Terms used in protected areas management as well as cultural resource management are defined. 'National park' is defined an area consisting of a relatively large land or marine area or some combination of land or sea containing natural and cultural features or scenery of national or international significance and managed in a manner to protect such resources and sustain scientific, recreational and educational

---

1033 Ibid.
1034 Antigua EPMA 2014, s 4.
1035 Ibid, s 7(5).
1036 Ibid, s 2.
1037 Ibid, s 54.
1038 Ibid, s 54(1)(b) (emphasis added).
1039 Ibid, s 54(1)(e).
1040 Ibid, s 76(1)(d).

activities on a controlled basis.[1041] 'Protected area' is defined as a national park, nature reserve, botanic garden, historic site, scenic site or any other area of special concern or interest designated under section 3(1) of this Act, which potentially contemplates public spaces.[1042] Protected area is therefore envisaged as an umbrella category. Notably though, the Minister is defined as 'the Minister for the time being charged with the subject of Development,'[1043] which is indicative of the policy objectives the act is expected to align with.

The Minister, in consultation with the Conservation Commission, designates an area as protected by notice published in the Gazette.[1044] The objectives of protected areas include the preservation of biological diversity; the protection of representative biological communities sustaining ecological processes; the protection of selected natural sites of scenic beauty or of special scientific, ecological, historic or educational value, including sites that are already degraded and need protection for restoration or sites that may become degraded if not protected; and the maintenance or restoration of historic sites of cultural, archaeological, scientific or educational value or interest.[1045] The duty to consult the general public is as extensive as that of the Vincentian legislation. All persons enjoying rights within the boundaries of a proposed protected area are invited to raise any claims and objections at a specified time and place.[1046]

The selection, management and administration of any protected area established under this Act is the responsibility of the Minister in consultation with the Conservation Commission.[1047] The Conservation Commission has representation from government and civil society across both islands in the state of St Kitts and Nevis. The functions of the Conservation Commission are to advise the Minister on the selection of protected areas, and the care and maintenance of such areas.[1048] The Commission is responsible for promoting conservation as part of long-term national economic development, and acts as trustee of any protected area, historic building or monument.[1049] The requirements for management plans and the contents of such plans are also addressed.[1050] Similar to the Vincentian legislation and the updated Antiguan EPM Act, the Kittitian legislation promotes a variety of mechanisms such as inventories and management plans, and the use of multipartite bodies to ensure representation is comprehensive. What is clear is that even in those countries that integrate natural and cultural resources in one piece of legislation, the management of these resources remains separate. The dichotomy between natural and cultural resources remains intact and requires coordination between different pieces of legislation and the institutions they establish such as the National Trust and other foundations to conserve these resources.

Park management remains under-developed due to the lack of involvement of local communities and the limited mechanisms for their representation – St Vincent is the

---

1041 NCEPA 1987, s 2.
1042 Ibid.
1043 Ibid.
1044 NCEPA 1987, s 3.
1045 NCEPA 1987, s 4.
1046 Ibid, s 5.
1047 Ibid, ss 7(1) and 8.
1048 Ibid, s 10.
1049 Ibid, s 11.
1050 Ibid, ss 13 and 14.

lone outlier in this regard and even this community involvement is regulated by the authorities. In Grenada, the national park system, despite the organisational structure created in legislation, has never been functional. There are attempts to recognise public spaces and commons, as in Antigua, but when public spaces are designed and managed in detachment from local communities, these resources are ultimately undermined because the relationship shared with these communities often plays a role in their effective functioning.[1051]

6.5 Conclusion

Parks and protected areas in the Caribbean exhibit a complex provenance, having emerged during colonialism as colonial reserves to sustain plantation agriculture and the lifestyles of the planter elite. Laws creating parks and protected areas are among the earliest forms of landscape protection, established to preserve pristine environments, while ironically ignoring that these areas were in fact man-made landscapes, modified over ensuing centuries through local land use, first by Amerindian populations, then by enslaved African and where relevant indentured Asian labour. This inherited preservationist approach continues to be applied to these spaces, excluding the general public in the interest of the environment, while ensuring access for elite or expert interests, such as tourists, developers and scientists. Legally, the public does possess access rights, but the design of parks, the complex layers of governance and the cost to access and use these spaces create obstacles to the embedding of ongoing relationships. Ultimately, this has implications for recreational activities, customary practices, livelihoods, recreational activities, community cohesion and local identity. In spite of recent recognition of the need for local participation, local communities are largely absent from parks law in the Lesser Antilles, which instead are being developed as tourism assets.

Dahlberg notes that the ideological and institutional legacy surrounding the conceptualisation of contemporary national park policy will influence its effectiveness.[1052] This institutional legacy is very much dependent upon the type of colony concerned. In this case, the blueprint for Caribbean slave colonies entrenches eco-imperialist institutions that are hard-pressed to recognise local community customs when they have been designed to expunge them. It is here that spatial justice becomes relevant, challenging the continuation of colonial ecological practices, and by extension, spatially unjust colonialism. True access requires a restructuring of parks, no longer as exclusive reserves but as public spaces, in order to give recognition to the relationship with local communities that maintain and use them. The next chapter discusses some high-profile conflicts in the Lesser Antilles that demonstrate these issues relevant to the protection of landscape as public space and highlight the problems concerning the legal framework in practice.

1051 See Andreas Philippopoulos-Mihalopoulos, who writes that spatial justice is understood in its simplest form as a geographically informed version of social justice', in 'Spatial Justice: Law and the Geography of Withdrawal.' *International Journal of Law in Context* 6(2010): 201-216, 201; Peter Bengtsen, 'Just Gardens? On the Struggle for Space and Spatial Justice.' *Australian Feminist Law Journal* 39 (2013): 79-92.
1052 Dahlberg 220.

7

Examples of Conflicts over Landscape as Public Space

7.1 Introduction

Cultural heritage law in the Lesser Antilles has not given rise to a rich body of case-law from which projections can be made about the implementation and enforcement of the law, save for instances where heritage protection is incidental, such as a challenge to a refusal of development permission where the site contains heritage resources, or an injunction to prevent the destruction of such resources where a building order has been violated.[1053] However, this chapter highlights examples of conflicts concerning public space that are worth analysing for the insight they provide into ongoing divergences between local and prescribed land uses, which in turn underscore the symbiotic relationship between heritage and landscape protection. Importantly, these examples also reveal the extent to which the legal framework for heritage and landscape in the Lesser Antilles is spatially just in practice.

Regulation of the landscape implicates not only heritage law, but planning and environmental legislation as well, so these examples often involve these conflicting spheres of law, which were reviewed in Chapters Four to Six. Emphasis is placed on how legal mechanisms are employed (or not) to resolve these conflicts. In some cases the administration of the law is a critical factor in successful implementation. Where mandates are broad or obscure, administrators can contribute to the development of policy, which in turn can strengthen law through successive amendments, making it more locally specific. Poor administration therefore functions as a barometer for the efficacy of legislation.[1054]

These examples demonstrate the challenges of current legislation to meet the needs of local communities. Significantly, communities are often the advocates for implementing sustainable heritage protection as part of a wider strategy to secure their livelihoods and way of life. The scenarios presented here are the most high-profile recent examples of spatial injustice concerning heritage resources. The example from Trinidad and Tobago highlights the challenges of protecting public spaces where the underlying framework is outdated and ineffective and serves as a useful introduction to the legal issues surroun-

---

1053 This is similar to other common law jurisdictions. See Petrie 188.
1054 Petrie 188.

ding protection of public spaces in the region. The Saint Lucia example focuses on the inherent tensions between policy and administration within heritage institutions. The first example from Grenada emphasises the shortcomings of the planning process where communities and heritage protection are concerned, while the case from St Vincent and the Grenadines serves as a valuable counterpoint. Finally, the second example from Grenada shows how implementation of appropriate parks law has become a springboard for spatial justice issues in that island, particularly as it relates to use and access. In all cases, it is clear that protection of the landscape, whether natural, cultural or public space, relies on coordinating various areas of law, which adds another layer of complexity and weighs against adopting a narrow approach to this issue.

7.2 Greyfriars Church of Scotland, Trinidad and Tobago

The Greyfriars Church of Scotland was a nineteenth century church located in Port of Spain, the capital of Trinidad and Tobago. Greyfriars was home to the first public library in the country, the location of the first meeting of the antislavery movement, and the first church to welcome all persons equally without regard to class or race, as well as permit parishioners to marry across religions.[1055] The church also became a sanctuary for refugees, namely displaced Protestants from Madeira, and has symbolised the integration of new cultures to the Trinidadian melting pot.[1056]

In addition, Greyfriars was a fixture of Woodford Square, a fountained square situated in the heart of Port of Spain. The Square is lined by architecturally significant buildings such as the Red House (whose restoration has been delayed by the discovery of Amerindian burial remains during excavations), Holy Trinity Cathedral, the Old Public Library and the Old Fire Station – the latter formerly home to Saint Lucian poet and Nobel laureate Derek Walcott's Trinidad Theatre Workshop. During the country's independence movement, led by Dr Eric Williams, the square was dubbed 'the University of Woodford Square' for its role as a forum for political gatherings.[1057] It was designated by the Trinidad and Tobago National Trust as a heritage district in 2015.[1058]

Greyfriars was one of two Anglican churches in the capital in need of refurbishment.[1059] Despite a series of renovations, the property was in an advanced state of disrepair and eventually sold to businessman and real estate developer Alfred Galy

---

1055 Kim Boodram, 'National Trust to take legal action' (*Trinidad Express*, 1 September 2015) <https://www.trinidadexpress.com/news/local/national-trust-to-take-legal-action/article_95cc-ba41-68d0-575b-8755-6a1e933f5da2.html> accessed 30 July 2018.

1056 Mark Clarke, 'Save our heritage for future generations' (*Trinidad Express*, 2 December 2014) <https://www.trinidadexpress.com/news/local/save-our-heritage-for-future-generations/article_d6dacaab-75c0-5b9d-bad1-de8b4a266f28.html> accessed 30 July 2018 and see also Angela Pidduck, 'Historic church in dire need of repairs and assistance' (*Trinidad and Tobago Newsday*, 3 October 2010). <https://archives.newsday.co.tt/2010/10/03/historic-church-in-dire-need-of-repairs-and-assistance/> accessed 30 July 2018.

1057 'Repurposing of Woodford Square' (*Trinidad and Tobago Guardian*, 23 November 2014) <http://www.guardian.co.tt/article-6.2.390758.5a110e2900>accessed 30 July 2018.

1058 Joshua Surtees, 'Trinidad's forgotten architectural gems' (*The Guardian*, 16 February 2015) <https://www.theguardian.com/travel/2015/feb/16/trinidad-port-of-spain-architecture-tour> accessed 30 July 2018.

1059 Pidduck, 'Historic church in dire need of repairs and assistance', (*Trinidad and Tobago Newsday*, 3 October 2010).

in August 2014.¹⁰⁶⁰ There was immediate outcry, pointedly at the Trinidad and Tobago National Trust for not listing the church, which would have given it legal protection against such a fate.¹⁰⁶¹ This prompted the TTNT to issue a statement on 13ᵗʰ August, 2014 in which they expressed concern at 'the sale of one of our architectural treasures.'¹⁰⁶² The Council of the TTNT stated that the church was recorded in its National Inventory of Cultural and Natural Heritage as a historical site, and was in the process of being listed in accordance with its legislation.¹⁰⁶³ The TTNT also advised that prior to the sale of Greyfriars, the National Trust through its member and technical adviser, the Historical Restoration Unit, of the Ministry of Works and Infrastructure, advised the Town and Country Planning Division on the management needs for the property as a built heritage monument, in keeping with conservation guidelines. Nevertheless the listing process was a protracted one, requiring extensive surveys, valuations and planning. ¹⁰⁶⁴

Mr Galy's response to the TTNT summarises the traditional approach to heritage in the region. He explained that of the two church properties, it was decided by church authorities that the other, St Ann's had more architectural merit and was therefore worth refurbishing.¹⁰⁶⁵ According to Galy, 'From a practical pragmatic position, they had to save one of the two in the city and they saved the better of the two, also a very old icon, which has architectural merit and lends itself more to restoration'.¹⁰⁶⁶ It is notable that he cites the architectural features of St Ann's as making it more deserving of protection, compared to the community and historical value of Greyfriars. He further justifies his proposed development of the site by stating that, 'The building was not habitable, and was not conducive to spiritual worship. That's why it fell into disrepair, and became over the past ten years, a place for druggies, for people to defecate and to do all manner of things.'¹⁰⁶⁷ He underscores his position by emphasising the vacuity of the space: 'When I purchased [Greyfriars], there were no artefacts, there were no religious symbols, all the stained glass, the organs were all removed…and the ritual of the deconsecration had taken place. There was nothing in it at all.'¹⁰⁶⁸

1060 Kalifa Clyne, 'Owner of Greyfriars: Toxic roof removed from church hall' (*Trinidad and Tobago Guardian*, 13 November 2014) <http://www.guardian.co.tt/article-6.2.390342.7e91ca0fce> accessed 30 July 2018.

1061 Mark Fraser, 'Greyfriars Church sold' (*Trinidad Express*, 12 August 2014) <https://www.trinidadexpress.com/news/local/greyfriars-church-sold/article_2b81668a-e44a-5bee-b54f-7738c63cb660.html> accessed 30 July 2018.

1062 'National Trust moves to protect historic Greyfriars Church' (*Trinidad Express,* August 2014) <https://www.trinidadexpress.com/news/local/national-trust-moves-to-protect-historic-greyfriars-church/article_75b7d56d-c75a-5320-8e9a-f9e476137a98.html> accessed 30 July 2018.

1063 See Chapter Four for a discussion of the listing process pursuant to the National Trust of Trinidad and Tobago Act.

1064 'Save Greyfriars Church' (*Trinidad Express*, 14 August 2014) <https://www.trinidadexpress.com/news/local/save-greyfriars-church/article_b04f74c8-f023-5fe8-9741-c64a96d5b47e.html> accessed 30 July 2018.

1065 Richard Charan, 'Too late for Greyfriars' (*Trinidad Express*, 24 August 2015) <https://www.trinidadexpress.com/news/local/too-late-for-greyfriars/article_3560b1be-c9e3-5c7f-a1ee-ca2e7224edc9.html> accessed 30 July 2018.

1066 Richard Charan, 'Too late for Greyfriars' (*Trinidad Express*, 24 August 2015).

1067 Charan, 'Too late for Greyfriars (*Trinidad Express*, 24 August 2015).

1068 Ibid.

Galy appointed a team comprising an architect and an engineer to advise him on the future of Greyfriars by mid-September 2014. He also stated that the National Trust should prioritise which buildings it intended to save since it was virtually impossible to save all the dilapidated historical edifices. 'Not all buildings are good for restoration. The Trust has to understand they cannot save everything.'[1069] The comments indicate a limited understanding of the role of the Trust, and its criteria for preserving historic properties. In Chapter Four it was noted that Trust legislation contains criteria for designating heritage as protected, which included sociological interest and association with well-known characters or events – Greyfriars certainly met these requirements.[1070] Mr Galy stated that he had submitted an application to the Town and Country Planning Division for the development of the site in a manner that 'will embrace culture, foods, our local foods, general business, sports and a range of business.'[1071]

Lack of architectural merit would reduce any available support under the Planning Act, already limited in criteria for assessing historic value and with weak protections in the form of preservation orders.[1072] Nevertheless, public dissatisfaction was expressed via a flurry of letters to the national newspapers. In November 2014, Minister Rodger Samuel received a petition with 2,000 signatures, calling on him to ensure the church was saved. 'I was surprised at the amount. We might not have recognised that so many people were interested in this country's history,' he added. Public pressure was the impetus needed to trigger the planning process, and he noted that his ministry would review the case, and had contacted the owner to state its intent of making Greyfriars an historic site. This involved preparation of a dossier on the site, publishing the information for public perusal and a final review by the Ministry of Legal Affairs.[1073]

However on 9th November, 2014, a contractor removed the roof of the church hall in what appeared to be the start of demolition. Protestors, mainly from the activist group Citizens for Conservation, which used its Facebook page to rally supporters, obstructed the demolition crew and occupied the church hall to prevent further progress.[1074] Galy subsequently denied that there were plans for demolition, stating that a preliminary health and safety assessment of the property was being conducted and the roof had been removed because it was filled with asbestos.[1075] The Port of Spain City Corporation (the Corporation) issued a stop order to Galy for initiating demolition without a proper permit, and he duly applied for the required demolition notice. The

---

1069 Mark Fraser, 'I felt compelled to buy Greyfriars' (*Trinidad Express*, 17 August 2015) <https://www.trinidadexpress.com/news/local/i-felt-compelled-to-buy-greyfriars/article_058b9f52-a7bc-53ba-8f27-80833b74137d.html> accessed 30 July 2018.
1070 National Trust of Trinidad and Tobago Act, second schedule, reg 4(c) and (e).
1071 Charan, 'Too late for Greyfriars' (*Trinidad Express*, 24 August 2015).
1072 See Chapter Five for a discussion of Trinidad and Tobago's planning legislation.
1073 Kalifa Clyne, 'State moves to save Greyfriars' (*Trinidad and Tobago Guardian*, 25 November 2014) <http://www4.guardian.co.tt/news/2014-11-25/state-moves-save-greyfriars> accessed 30 July 2018.
1074 Mark Fraser, 'Protesters block demolition crew: confrontation at Greyfriars Church' (*Trinidad Express*, 10 November 2014) <https://www.trinidadexpress.com/news/local/protesters-block-demolition-crew/article_80a66872-36ba-54c8-865b-7b54aa1ab2c3.html> accessed 30 July 2018.
1075 Ibid.

city engineer's office advised that the notice was on hold as the corporation was in discussions with Galy and the Town and Country Planning Division.[1076]

Two weeks later, Galy returned to the site and resumed demolition works, resulting in an injunction being filed by the Corporation to compel him to desist. Following his 4th January, 2015 court appearance, the parties agreed to attempt to settle the matter out of court.[1077] Notably, the injunction, which resulted in an action before the High Court, concerned not the TTNT's notice of intent to list the property as protected heritage, but the illegal demolition of the site as Mr Galy had not been granted a permit.[1078] According to the Municipal Corporations Act, no person may pull down or remove from its site any building within any municipality unless, not more than 14 days and not less than two days before such removal, he gives notice in writing. Any person who pulls down or removes any building from its site, and any owner of any such building who causes or permits any building to be removed from its site without having first given the notice would be liable to a fine of TT$4,000.[1079]

Three months after he was ordered to halt the demolition, Mr Galy submitted a method statement on 12th February, 2015 to the Port of Spain City Corporation outlining his plans for clearing the site.[1080] Nevertheless, the Council of the National Trust had gazetted its intention to list the Greyfriars Church of Scotland as a heritage site on 8th December, 2014. On 29th August, 2015, eight days after the Trust had listed the building, the demolition was completed.[1081] This is unfortunate as listing does not preclude development of a site; it was the developer who considered the intention to list a threat to his development plans.[1082] The TTNT explained that the effect of the listing meant that Mr Galy had to obtain permission from the Port of Spain Corporation and the Town and Country Planning Division to undertake any alteration, demolition or destruction of this listed property, as well as that of the National Trust. This was never granted, and the Trust intended to seek redress from Mr Galy.[1083]

1076 Michelle Loubon, 'Galy defends demolition: Church a danger to the public' (*Trinidad Express*, 31 August 2015) <https://www.trinidadexpress.com/news/local/galy-defends-demolition-church-a-danger-to-the-public/article_14008d6d-bafa-5a4c-8451-65936f0345dc.html> accessed 30 July 2018; Clyne, 'State moves to save Greyfriars' (*Trinidad and Tobago Guardian*, 25 November 2014).

1077 'Bid to settle Greyfriars out of court' (*Trinidad Express*, 5 January 2015) <https://www.trinidadexpress.com/news/local/bid-to-settle-greyfriars-demolition-out-of-court/article_857e6357-3494-502e-a423-c29ae55b42d3.html> accessed 30 July 2018.

1078 Anna Lisa Paul, 'Greyfriars owner submits demolition plan' (*Trinidad and Tobago Guardian*, 22 February 2015) <http://www.guardian.co.tt/news/greyfriars-owner-submits-demolition-plan-6.2.375536.45d102b5ce> accessed 30 July 2018: Adding that their concern did not lie with Galy's decision on whether or not he intended to preserve the remaining structure, the official said: 'The Corporation is concerned with the structural and safety aspects…' Discussions are said to be continuing between Galy and the Ministry of Diversity to determine the next step.

1079 The Trinidad and Tobago Municipal Corporations Act 2015, s 164 (1), (2) and (3). See also Paul, 'Greyfriars demolition stopped' (*Trinidad and Tobago Guardian*, 12 November 2014) <http://www4.guardian.co.tt/news/2014-11-12/greyfriars-demolition-stopped> accessed 30 July 2018.

1080 The official revealed that Galy had addressed several issues, including how he plans to safely approach further demolition, clear the site of rubble and other debris, safe removal of the asbestos roof and other conditions he would adhere to if he continued with the demolition. Paul, 'Greyfriars owner submits demolition plan' (*Trinidad and Tobago Guardian*, 22 February 2015).

1081 Charan, 'Historic church falls' (*Trinidad Express*, 30 August 2015).

1082 'Greyfriars owner hires engineer' (*Trinidad Express*, 5 December 2014).

1083 Kim Boodram, 'National Trust to take legal action' (*Trinidad Express*, 1 September 2015).

The Mayor of Port of Spain, Tim Kee, confirmed that Greyfriars Church was not protected. The building was situated on freehold land and not listed as a protected property and as such, the Port of Spain City Corporation could not control Galy's actions.[1084] However, there are indications that Galy was not negotiating in good faith, as an intention to list the property was served on him in November by the TTNT,[1085] and he had attended meetings with Citizens for Conservation and other stakeholders for two weeks prior to demolition. Minister Samuel stated that the Town and Country Division had been in talks with Mr Galy concerning preservation of the church and that 'no demolition approvals were granted by the Port of Spain City Corporation' for the action.[1086]

The TTNT attempted to demonstrate to the owner that the Greyfriars historical site could be developed sensitively and still operate as a viable business.[1087] Galy acknowledged that several meetings had been held with the National Trust and public authorities before demolition began, and there were discussions about retaining and restoring the property. However, he believed the lack of listing by the TTNT up to September 2014 and its subsequent listing following his purchase of the property reflected an inconsistent stance on the TTNT's part.[1088] He admitted that the intention to list triggered the partial demolition, citing it as a 'red flag'.[1089]

Nevertheless, the Council of the National Trust had gazetted its intention to list the Greyfriars Church of Scotland as a heritage site on 8th December, 2014. The Notice of Intention to List was signed by chairman of the Trust Professor Winston Suite. The church was to be named as part of the Woodford Square Historical District.[1090] The owner was notified when the Intention to List was gazetted and the Notice was also published in all three national newspapers.[1091] As of 2018, the Greyfriars property was listed as demolished on the Heritage Asset Register of the TNTT.[1092]

The TNTT's inability to identify, manage and protect a site valued by the public, and private landowners' ability to override any concerns in spite of opportunities for

---

1084 'Government to rescue Greyfriars Church' (*Trinidad Express*, 26 November 2014) <https://www.trinidadexpress.com/news/local/govt-to-rescue-greyfriars-church/article_e8c46649-8e93-5415-9890-ff60bd1a6643.html> accessed 30 July 2018.

1085 Subsequently gazetted – see the Trinidad and Tobago Gazette No. 156 of 2014, 8 December 2014.

1086 Lisa Allen Agostini, 'No surprise here' (*Trinidad and Tobago Guardian*, 2 December 2014) <http://www.guardian.co.tt/article-6.2.391123.c15833cc9e> accessed 30 July 2018.

1087 Kim Boodram, 'National Trust to take legal action' (*Trinidad Express*, 1 September 2015).

1088 Charan, 'Too late for Greyfriars' (*Trinidad Express*, 24 August 2015).

1089 Mark Fraser, 'Greyfriars owner hires engineer' (*Trinidad Express*, 5 December 2014) <https://www.trinidadexpress.com/news/local/greyfriars-owner-hires-engineers/article_dac1ab5f-3c5f-5a37-8144-39f664e96470.html> accessed 30 July 2018.

1090 Trinidad and Tobago Gazette No 156 of 2014, 8 December 2014; Anna Lisa Paul, 'Greyfriars owner submits demolition plan' (*Trinidad and Tobago Guardian*, 22 February 2015) <http://www.guardian.co.tt/news/greyfriars-owner-submits-demolition-plan-6.2.375536.45d102b5ce> accessed 30 July 2018.

1091 Trinidad and Tobago Gazette No 82 of 2015, 4 August 2015; Kim Boodram, 'National Trust to take legal action' (*Trinidad Express*, 1 September 2015).

1092 Prior to this, Greyfriars Church was a listed property of interest, at stage 7 of the listing process (Gazette Notice & inform owner of Intention to list as a Heritage Site & publish in at least three issues of a daily newspaper) according to the Trust criteria. Richard Charan, 'Historic church falls' (*Trinidad Express*, 30 August 2015) <https://www.trinidadexpress.com/news/local/historic-church-falls/article_e571c8db-4468-5467-a683-f3c282a36481.html> accessed 30 July 2018.

collaboration, is an example of the challenges posed to heritage protection. Perhaps Greyfriars has served as a cautionary tale, since other Woodford Square properties such as the Gingerbread House have subsequently been restored rather than abandoned to suffer the same fate.[1093] Nevertheless, the failure of heritage law to protect heritage sites is apparent in the financial and political constraints placed on heritage institutions, the outdated process for listing and protecting, as in this case, the TTNT's register of heritage sites,[1094] and the absence of procedural mechanisms for protecting heritage sites by recognising place-protective behaviour of communities affected by the loss of heritage as participatory decision-making, as well as the use of preliminary assessments of the impact of development on heritage sites, and the application of the principle to make good where damage has been incurred.

While Mr Galy was roundly criticised, and the TNTT threatened legal action for the breach of the National Trust Act,[1095] it has been noted that the final demolition was a calculated risk on his part, as the minimal fine for proceeding without a permit was hardly a punitive figure when one considers that the development was worth over TT$30 million. The disparities that exist today with regard to fines and modern development signal the need to update legislation and revise listing criteria to accommodate public spaces as significant heritage in National Trust legislation. In addition, the TTNT at the time of the November partial demolition had no functioning board. One was subsequently appointed by Cabinet the week prior to the partial demolition, but it was not expected to be fully operational until the week following the partial demolition.[1096] The City Corporation of Port of Spain was also criticised for failing to set appropriate development guidelines for new owners of historic sites.[1097] The Government of Trinidad and Tobago was aware of the Church's dilapidated state for a number of years, yet had made no decision concerning its protection. The lack of synchronicity in the planning and heritage legislation, reflected in the inadequate institutional arrangements of the TNTT and the planning authorities, also hindered the process and ultimately failed to protect a public space from its lawful owner.

This case demonstrates the conflict between heritage and planning law, as planning law often facilitates development. Where planning law mechanisms such as notices and injunctions are deployed, it is often in the developer's interest to ignore these measures, because enforcement is often limited and lacking teeth. The narrative surrounding Greyfriars also illustrates the postcolonial planning process, which is intolerant of other spatial uses, and focused on clearing clutter, evacuation of space and treating former residents/stakeholders as transgressors through ejection of protesters. While Mr Galy engaged in talks with stakeholders, and was open to some insertion of the cultural heritage, this would be on his terms.[1098] Notably, Mr Galy contrasted the value of

---

1093 Jewel Fraser, 'A Heritage Building lives on in Trinidad' (26 March 2015, *The New York Times*) <https://www.nytimes.com/2015/03/27/greathomesanddestinations/a-heritage-building-lives-on-in-trinidad.html> accessed 30 July 2018.
1094 See <http://nationaltrust.tt/heritage-sites/heritage-asset-register/>
1095 Kim Boodram, 'National Trust to take legal action' (*Trinidad Express*, 1 September 2015).
1096 Clyne, 'Owner of Greyfriars: Toxic roof removed from church hall' (13 November 2014, *Trinidad and Tobago Guardian*).
1097 'Slap on the wrist for Greyfriars Church demolition' (*Trinidad Express*, 10 December 2014).
1098 Charan, 'Too late for Greyfriars' (*Trinidad Express*, 24 August, 2015).

the 'architectural icon' that Planning would be amenable to preserving, with Greyfriars, which, despite its equally relevant value, had become publicly unsafe, both in terms of environmental health and crime due to 'placeless' vagrants, recalling both the expulsion and alienation of commoners in England, and Herzfeld's summation of postcolonial planning law's approach to demolishing suspect sites and cleansing these spaces of unacceptable denizens who are now considered interlopers, in the name of progress.[1099]

7.3 Saint Lucia National Trust and Maria Islands Nature Reserve, Saint Lucia

Even where there are instances in which a heritage institution is functioning and has a management framework in place, public spaces can still be threatened. This example from Saint Lucia demonstrates challenges associated with an evolving heritage institution that is attempting to protect public spaces in a manner that challenges traditional notions about the role of heritage in the authorised heritage discourse.[1100]

The Saint Lucia National Trust (SLNT) is charged with the conservation and sustainable use of Saint Lucia's natural, built and cultural heritage, and is a leading heritage actor in that island. The Trust manages 25 heritage sites with over 240 hectares conserved. In particular, it holds a 99-year lease of Pigeon Island and owns the Maria Islands Nature Reserve.[1101] The Government of Saint Lucia designated Pigeon Island as a National Park in 1979 and as a National Landmark in 1992 under the auspices of the Trust.[1102] The site was occupied by Amerindians followed by the British and French, and there are several defence heritage sites on its grounds.[1103]

The Maria Islands Nature Reserve was declared a Nature Reserve in 1982 by the Government of Saint Lucia in recognition of the special function of the islands as a wildlife habitat and their unique flora and fauna. There are over eighty plant species found on Maria Islands, and the island is home to five endemic reptile species. The islands are comprised of Maria Major, which is 10.1 hectares and Maria Minor (1.6 hectares). The Reserve is also a major nesting site for migratory birds that travel thousands of miles from the west coast of Africa to nest annually. The Saint Lucia Forestry Department of the Ministry of Agriculture provides support by monitoring the birds' migratory patterns to determine closed seasons.[1104]

1099 Herzfeld 139, 142.

1100 See Chapter Four, which describes how heritage institutions can uphold certain regimes of power, especially the status quo. In situations where the interests of communities and governments may not be compatible, non-state heritage actors are offered expected to assimilate. Laurajane Smith has critiqued this control of heritage in *The Uses of Heritage* (Routledge 2006) 44.

1101 Saint Lucia National Trust, 'Proposed elimination of government's annual contribution to the Saint Lucia National Trust for the 2017-18 financial year' [press release] 24 April, 2017, 2.

1102 Pigeon Island National Park Bylaw (S.I. No. 47 of 1982) implements s 16 of the Saint Lucia National Trust Act 1975, and addresses the management and control of the Pigeon Island National Park. It regulates the opening hours of the Park, prescribes entrance fees, lays down rules for the conduct of persons in the park, provides for the protection of plants and wildlife and the soil, and prohibits use of vehicles and introduction of animals in the Park without permission.

1103 Tom Dart, 'Derek Walcott museum closes amid row over Caribbean tourist developments' (*The Guardian*, 21 June 2017) <https://www.theguardian.com/books/2017/jun/21/derek-walcott-museum-st-lucia-caribbean-tourism> accessed 30 July 2018.

1104 <https://slunatrust.org/sites/maria-island-nature-reserve/> accessed 9 November 2018.

Unlike many of its counterparts in the Lesser Antilles, the SLNT enjoys a substantial subvention from the Government of Saint Lucia. For twenty years, the Government's annual contribution to the SLNT has been EC$500,000, which the Trust has put towards programmes and operations. Since 2000, this amount was further augmented by an EC$200,000 special annual contribution to help the SLNT fund the establishment of its head offices.[1105] Along with the Saint Lucia Archaeological and Historical Society, the SLNT was designated a Referral Body under the Planning and Development Act of 2002, with the goal of assisting the Planning Department and the Development and Control Authority (DCA) in approving repair, restoration, and maintenance projects on structures of architectural or historic interest within designated national parks or national monuments.[1106]

The SLNT's subvention was cut during the year 2017-2018, the Government of Saint Lucia citing severe budget constraints, and the SLNT's failure to develop its sites. The SLNT believed this was a retaliatory response to the Trust's vocal objections to projects that would affect these two protected areas – the Maria Islands Nature Reserve, one of only two wildlife reserves on Saint Lucia, and the Pigeon Island National Landmark.[1107] The SLNT had expressed opposition to the 'Pearl of the Caribbean' project proposed by international investors, which they believed posed a serious threat to the country's ecological, cultural and archaeological heritage. The developers intended to construct a causeway linking the Maria Islands Nature Reserve to the mainland, which could potentially threaten the coastline and the endemic species within the reserve.[1108] In addition, the SLNT objected to a planned dolphinarium at the Pigeon Island National landmark in the north of the island. With the loss of the subvention, the Trust was forced to close other historic properties, such as the Derek Walcott Museum.[1109]

The Government of Saint Lucia addressed the removal of the subvention in the annual budget speech of 2017-2018:

> *The Trust is charged with conserving the natural and cultural heritage of Saint Lucia. It is an advocacy group and is responsible for developing the sites which have been vested in it. As an advocacy group, the Trust performs that function reasonably well. The Trust has, however, not performed well in developing the sites that are vested in it. The Government has supported the Trust through an annual subvention as well as through the vesting in the Trust, premier heritage sites. These valuable national assets can and should be leveraged to generate more significant revenue to sustain its operations, and thereby the Trust is being asked to revise its business model to become financially independent. As a result, the*

1105 Saint Lucia National Trust, press release 24 April, 2017, 1.
1106 Milton Branford 'Saint Lucia' in Siegel and Righter 72-75, 73; Saint Lucia National Trust, Press release, 3.
1107 'St Lucia Prime Minister cuts funding for National Trust' (*Antigua Observer*, 26 April, 2017) <https://antiguaobserver.com/st-lucia-pm-cuts-funding-for-national-trust/> accessed 3 July 2018.
1108 Dart, 'Derek Walcott museum closes amid row over Caribbean tourist developments' (*The Guardian*, 21 June 2017).
1109 Ibid.

annual subvention will be discontinued. However, the government will continue to provide support to initiatives the Government believes has merit in supporting the development objectives of the state.[1110]

Several observations may be made here. The Government of Saint Lucia views nature reserves and other such spaces as elements of the broader national development strategy, aligned with tourism development and the private sector. Heritage appears to have purely commercial value, without consideration for the social linkages the public may have with these spaces. The Government suggests that these heritage assets must be positioned as major income earners, but there is no mention of the community valuation of these sites as they are historically, environmentally and culturally significant, only the vague criterion of 'merit' in meeting the development objectives of the state. This is a conservative approach to heritage and implies that the state defines the role of these resources for the community, which the SLNT appears to contest in its challenges to the development of public spaces.

The SLNT was criticised for poor management of heritage properties such as Maria Islands and Pigeon Island. However, there was no positive move on the Government's part to enhance the SLNT's capacities to perform these functions as defined in the Saint Lucia National Trust Act, such as increasing technical capacity in heritage management or community involvement. This would be well within the State's duties to provide an enabling environment for the protection of cultural rights, ensuring preconditions for participation, facilitation and promotion of cultural life, and access to and preservation of cultural goods via cultural heritage institutions such as the Trust, as discussed in Chapter Three.[1111]

Finally, in calling on the SLNT to become financially independent, the Government of Saint Lucia nevertheless withdrew the SLNT's funding without consultations between the two parties, and with no proposal to restructure and upgrade the SLNT on a phased basis. The future of the SLNT therefore appears uncertain now that its ability to administer and implement the law is impaired. Other administrative processes that affect heritage protection concern the conduct of Environmental Impact Assessments, as with Lower Sauteurs (Grenada) and Argyle (St Vincent and the Grenadines).

7.4 Lower Sauteurs EIA Process /St Patrick's Breakwater, Grenada

The construction of the St Patrick's breakwater in Sauteurs, on the northeastern coast of Grenada, demonstrated the critical need for engaging communities residing near or amongst heritage resources, who maintain these resources because they regard them as their own.

The coastal community of Sauteurs relies on the sea for food security and their livelihoods. The area is also home to Leapers' Hill, an important location in

---

1110 Government of Saint Lucia. 'Annual Budget Speech for the financial year 2017-2018', delivered by Hon. Allen Chastenet, Prime Minister and Minister for Finance, Economic Growth, Job Creation, External Affairs and the Public Service, 9 May 2017, 42 (emphasis added).

1111 Interestingly, Saint Lucia is the only state in the Lesser Antilles not party to the ICESCR, but it is a WHC party and signatory to the Escazú Agreement.

Grenadian history due to its association with the reputed last stand of the Kalinago people against French colonisers. Trapped by the French in a retreat, the story goes, some forty Kalinago warriors jumped from Morne du Sauteurs into the sea, where they perished.[1112] It is an important archaeological site, one of many documented in the early 1980s by the Foundation for Field Research (FFR) and the University of Florida. Around eighteen human burials were excavated and transferred to the Grenada National Museum at that time.[1113] This was prior to the existence of heritage legislation and an extensive planning framework in the country.[1114] Nevertheless, the discovery failed to inspire efforts to secure the site.

Erosion caused by intense wave action exposed what appeared to be an Amerindian burial ground at Sauteurs during the first weeks of 2018. The Sauteurs community had reported skeletal remains and artefacts washing up on the beach, and expressed concerns that the nearby breakwater project was responsible for the exposure of the site. This breakwater was built as one of a number of mitigation efforts recommended by a 2013 EIA study for the Lower Sauteurs area.[1115] The EIA had been undertaken as part of the development of a Climate Change Adaptation (Disaster Management) Plan for the Coastal Communities of Lower Sauteurs, Grenada. The plan was intended to strengthen community capacity to address climate change impacts, but did not substantively consider the cultural heritage implications of the project for the community, despite the use of participatory methodologies. However, it must be noted that this was not a requirement of the original terms of reference.

While the EIA identifies Sauteurs as a historic site, it delved no deeper into the significance for the community. There were community consultations, but the questionnaire forms indicate that no questions addressed the protection of the local heritage.[1116] While this was in keeping with Grenada's physical planning legislation, which has no guidance on EIAs for archaeological sites, the Act at the time did call for a liberal and purposive interpretation of the legislation, which included an objective to protect the cultural and natural heritage, and had established an Advisory Committee on Cultural and Natural Heritage.[1117] Although this law was referenced in the report, these provisions were not addressed.[1118]

The failure to consider community linkages to the heritage site subsequently had implications for the protection of Amerindian heritage, which is noteworthy because at the time, the National Heritage Protection Act 1990 made provisions for the protection of Amerindian

---

1112 Melanie Newton, 'The Race Leapt at Sauteurs: Genocide, Narrative and Indigenous Exile from the Caribbean Archipelago' *Caribbean Quarterly* 60(2) (2014) 5-28.
1113 Curlan Campbell, 'Amerindian burial site under siege' (*Now Grenada*, 1 March 2018) <https://www.nowgrenada.com/2018/03/archaeologists-saving-amerindian-burial-site-under-siege/> accessed 15 November 2018.
1114 Chapter Four explains that the Grenada National Museum was only established by an Act of Parliament in 2017.
1115 Government of Grenada. Climate Change Adaptation (Disaster Management) Plan for Lower Sauteurs. Grenada. Prepared by OECS/Geotechnical Investigative Services, 2013, 5.
1116 Government of Grenada. Climate Change Adaptation Plan for Lower Sauteurs – Appendix 1: Vulnerability Survey Documents. Grenada. Prepared by OECS/Geotechnical Investigative Services, 2013.
1117 The Physical Planning and Development Control Act 2002 was repealed in 2016 and replaced by the PPDC Act of 2016. The latter was discussed in Chapter Five.
1118 Government of Grenada. Report of the Climate Change Adaptation Plan for Lower Sauteurs 13.

heritage and outlined a process for the involvement of the National Trust. Under this act, two nearby Amerindian heritage sites Pearls and Grand Bay, had been scheduled, as part of the wider Amerindian landscape.[1119] These laws were not referenced in the report.[1120] While the Physical Planning Unit did conduct a site visit with the Ministry of Culture during a rescue excavation involving community volunteers, no strategy was prepared for protecting the site, in spite of the recent enactment of museum legislation.

The 2004 Akwé: Kon Voluntary Guidelines provide a baseline for considering the impacts of EIAs on landscapes and were discussed in Chapter Three. The range of cultural aspects of Sauteurs that could have been considered included traditional knowledge about the history of the site,[1121] which may have flagged the possibility of undiscovered archaeological sites, before the human remains were discovered. This could have been supported by the Museum, which was in possession of remains previously retrieved from the same site. Possible impacts on customary use of the area, community practices, as well as associated ceremonial activities were addressed via only one question on the community questionnaire.[1122] Social aspects that should have been considered included impacts on land use practices, and other traditional systems of natural resources and access to biodiversity resources, particularly the ocean environment as it was a coastal community, and the effects on the social cohesion of the community. Only the economic considerations from potential loss of fisheries and traditional medicine sources were touched upon cursorily in the questionnaire.[1123]

The implications for underlying values, following impacts of potential change to the area, and evolving views of the local community regarding their future and ability to achieve future aspirations were not explored.[1124] The Lower Sauteurs coastline includes beach area that functions as a public space to commemorate holidays and other special functions. Loss of beach area does not simply represent loss of sand, but loss of identity of the community, their practices, livelihoods, and ways of life. While the project was intended to bolster existing infrastructure and render the area climate-resilient, this is precisely why the impact assessment process should have been as comprehensive as possible, to incorporate consideration of the social and cultural dimensions of the area, which reflect the community's valorisation of coastal resources. Identifying the full range of stakeholders, beyond the settlement nearest to the breakwater site, to include all inhabitants of the wider Sauteurs landscape (not just Lower Sauteurs), as well as ensuring ongoing public participation in the EIA process, during construction, could have provided critical information. This extensive participatory process

---

1119 Repealed in 2017.
1120 Government of Grenada. Report of the Climate Change Adaptation Plan for Lower Sauteurs 13.
1121 Three general questions of relevance on the community risk assessment addressed whether risks to the protection of social and economic assets, and the protection of cultural and ecosystem assets had been identified, and the vulnerability of indigenous flora and fauna. There were three questions on the community questionnaire asking respondents to identify any cultural resources, community livelihoods and cultural rituals. See the Climate Change Adaptation Plan for Lower Sauteurs – Appendix 1: Vulnerability Survey Documents. It is unclear whether the 2004 Akwé: Kon Voluntary Guidelines were consulted.
1122 Akwé: Kon Guidelines, para 27.
1123 Ibid, para 43.
1124 Ibid, paras 44 and 45.

and attending to the cultural, social and environmental nuances of communities was addressed in the Escazú Agreement, discussed in Chapter Three.

Concerns for sustainability, where development occurs in proximity to, takes place on, or likely impact heritage resources appear to be lacking. A sustainable approach should require that the impact assessment process while maintaining a balance between economic, social, cultural and environmental concerns, on the one hand, also enables, where appropriate, opportunities for the conservation and sustainable use of biological diversity, the access and equitable sharing of benefits and the recognition of traditional knowledge, innovations and practices are maximised.[1125]

While the EIA was intended to inform the preparation of a community plan to strengthen community capacity to address climate change impacts, the failure to accurately assess and define the social and cultural aspects of the space, notwithstanding the use of participatory methodologies, ultimately affected the siting and design of the breakwater with implications for the future of the community. While this was not a requirement of the original terms of reference, existing relevant legislation at the time was not applied. The problems were further exacerbated by the response of the government, which did not seek to engage the community in new consultations. In spite of these archaeological discoveries, the enactment of new legislation, and a new cultural policy calling for increased protection of heritage sites,[1126] the site was not secured and there is no management structure currently in place for its protection. While there is community interest, and laws in place, implementation is a challenge. The Museum, with no board or staff, was unable to assemble a team to investigate, document and mitigate the situation.[1127] Nevertheless, community members publicly queried the siting of the breakwater and took part in the excavations to rescue endangered heritage.

The Lower Sauteurs Grenada case represents the culmination of a number of pressing underlying issues concerning the protection of heritage. When the government and its institutions fail to consider the wider meaning of the landscape, they are likely to be ineffective in protecting cultural heritage. The impact can be seen in the St Patrick's breakwater situation, which affects coastal communities, their spaces and livelihoods. Despite noting that the area has an important cultural site, mechanisms such as consultations, surveys and EIAs are rendered purposeless because they neglect to substantively integrate cultural and social factors into the process.[1128] Grenada subsequently repealed its 2002 physical planning legislation in 2016, and the new law has conservatively redrafted many of the provisions concerning national heritage protection, reflecting in many ways the reassertion of private property rights to the detriment of communal heritage.

This failure to invoke and implement both heritage and planning legislation may be contrasted with the success of the St Vincent and the Grenadines National Trust and Vincentian planning authorities, which were actively involved in the EIA process for Argyle International Airport.

1125 Ibid, para 56.
1126 The Government of Grenada. Grenada National Cultural Policy 2012, Positions 2.4 (Museum) and 2.5 (Historical and Archaeological Sites) respectively. See Chapter Four.
1127 Curlan Campbell, 'Amerindian burial site under siege' (*Now Grenada*, 1 March 2018).
1128 Akwé: Kon Guidelines, para 23.

7.5 Argyle International Airport EIA Process, St Vincent and the Grenadines

With St Vincent and the Grenadines, the limitations of planning legislation to manage and protect heritage, namely through the absence of progressive mechanisms for recognising community linkages to that heritage, were addressed in creative ways during the EIA process for the Argyle International Airport. In 2007, plans for the construction of an international airport at Argyle on the Windward coast of the island were announced.[1129] This would upgrade existing facilities to accommodate increased tourist traffic. The topography of St Vincent limits its options for siting a new international airport, as it is a very rugged island with only a narrow strip of relatively flat land between the sea and the mountains. This is the only location suitable for an airport capable of handling large jet aircraft and unfortunately placed the Yambou Valley petroglyphs and colonial heritage directly in the path of destruction.[1130]

The Yambou Valley area represents 2000 years of landscape change in St Vincent.[1131] The proposed airport construction would endanger the petroglyphs, require destruction or relocation of a Catholic church to make room for the new runway, as well as the removal of the ruins of a sugar factory near the site.[1132] These petroglyphs were part of a group of Vincentian petroglyphs under consideration for UNESCO World Heritage status.[1133] In addition, the Our Lady of Lourdes Catholic Church was built by Dom Charles Verbeke, and is a mixture of Byzantine, Flemish, and Romanesque architectural styles that has made the cathedral one of the finest examples of ecclesiastic architecture in the Lesser Antilles.[1134] The sugar factory site has an intact water wheel among its components.[1135]

The public announcement in the local newspaper on 28th September, 2007, which reported that the Vincentian government, through the International Airport Development Company (IADC), would construct the new airport, elicited responses from all sectors of society.[1136] The St Vincent and the Grenadines National Trust (SVGNT) raised the issue of preserving the site with the CEO of the International

---

1129 Richard Callaghan, 'St Vincent and the Grenadines: Recent Efforts in Protecting Heritage' in Siegel and Righter 83-86, 83.
1130 Ibid, 85.
1131 The St Vincent and the Grenadines National Trust notes that the old sugar mill at Escape, Argyle, will be the centrepiece of a new heritage landscape on the Windward side of St Vincent. The mill had been buried in the forest overgrowth, until it was rediscovered by engineers working on the new airport in 2007. The mill was water-powered and a large water wheel is still in location. There were several ruined buildings on the site ready to be restored into a working museum of St Vincent's agricultural history. Also at the site were the Yambou 1 petroglyphs, which will be moved the half-mile from their current location at the Argyle Airport site. When the site is complete, visitors can walk through 2,000 years of Vincentian history in one afternoon. See the website of the SVG National Trust <http://www.svgnationaltrust.moonfruit.com/escape-heritage-park/4568200610> accessed 31 July 2018.
1132 Paul Lewis 'St Vincent and the Grenadines' in Siegel and Righter 76-82, 80.
1133 UNESCO Tentative List of St Vincent and the Grenadines: <https://whc.unesco.org/en/tentativelists/5749/> accessed 15 October 2019.
1134 Lewis 80.
1135 Website of the SVG National Trust < http://www.svgnationaltrust.moonfruit.com/> accessed 31 July 2018.
1136 Lewis 80.

Airport Development Company.[1137] Following a slew of newspaper articles and television interviews, and statements by the SVGNT and the Roman Catholic Church, the Vincentian government announced late in October 2007 that they had hired a German firm, Kocks Consult GmbH of Koblenz, Germany, to conduct an assessment of the area. The study was presented to the public approximately three months after its release to the government, but only one of the three volumes that comprised the report was released, and no public discussion of its contents was held.[1138]

Paul Lewis writes that the original course contemplated would have condoned state destruction of the site to accommodate the airport. The government did not originally intend to conduct an EIA, but reluctantly complied as they realised the potential negative public feedback could have for the project. Plans for the removal/repositioning of the affected sites were subsequently implemented by a multinational team of experts in collaboration with the SVGNT.[1139] In addition, archaeologist Richard Callaghan notes that although only impacts on natural resources were included in the scope of the EIA, Kocks Consult elected to include a discussion of the potential impacts on heritage resources given the importance of the site to the local community.[1140]

Callaghan notes that government efforts to mitigate the effects of the construction on the site were conducted in the prefeasibility, construction and post-construction phases of the project. Construction plans were examined to determine if the runway could be redesigned to avoid the site. This would have required extending the runway into the sea, adding a prohibitive cost to the airport project. As an alternative, the IADC funded the transfer of the petroglyphs, and the production of high-quality reproductions. This was accomplished with the support of the SVGNT, with a relocation team that included archaeologists and restoration specialists as well as senior engineers.[1141] The SVGNT invited a team of archaeologists from Leiden University, led by Corinne Hofman to conduct the rescue excavation.[1142] The excavation uncovered the first complete early colonial Island Carib settlement in the Lesser Antilles.[1143] Other proposed mitigation efforts included preparation of an archaeological display in the airport terminal[1144] as well as a park as a new public space, showcasing the features of the archaeological landscape such as the excavated settlement. The Leiden University

---

1137 Callaghan 83.
1138 Lewis 80.
1139 Ibid. See also 'IADC National Trust working on petroglyphs solution' (*Searchlight*, 12 October 2007) <https://searchlight.vc/searchlight/news/2007/10/12/iadc-national-trust-working-on-petroglyphs-solution/> accessed 30 July 2018.
1140 Callaghan 85.
1141 Ibid. See also 'SVG National Trust saves petroglyphs at Argyle' <https://searchlight.vc/searchlight/news/2007/06/29/svg-national-trust-saves-petroglyphs-at-argyle/> (*Searchlight*, 29 June 2007) accessed 30 July 2018.
1142 See also Arie Boomert, 'From Cayo to Kalinago: Aspects of Island Carib Archaeology' 291-307 at 291 and Alistair Bright, "Removed from off the face of the island': Late pre-Colonial and early Colonial Amerindian society in the Lesser Antilles' 307-325 at 317 in Corinne Hofman and Anne van Duijvenbode (eds) *Communities in Contact: Essays in Archaeology, Ethnohistory & Ethnography of the Amerindian Circum-Caribbean* (Sidestone Press 2011).
1143 Corinne Hofman and Menno Hoogland, 'Caribbean Encounters: Rescue Excavations at the Early Colonial Island Carib Site of Argyle, St. Vincent' 63-76 at 64, in Corrie Bakels and Hans Kamermans (eds), *Analecta Praehistorica Leidensia: The End of Our Fifth Decade*. Publication of the Faculty of Archaeology, Leiden University 2012.
1144 Callaghan 85.

archaeologists also worked with local experts to reconstruct this Amerindian village, which was completed in 2016.[1145] The design and construction of the village included input from descendants of the indigenous communities from Saint Vincent and nearby islands, as well as stakeholders from government, civil society and other members of the public.[1146] Clearly the significance of the site, the public pressure and the international attention served to encourage a level of scrutiny hitherto not provided for in the planning legislation or current policy.[1147]

In the summer of 2019, two indigenous communities actively involved in the construction of the Amerindian village returned to the site to call attention to the need for its restoration, and to share proposals for its maintenance and resolving ownership issues. As a result, the Government of St Vincent and the Grenadines affirmed its commitment to the Amerindian Village and communicated that contractors were being sought to properly manage the site and enhance its facilities.[1148] This demonstrates the power of communities to protect landscapes by (re)defining and defending their spaces, through physical action and as a matter of policy intervention. The model village is now a landscape of importance to Amerindian and national heritage in that island.

A major impediment to heritage protection is the lack of procedures governing development located near archaeological sites and other heritage resources. As Lewis notes, EIAs are only undertaken where the public become aware of such projects and place public pressure on the government to take this step.[1149] With the recent dispute over the proposed destruction of petroglyphs at the site of the new international airport in Argyle, which Lewis cites as evidence of the government's insensitivity to historical and cultural issues and heritage protection in general,[1150] the planning process was made more spatially just by integrating considerations of the community linkages to the site, as advocated for by the SVGNT.

While cultural resources management is in its infancy on St. Vincent and the Grenadines, the Argyle airport project has demonstrated vast improvements in the approach to these resources. A decade ago, there was little organised interest despite the best efforts of some individuals. Recently, interest in cultural heritage has increased dramatically. This is exemplified by the support of the IADC even though the sites involved had not yet attracted protected status when construction plans had been an-

---

1145 'Reconstruction of Amerindian Village St. Vincent – Completed by local volunteers' (29 June 2016) <https://www.universiteitleiden.nl/nexus1492/news/reconstruction-of-amerindian-village-st.-vincent-%E2%80%93-completed-by-local-volunteers> accessed 6 December 2019.
1146 Tibisay Sankatsing Nava and Corinne Hofman, 'Engaging Caribbean Island Communities with Indigenous Heritage and Archaeology Research.' *Journal of Science Communication* 17(4) (2018): 1-10, and Corinne Hofman and Menno Hoogland, 'Connecting Stakeholders: Collaborative preventive archaeology projects at sites affected by natural and/or human impacts.' *Caribbean Connections* 5(1) (2016): 1-31. See also 'Start of Reconstruction of indigenous village in St. Vincent' (8 February 2016) <https://www.universiteitleiden.nl/nexus1492/news/start-of-reconstruction-indigenous-village-in-st.-vincent> accessed 6 December 2018.
1147 Callaghan, 84.
1148 Kenville Horne, 'Indigenous people await Village restoration' (*The Vincentian*, 9 August 2019) <http://thevincentian.com/indigenous-people-await-village-restoration-p17710-135.htm> accessed 4 December 2019.
1149 Lewis 79.
1150 Ibid.

nounced.[1151] The SVGNT played an important role in facilitating the planning process where sites are potentially at risk due to development. In the absence of clear legislation, the Trust has developed practices to protect the national heritage in cooperation with the government, and by involving international partners, thereby improving administration of the planning law.[1152] Where legislation is absent or unenforced and the EIA process obscure, communities also attempt to engage in place protection in a variety of ways, as can be seen with Camerhogne Park in Grenada.

7.6 Camerhogne Park Relocation, Grenada

Camerhogne Park provides an illustration of how public spaces are contested in the absence of participatory mechanisms in the law and how parks can play a role in the protection of the national heritage.

7.6.1 Historical Background

Camerhogne Park (hereafter the Park) is located on Grenada's most popular beach, Grand Anse beach, which is situated on the island's south coast in the heart of the tourism belt bearing the same name. The name Camerhogne is an Amerindian term for Grenada in the Kalinago language.[1153] Historically, the area was known to have been a coconut plantation as part of the larger Grand Anse estate in the colonial period, but during the construction of the Coyaba and Allamanda resorts, Amerindian graves were unearthed, suggesting it was inhabited much earlier than previously thought.[1154] A number of surveys have been conducted in the past three decades that are indicative of the site's archaeological potential.

The Park was proposed by consultant Leon Taylor in the 1980s during an OAS study of the beach area,[1155] as a means of defusing social tensions between residents and tourists. Grenadians had objected to what they considered a reduction in community access to the major recreational area, during the construction of the Allamanda and Coyaba resorts on the beach. Public access to the coast, though not framed as such, has been in evidence since the colonial period, when beach and backshore areas were considered of little economic value to the plantation and allocated for use by the enslaved population.[1156] As originally planned, the Park would take up a vacant area of ten acres west of an old hotel, the Riviera; it was eventually designed and established on 2.5 acres of land, in order to accommodate the Allamanda and Coyaba hotels. The

---

1151 Callaghan 85-86.
1152 Ibid, 85.
1153 John Angus Martin, *A-Z of Grenada Heritage*, 2nd edn (forthcoming).
1154 Interview with Mr Michael Jessamy, Heritage Officer, Ministry of Tourism, Civil Aviation and Culture (St George's, Grenada, 1 April, 2016).
1155 L Taylor, 'Leave Camerhogne Park Alone' (Letter to the editor). *New Today* (St George's, 23rd December, 2015). On file with the author.
1156 Christine Toppin-Allahar, "De Beach Belong to We!' Socio-economic Disparity and Islanders' Rights of Access to the Coast in a Tourist Paradise.' *Oñati Socio-legal Series* 5 (1) (2015): 298-317, 302. Toppin Allahar also notes, at 311, that the right of public access to the coast through a reserve defined as 'three chains above the high water mark' was enshrined in colonial laws in Tobago and a number of OECS countries. The statutory basis is not always clear today, but the right of public access to the coast appears to have been preserved.

National Parks and Protected Areas Act[1157] was enacted to support development of the national parks system, and Camerhogne Park has been managed by the Ministry of Tourism and Culture ever since.

Today Camerhogne Park is a public park hosting a range of activities by various user groups. It has beach frontage, and provides residents with access, parking, picnic and leisure facilities, while at the same time regulating development on the beach and minimising environmental impacts.[1158] Park activities include picnicking, yoga, exercising, and sunbathing. The park also functions as a transit area, muster point and meeting space for social functions and events such as film festivals, public education initiatives, marathons and charity walks. It is also close to transportation, shopping and entertainment venues and the playing field which parallels that section of the beach.[1159] Employees from those various businesses nearby meet to eat lunch in the park. The tensions between tourists and residents have largely dissipated as both user groups make use of the park.[1160] As is typical of national parks, it is multifunctional and subject to a variety of spatial definitions, representing that balance between ideals in a recreative commons.[1161]

7.6.2 The Proposal to Replace Camerhogne Park

In 2015, it was announced that Egyptian developer Naguib Sawiris would be investing EC$270 million in a new hotel project, which would include lands formerly occupied by the Riviera hotel. The first phase would see the construction of a new hotel, Silver Sands, which is expected to be a 400-room facility with a casino, and provide employment for 260 Grenadians when the hotel becomes operational, with employment for 100 persons during the construction phase.[1162]

During its second phase, the proposed project could absorb land currently designated as Camerhogne Park, which borders the Riviera property. The developer proposed a new green space in the Grand Anse area, with neighbouring facilities for the community such as the vendors' market, basketball and tennis courts. This was widely protested and generated a wave of discussions on the significance of the park. It should be noted that access to the project documents has not been granted, so it is unclear whether an environmental impact assessment has been undertaken, or even if Sawiris had indeed purchased the Riviera property at that time. Mechanisms for protecting the heritage, such as the Heritage Advisory Committee in the Physical Planning Unit and EIAs, were not deployed, at least to the public's knowledge.

The Prime Minister announced that Camerhogne Park would be moved to another location along Grand Anse beach, as it would allow for Grenadians to continue with

---

1157 Discussed in Chapter Six.
1158 'Press release: 'The Save Camerhogne Park Committee finalises resolution for signing by political parties' (*Now Grenada*, 11 January 2018) <http://www.nowgrenada.com/2018/01/the-save-camerhogne-park-committee-finalises-resolution-for-signing-by-political-parties/> accessed 8 February, 2018.
1159 Letter of Leon Taylor (*The New Today*, 23 December 2015).
1160 Ibid.
1161 Dahlberg et al, 220; Colin Hall and Warwick Frost (eds), *Tourism and National Parks: International Perspectives on Development, Histories and Change* (Routledge 2009) 307. See also Olwig, 'Commons & Landscape' 20 in Chapter Six.
1162 Linda Straker 'Camerhogne Park to be relocated' (*Now Grenada*, 6 January 2016) <http://www.nowgrenada.com/2016/01/camerhogne-park-relocated/> accessed 8 February 2018.

their own activities without disruption or limits imposed by the hotel property, but this was also protested as the proposed location abuts a cemetery. It is noteworthy that this new park will be even smaller, with no beach frontage. No reference was made to the National Parks legislation and the process for designating such a park, and whether the park could be transferred, although legal minds in the community publicly supported the idea because it was in the 'national interest'.[1163]

A number of petitions were signed in favour of Camerhogne Park remaining in its original location and shared on social media. Demonstrations were also held in the park and supported by the Opposition in Parliament.

7.6.3 The Legal Status of Camerhogne Park

National parks legislation was passed in 1991 with the National Parks and Protected Areas Act. Prior to the passage of this law, a handful of laws addressed the establishment of other protected areas on an individual basis, such as the Grand Etang Reserve Act, or on a thematic basis, such as marine reserves, parks, and sanctuaries under the Fisheries Act.

Although the park has been in use since the 1990s, and was landscaped with appropriate signage and public facilities such as toilets, showers, tables, and trash receptacles for picnicking, the park was never legally designated pursuant to the National Parks and Protected Areas Act. However, that legislation has never had implementing regulations to outline the details of the designating process for parks. Nevertheless, the park is managed by the Ministry responsible for national parks, the Ministry of Tourism and Culture. A report in 2009 in support of the OECS Protected Areas and Associated Sustainable Livelihoods (OPAAL) project, to develop protected areas in the Eastern Caribbean, proposed a national system of parks and protected areas for Grenada. The report recommended that parks in Grenada be formalised if they fell into one of the following two categories: where it has been widely accepted as a park area based on administrative and management arrangements, or land that has been identified by other completed and accepted land use studies as priority areas of interest. The plan identified Camerhogne as belonging to the former category and suggested it be formally gazetted under the National Parks and Protected Areas Act.[1164]

7.6.4 Camerhogne Park as a Contested Public Space

On 25th November, 2015, during a sitting of the lower house of Parliament, Prime Minister Dr Keith Mitchell announced in the Budget speech that the Park would be relocated.[1165] He stated that Camerhogne Park would be moved to another location along Grand Anse beach, and that the developers would provide upgraded facilities

---

1163 Arley Gill, 'Relocate park and build hotel' (*Now Grenada*, 14 March 2016) <http://www.nowgrenada.com/2016/03/relocate-park-build-the-hotel/> accessed 8 February, 2018.
1164 Government of Grenada. Grenada Protected Areas System Plan Part 1: Identification and Designation of Protected Areas. OECS/Mel Turner, 2009, 27 and 32.
1165 Linda Straker 'Camerhogne Park to be relocated' (*Now Grenada*, 6 January 2016); Government of Grenada, '2016 Budget Statement', presented by Dr the Rt Hon Keith C Mitchell, Prime Minister and Minister of Finance and Energy, 25 November 2015, 51.

such as a new vendors' market, and basketball and tennis courts. No reference was made to the legislation and the process for designating such a park.[1166]

There was public outcry and the administration immediately retracted its stance, stating that no firm decision had been made concerning the park.[1167] The administration agreed to work with communities to address the matter, and Health Minister Nickolas Steele subsequently announced that a committee with broad representation from society would be established to explore the possibility of improving Camerhogne Park.[1168] Nevertheless, there were no attempts to coordinate with the planning authority, which can designate environment protection areas, and has an advisory committee on the natural and cultural heritage to vet applications for planning permission and make recommendations for the protection of heritage resources.[1169]

Both former Attorney General Sir Lawrence Joseph and former Senator Arley Gill publicly supported the project, citing it as in the nation's interest, framing the matter as a choice between 'preservation or development', and appealing to the public to avoid letting 'emotionalism' hold sway.[1170] Both writers, practicing lawyers by profession, failed to make reference to environmental law and the existence of parks legislation in Grenada. There was no discussion of the function of parks or the role they play in national development. There was no reference to the natural heritage or historical significance of the site, except in dismissing such value. In fact, Mr Gill pronounced the park of 'no remarkable historical significance' but cited no research or study that would validate his statement.[1171]

Consultations continued between the developer and various interest groups across Grenada, including civil society and the private sector.[1172] During this time, the park continued to be accessed by the public. A petition to save the park drew 15,000 signatures, not an insignificant figure on a small island of 100, 000 people.

The issue became increasingly politicised when the Opposition Party took up the mantle. A town hall meeting was held,[1173] locally and within the Grenadian diaspora, as meetings were held in Brooklyn, New York on 13th March, 2016.[1174] There was an 'Occupy Camerhogne Park' sit-in demonstration. A 'Save Camerhogne Park' committee was established and a 'People's resolution' prepared in January 2018, which was disseminated to political parties throughout the nation for signing as evidence of

---

1166 Arley Gill, 'Relocate park and build hotel' (*Now Grenada*, 14 March 2016).
1167 'No decision on Camerhogne Park' (*Now Grenada*, 13 January 2016) <http://www.nowgrenada.com/2016/01/no-decision-camerhogne-park/> accessed 8 February 2018.
1168 'Government to work along with Critics on Camerhogne Park' (*Now Grenada*, 15 January 2016) <http://www.nowgrenada.com/2016/01/government-work-along-critics-camerhogne-park/> accessed 8 February 2018.
1169 See the Grenada PPDC Act discussed in Chapter Five.
1170 Sir Lawrence Joseph 'Camerhogne Park and the national interest' (*Now Grenada*, 7 March 2016) <http://www.nowgrenada.com/2016/03/camerhogne-park-and-the-national-interest/> accessed 8 February, 2018.
1171 Arley Gill, 'Relocate park and build hotel' (*Now Grenada*, 14 March 2016).
1172 'Government consultations on Camerhogne Park' (*Now Grenada*, 5 March 2016) <http://www.nowgrenada.com/2016/03/government-consultations-on-camerhogne-park/> accessed 8 February 2018.
1173 Press release: 'NDC Statement on Town Hall Meeting for Camerhogne Park' (*Now Grenada*, 16 January 2016) <http://www.nowgrenada.com/2016/01/22054/> accessed 8 February 2018.
1174 Kellon Bubb, 'Camerhogne Debate reaches Brooklyn' (*Now Grenada*, 17 March 2016) <http://www.nowgrenada.com/2016/03/camerhogne-park-debate-reaches-brooklyn/> accessed 8 February 2018.

commitment to protecting the park for recreational use for future generations.[1175] The title is 'Protect Camerhogne Park in perpetuity: People's Resolution, January 31st, 2018'.[1176] The committee therefore references the people of Grenada as the authority to publish the resolution, and focuses on the long-term preservation of the park, 'in perpetuity'.

The Camerhogne Park resolution attempts to be authoritative by making use of quasi-legal language. It documents the conflict relating to Camerhogne Park and the concerns of the interested parties, situating both within the historic and environmental context. Prime Minister Mitchell's speech is referenced, in which he announced a new park would be developed by the investors. Environmental threats such as climate change are mentioned, including the particular threats for small island developing states such as Grenada, and their coastal vulnerabilities. The resolution highlights the purpose of the Park as the solution to conflicting uses, and the fact that the Park's original size had been reduced in order to accommodate hotel development.

The resolution makes reference to the Constitution of Grenada, the highest law of the land, which protects the rights of its citizens to own property; that the Government of Grenada has a responsibility to protect the national assets and national patrimony for the use and enjoyment of its citizens now and in the future. Importantly, the resolution refers to Camerhogne Park and Grand Anse beach as forming part of the 'patrimony' of Grenada. Though not a legal term in the common law, nevertheless it is one charged with meaning, as it connotes property inherited from one's ancestors, not inappropriate given that the park's name, Camerhogne, can be taken to mean Ancestral Grenada. The resolution concludes with an appeal for signature as evidence of the 'irrevocable commitment to protect and preserve, in perpetuity, Camerhogne Park, at its current location as public green space for the use and enjoyment of the people of Grenada'.[1177] The current administration did not sign the resolution.

Nevertheless, the public occupation of the Camerhogne Park space, and resort to quasi-legal means through the establishment of a committee and its resolutions, are evidence of a public position. The community saw the park as a public space that was important to their identity and their well-being. The government ignored or was unaware of the significance of the park to serve both tourists and residents, believing it to be a politicised issue on the part of the opposition, and appealing instead to the nation's need for development and growth via foreign revenue injection that a new high-end resort would offer. At no stage in the discussions were park laws referred to, only the fact that people viewed the park as established and that it was a public space for all to use.

1175 Press release: 'The Save Camerhogne Park Committee finalises resolution for signing by political parties' (*Now Grenada*, 10 January 2018) <http://www.nowgrenada.com/2018/01/the-save-camerhogne-park-committee-finalises-resolution-for-signing-by-political-parties/> accessed 8 February 2018.

1176 See Camerhogne Park final resolution dated January 10th, 2018, available at <http://www.nowgrenada.com/2018/01/the-save-camerhogne-park-committee-finalises-resolution-for-signing-by-political-parties/> accessed 18th February 2018.

1177 The Save Camerhogne Park Committee, 'People's Resolution: Protect Camerhogne Park in perpetuity', January 31st, 2018, available at <https://www.nowgrenada.com/wp-content/uploads/2018/01/Camerhogne-Park-Final-Resolution-Updated-10-1-18.pdf> accessed 18th February 2018.

7.6.5 Virtual Enclosure and Spatial Injustice in Camerhogne Park

The spatial logic of virtual enclosure is based on much older ideas of land as property and landscape as scenery, which can lead to spatial injustice. As Olwig notes, virtual enclosure extinguishes the commons, creating a shift not just physically with the spatial definition of land as property[1178] but psychologically in the way land is comprehended, accompanied by the rise of the perception of land as scenic space.[1179] When nature becomes landscape scenery, it is rendered perfectly scalable and transferable.[1180]

The idea that space is a result of the struggle between different spatial definitions, which co-exist and challenge one another, can be linked to the concept of spatial justice, which Andreas Philippopoulos-Mihalopoulos has explained as requiring withdrawal.[1181] When more than one body seeks to occupy the same space at the same time, 'a conflict of bodies that will never be sated' occurs. A way to negotiate this conflict is through a 'permanent state of oscillation', where the parties with their individual legitimate claims alternate in taking possession of the space and retreating from that claim.' As noted in Chapter Two, spatial justice thus 'demands a radical gesture of withdrawal'. [1182]

The multifunctionality of parks is an inherent characteristic of socially constructed and contested spaces.[1183] Bengsten notes that giving priority to certain groups is a way to minimise the claims of others.[1184] Practically speaking, another park could have been designated, but the historical and cultural use of Camerhogne Park was dismissed. The physical characteristics of the park are also reflective of the people's desires, normativities and agency, as well as legal structures. Removal can therefore be associated with the determination to establish a space of law through the formal sale to the resort developers.[1185]

The government reserved the right to define the space of the park, yet this was contested by the public. The government therefore retreated from its claim, and this 'radical gesture of withdrawal'[1186] is in fact evidence of spatial justice. The presence or absence of regulation does not lead to spatial justice necessarily.[1187] Although the park was never legally designated, Bengsten has written that this is not conclusive – multiple spaces can co-exist without the need for structural interventions and formal regulation.[1188] The park had been in use since 1990, with signage declaring it a park, and public facilities maintained by the Government of Grenada via the Ministry of Tourism, Civil Aviation and Culture. The government by its actions therefore tacitly recognised and supported the park and its use by communities.

1178 Olwig, 'Virtual Enclosure and Alienation' 256.
1179 Ibid, 254.
1180 Ibid, 258.
1181 See Andreas Philippopoulos-Mihalopoulos, who writes that spatial justice is understood in its simplest form as a geographically informed version of social justice', in 'Spatial Justice: Law and the Geography of Withdrawal.' 201.
1182 Bengsten 81.
1183 Hall and Frost (eds), *Tourism and National Parks* 307 as cited by Dahlberg et al 220.
1184 Bengsten 89.
1185 Ibid, 81.
1186 Andreas Philippopoulos-Mihalopoulos, 'Spatial Justice: Law and the Geography of Withdrawal' 202.
1187 Bengtsen 90.
1188 Ibid, 92.

Spatial justice is thus a process that is evident when spatial definitions continuously alternate between a dominant and more subordinate position. Public contesting of the government's definition of Camerhogne Park occurred over a three-year period. People can reclaim the right to define space, and there is ample evidence of Grenadians occupying and using the park during the protest period. Examples of space occupation include watching movies and yoga, continuing to use the park daily, along with the more obvious demonstrations within the park.[1189]

Thus particular spatial definitions have been established that complement each other. This is evidence of the existence of a type of commons, because the commons tend to be contested places where differences must be worked out in the common interest.[1190] The Prime Minister's statements about moving the park can be taken as an attempt to shift the approved spatial definitions of Camerhogne Park by appealing to national development and the vaunted attractiveness of the new space. The aim was to establish a particular space without the need for community consultation.[1191] The letters of the former Attorney General and a former Senator calling for relocation of the park 'in the national interest', strengthened the administration's efforts. It was clear which user was being given priority:[1192] the wealthy foreign party, in a country with a history of foreign exclusive ownership of land (the approved spatial definition of land).

Through the attempted dissolution of a national park, the administration was engaging in virtual enclosure; enclosing land understood as visual space,[1193] rather than landscape. Spatial justice – access to space – is dependent upon the historical settings and ideological contexts in which the institutions controlling national park management have evolved. The conservation framework is directly related to how we perceive landscapes and by extension value them, and will reflect the views of those who make the decisions. Conservation therefore continues to be related to issues of power and justice.[1194]

Parks and protected areas legislation has not considered the needs of local communities, and the institutional arrangements that best reflect their relationship to the resources being protected, because of the region's colonial past and entrenched institutional arrangements that underpin park governance. Traditional protected area legislation can only do so much because it was never intended to account for human presence – parks and protected areas are frozen in time, while landscapes are dynamic and reflect the community relationship with natural resources/community-nature interaction. The failure to allocate roles and responsibilities to manage heritage resources reflects the bewilderment on the part of the authorities in identifying and recognising heritage as a resource necessary for sustainable development of small island states. The result is a 'clash between two different cultural views of conservation… representing the government and the public.'[1195]

1189 Bengsten 83.
1190 Olwig, *Landscape, Nature and the Body Politic* 224.
1191 Bengsten 86.
1192 Ibid, 89.
1193 Ibid, 90.
1194 Dahlberg et al, 209.
1195 Ibid, 215.

Martin and Scherr have noted the ways that legal frameworks, particularly those governing the use of public space, work to shape landscapes by restricting access to space for some people. For example, laws designed to maintain public order and cleanliness have in effect legislated the homeless out of space. Through a focus on public safety, these laws essentially render public space accessible only to some persons: those who already enjoy full access to and benefits of private spaces (such as homes, restaurants and the like) through their economic standing. Thus, 'public space' becomes exclusionary rather than a common ground for all persons, and the landscapes of public spaces are to some degree 'cleansed' of social difference.[1196]

Restricting public space eventually leads to virtual enclosure. Space then becomes accessible only to the richest, because they are likely to be the user group that can afford to enter the area and so the multiplicity of spatial definitions are erased. Thus the increasing privatisation of public space is defaulting to the colonial style practice in which land is malleable, enclosable space, where colonialism promotes spatial privilege for the elite, at the expense of the general populace. There is a need to reform these institutional structures that arose in previous ideological contexts and develop the capacity to devolve control and decision-making powers to a local level.[1197]

The administration ignored usage, practice and tradition when it proposed a new park space. The purported sale of Camerhogne Park is not a regulatory way of restoring spatial justice; instead it stifles a recreational space, by establishing boundaries in that public space that exclude the public. This is law reducing space to a controlled context.[1198] Eliminating the space impedes the activities of the public and their use and definition of the area, while the offer of an alternative space controls access to certain spaces and certain spatial definitions.[1199] The Grenadian public challenged virtual enclosure and enacted their own justice – promoting group rights and common practices through the 'people's resolution', appealing to the idea of 'patrimony' and viewing the natural heritage as an inheritance for future generations against damage and loss.

Without this perspective, the view of nature as blind to or separate from the existence of cultural landscapes and which subsequently became embodied in the purpose of national park management will prevail. This spatially unjust approach resulted in laws that provide for 'state controlled commons governed by centralised institutions with top down management structures that ignore local people or regard them as the problem'.[1200] As Dahlberg writes, 'attempts at change are often met with official resistance or lose out in competition with market forces aimed at increasing tourist access, tourists being perceived as less harmful to environment than land use custom of local communities.'[1201] By contrast, a landscape approach acknowledges these diverse interests that are not represented in property law.

These tensions are captured in Camerhogne Park, despite the existence of a parks framework and the park's significance as a public space. The presence or absence of regulation is not dispositive – spatial justice must be considered on a case by case

---

1196 Martin and Scherr 380-381.
1197 Dahlberg 221.
1198 Bengsten 88.
1199 Ibid, 90.
1200 Dahlberg et al, 219.
1201 Ibid, 220.

basis.[1202] While the Government of Grenada defined the park in terms of a space created solely in law, in these legally grey areas, people enact their own justice by engaging in place-protective behaviour and appealing to a range of authorities – legal (the Constitution) and moral (the people/patrimony) as represented in the Camerhogne Park resolution. As of June 2016, the Prime Minister has indicated that the Park will not be absorbed or enclosed by the new resort.

7.7 Conclusion

These examples from the Lesser Antilles illustrate the contemporary challenges facing heritage protection, where public spaces are not recognised within the law and are undermined to reinforce private property interests. The result is that land is ascribed fixed spatial definitions that are colonial in character, yet landscapes by their very nature are contested places. The law does not accommodate the range of communal interests that landscape represents, so the multiplicity of uses of public space remains unrecognised. Because it cannot accommodate various spatial definitions, there is friction between heritage protection and the law. This spatial blindness has resulted in a convoluted institutional framework and poor administration of the law, to which the OAS Heritage Legislation Survey alluded to, as discussed in Chapter One. As a result, landscape protection is not a priority, to the detriment of communities who are the bearers and creators of cultural heritage. In addition, current international best practice in the preparation of EIA reports which recommends the use of participatory processes is often deviated from, underscoring conservative and at times retrogressive positions on heritage protection, in order to entrench State interests.

Many of these examples reflect the tension between the land use planning process and heritage protection. The Saint Lucia National Trust found itself in the crosshairs of the government when it was reprimanded for not maximising the 'development' potential of heritage 'assets', despite its legislative limits. The Trinidad and Tobago example also illustrates this well. In spite of Greyfriars being part of a proposed heritage district, the site was not considered 'unique' or aesthetically pleasing, as there was another Anglican church in existence, ignoring Greyfriars' value as a public space and the criteria in the legislation for designating such spaces. As a result, the TTNT could not leverage support to protect Greyfriars, in spite of its attempts to list the site, challenge the developer in court, and the public calls for the site's protection.

Planning and heritage law thus rarely work in alignment, unless heritage actors can make use of creative strategies, such as with the Argyle EIA process in St Vincent and the Grenadines. Here the SVGNT found the Airport Authority receptive to mitigation measures for heritage, in spite of limited legislative protection available in planning law. Recommended measures included a rescue excavation, the production of replicas and the relocation where possible of some of the archaeological resources. The SVGNT advocated for the insertion of consideration of the impacts on heritage resources in the EIA process, facilitated the rescue excavation, and supported the creation of a heritage village as an alternative public space to protect some of the petroglyphs, developed through a participatory process with input from communities. Indigenous

---

1202 Bengtsen 90.

groups have occupied the village peacefully since its construction in order to advocate for its upkeep, an indication of its significance to the community and efforts to regulate use and access to this new space for future generations.

While St Vincent has benefited from the presence of an active Trust, which advocated for the protection of a prominent site, and an extant indigenous population that gave these heritage resources contemporary resonance, in Grenada the Trust and Museum played no vital part in the discussions surrounding the Lower Sauteurs EIA, in spite of existing legislation and the site's heritage value. The Lower Sauteurs EIA gave minimal consideration to the heritage significance of the site since it was not the focus of its terms of reference, but the EIA prepared for Argyle reflected the fact that the authorities had succumbed to community pressure and assessed the impact of the airport development on the cultural heritage of the area. Interestingly, while St Vincent attempted to address the concerns of the community and the impact on the heritage resources during the planning process, Grenada did not seek innovative approaches to this issue, despite having a policy and legislative framework that promoted conservation of historic sites. Even though it was within the ambit of the planning authority to consider the impact of the breakwater on the natural and cultural heritage and the coastal community of Sauteurs, it refrained from doing so. While it does recognise the existence of the cultural heritage, the authority failed to deploy protective measures because these sites have no perceived contemporary value in the face of pressing economic considerations.

Deploying the spatial justice lens in the Camerhogne Park example allows us to view contested access to parks and public spaces not merely as challenges to government authority but as place-protective behaviour derived from community bonds with place, and locally specific views on how places should change over time, as was discussed in Chapter Two. Such protests can be indicative of community practices tied to land that are not accommodated by statute. They question the adequacy of parks law to regulate public spaces, presenting an opportunity to consider the ways in which the law, by ignoring or devaluing space, is ultimately effective. Spatial justice can therefore be enacted by the public, regardless of the existence of regulations. The Grenadian public challenged virtual enclosure and enacted their own justice – by demanding that these alternatives to private property be recognised as legitimate land use. These efforts are attempts to localise the law to effectively respond to current needs and conditions.

Where cultural heritage law, environmental law and planning law interact, the process is far from harmonious. Yet while standing is only extended to private property owners, non-State heritage actors, whether communities or groups or institutional actors, are attempting to challenge current spatial definitions to protect heritage, whether this means defending access to space or the right to define such spaces. When the public is not excluded from decision-making concerning public spaces, as with the creation of a new park in St Vincent, the reaction is different from situations in which the public has no opportunity to (re) define spaces, as in Grenada and Trinidad and Tobago. In assessing these scenarios of heritage and landscape conflicts in the Lesser Antilles, Layard's proposed test for determining whether spatial justice has been met (as outlined in Chapter One) – whether aspatiality, the dismissal of space 'is a defeat for citizens, localities, and place' has proven highly relevant.

8

Conclusion

In reviewing the legal framework for heritage protection in the Lesser Antilles, this research has drawn on new perspectives in the legal geography and legal anthropology fields to better understand the role of law, its strengths and weaknesses, and opportunities for improving implementation in this region. The concept of landscape as a term in legal geography has been explained herein as a place in which a community interacts with their natural and cultural environment in such a way as to define their relationships with the land and each other, prescribe the use of shared resources for those belonging to the land, and codify the practices and rituals that arise so that they can be transmitted over time to sustain the community. Because each environment is different and change is inevitable, the people, the practices and the institutions as shaped by this relationship will always be distinctive, and always tied to place – as a result, cultural identity has a particular spatial location. As 'cultural nature', landscape is the locus of cultural heritage, a public space or a common good, and its continued existence is relevant to the sustainability of heritage.

Crucial therefore to the effectiveness of heritage law is spatial justice, because acknowledging the spatial setting ensures that law accommodates local conditions, and legal rules are embedded in local conditions of existence, rather than abstract conceptions of universal application. Universal rules can contribute to spatial injustice by erasing the local specificities of place – this was typically practised during colonialism when various territories around the world were invaded by European settlers and subjugated to an imposed system of law, which remade these places into spaces that reflected the images, beliefs, practices and environments of Europeans, despite the fact that they were not located in Europe at all. The impact of the colonial enterprise on the landscapes of the Lesser Antilles was outlined in Chapter Two and is worth recalling here before considering the findings.

Slave colonies require the total erasure of place, any social linkages to the land, and any human presence in order to embed plantation agriculture. Laws were developed to protect spaces but only in the furtherance of imperial pursuits. These laws never considered the features of local natural resources, or the significance to communities, as by this time, all non-Europeans had restricted access to space. This impacted the Caribbean environment and the communities that depended upon them, which was explored in Chapter Two. St Vincent's King's Hill Forest Act was the first law enacted in this context to establish a colonial reserve to sustain the functioning of the plantation system at the expense of Amerindian communities. It is representative of the legislation that would be enacted throughout the region.

The idea of the Caribbean as a placeless void enabled a legal system that prioritised abstract rules at the expense of local communities and customs. Regulation of the landscape was fraught with obstacles to heritage protection, because these heritage resources emanated from the land which was now subject to private property rights. Colonialism in particular ensured that no other land use was permitted under the common law. Early common law in the Caribbean therefore developed features that have consequences for cultural heritage in the Lesser Antilles today. This leads to the following four findings.

The first finding of this analysis is that heritage institutions tend to uphold a colonial-era approach to heritage, because they are often not embedded in the communities they serve. National Trusts and state museums, the major heritage institutional actors, remain passive since they form no part of an integrated approach to protect public spaces. Trusts have limited language for recognising vernacular heritage and their legislation reflects the colonial-era National Trust law that prioritised private interests and the dominant class's perception of heritage. As Chapter Seven has shown, the National Trust of Trinidad and Tobago was unable to save Greyfriars Church of Scotland, a public site important to the abolition of slavery and independence from being demolished, despite having criteria in its legislation for listing and protection, and serving in an advisory capacity to the Government of Trinidad and Tobago. The same was true of Grenada when an Amerindian burial ground was discovered. Where Trusts attempt to challenge the State approved definition of heritage, they are often rendered ineffectual, as was the case in Saint Lucia. A landscape approach requires the decolonisation of heritage institutions, the practices of which have prioritised Eurocentric heritage, and overlooked the significance of landscapes to defining heritage, relying instead on arbitrary definitions for classifying artefacts. Without place-based knowledge, these laws are unable to devise locally specific or place appropriate strategies for protecting heritage.[1203]

Heritage laws are often subject to the prerogatives of planning law, which leads to the second finding – that the planning process via EIAs can precipitate heritage destruction, because heritage is not considered an approved use of land in planning law. Planning law is directing development of post-industrial Britain, not the post-colonial Lesser Antilles. This is literally law for a different space and time, which makes use of listed buildings and preservation orders because heritage is viewed only as a visual accent to land, and only private property interests are protected as development is promoted. Industrial Britain's idea of heritage was aestheticised in order to provide a contrast to the perceived evils of urban London – this conceptualisation is irrelevant to the Lesser Antilles. These laws continue to promote development as construction, which can displace or disproportionately impact communities, as seen in the Lower Sauteurs EIA process in Grenada, where, in spite of having legal provisions for the protection of the cultural heritage, and implementing language for the WHC, the legislation was not relied upon and scant attention was paid to heritage resources in the final EIA report.

1203 Bartel 347.

Planning law often prioritises health and safety as a pretext for cleansing spaces of heritage resources, while upholding the rights of private landowners. Only aesthetic aspects of heritage such as facades of listed buildings are considered for preservation. The example of Greyfriars Church demonstrates this approach, as the developer alluded to the architectural merits of another church of similar denomination as justification for demolishing Greyfriars, ignoring its contribution to Trinidad's independence movement and value as a refuge for diverse immigrants and former slaves, ancestors of modern Trinidadians. Here the developer was challenged, not for the actual destruction of an important public space, but for failure to secure approval for demolition as outlined in the law (and which was later granted). The planning authorities explicitly stated that their concern was not the historic significance of the site.

Spatial cleansing narratives continue to drive 'development', often aligning with the laudable goals of promoting health and safety. Evacuation of space upholds Western notions of development, as planning was first practiced in the Lesser Antilles through virtual enclosure, evicting undesirable peoples to acquire private property for the colonisers for sugar plantations. Such laws extended the practices of industrial Britain without recognising the Caribbean as a diverse environmental and cultural space. The Greyfriars developer justified his demolition by characterising it as a 'crime-ridden' space infested with drug addicts – the focus was on clearing space, not maintaining community memory.

The EIA for the Lower Sauteurs area in Grenada did acknowledge the importance of the historic Leapers' Hill site, but never substantively addressed the wider significance to the landscape and to community vitality during its community consultations, or in the design of the breakwater. When an Amerindian burial ground was later revealed along the same shoreline, impacting the local coastal communities and other archaeological sites, their spaces and their livelihoods, there was no recognition of the existing modalities in place for planning authorities to coordinate with heritage institutions or communities, perhaps because it would be onerous to do so. By contrast, in the case of St Vincent and the Grenadines, the planning authorities acquiesced in the inclusion of a heritage impact study that recommended as a mitigation measure an alternate space for the threatened heritage resources, to be opened to the public as a model Amerindian settlement. In this case, the SVG National Trust worked alongside the planning authorities to represent the public interest, and was likely successful because the Amerindian Village presented no obstacle to the continuation of the development project.

The third finding is that where national parks and protected areas legislation are in force, the type of conservation that is promoted for public spaces is often exclusionary, in the spirit of the colonial reserves established to sustain plantation agriculture. This is demonstrated by the fact that many parks are managed with a preservationist approach, to protect pristine natural environments, rather than supporting sustainable relations between places and local residents. This is because parks are defined as tourism assets and managed by the Ministry of Tourism (in Antigua and Barbuda, Grenada and St Kitts and Nevis) which means that foreign access to pristine environments is prioritised over local access. While communities legally have access rights to these spaces, they very rarely have a say in their designation or development, because consultation mechanisms are underdeveloped. This was demonstrated during the proposed relocation of Grenada's Camerhogne Park, which the public protested until the authorities relented. In the absence of access to public spaces, communities who object to the law's attempts to privatise public space will enact spatial justice through informal means to defend their traditions and practices. The example of Camerhogne Park demonstrates the capacity of the public to reclaim space – making use of quasi-legal means because their participatory and other procedural rights are limited in the law. Spatial justice is thus a process that is evident when spatial definitions continuously alternate between a dominant and more subordinate position. The protection of such places ensures that various community uses can continue to develop and interact in multiple ways in relation to these resources, as is characteristic of the commons.

Place is therefore the crosscutting factor that these laws neglect to address, leading to regulatory glitches in heritage protection. Chapter Seven provided examples of the erosion of heritage institutions and ineffective implementation of heritage law, as well as public actions to defend heritage resources outside the formal legal framework. The public has engaged in place-protective behaviour that challenges or varies the application of these laws. Mechanisms and procedures are supplemented by protests and petitions, which in turn are evidence of informal customs, social conventions and norms governing use and definition of these spaces.[1204] The Saint Lucia National Trust challenged the Government of Saint Lucia via press releases. In Grenada, letters, petitions, protests and declarations were used to demonstrate conflicts over public space. In other circumstances, stakeholders find ways to collaborate with the government, civil society and academia to preserve spaces, as with Argyle in St Vincent and in a more limited fashion, Sauteurs in Grenada.

The ways in which non-State heritage actors are challenging national approaches to cultural heritage represent in varied form the rebuke of private property definitions of public space, and evidence of landscape reasserting itself. None of these heritage laws is sufficiently participatory to ensure that communities are adequately represented and engaged where their interests in heritage resources may be under threat. This reflects the regional pattern of community challenges to protect these places, suggesting a regional approach to landscape might be necessary. Given the example of the Council of Europe Landscape Convention, which poses challenges for developed states despite its successes, and the potential problems with a Global Landscape Convention, such a treaty may not be forthcoming in the near future. Nevertheless, there are alternative ways to address place protection should such an instrument prove infeasible. This leads to the fourth and final finding – that procedural environmental rights may provide communities in the Lesser Antilles an opportunity to formalise their rights of access and use, and by extension support landscape protection.

While there is no substantive right to landscape in law because of the narrow definition of property, international law is proving to be progressive in landscape protection, by offering mechanisms that support community access, engagement with and definition of the cultural heritage. The Eurocentrism of international cultural heritage law that favoured monumental and iconic heritage has been challenged in the last few decades, so that international law has evolved to embrace a broader anthropological approach to culture and cultural heritage, recognising communities' role as heritage creators and stewards. The Council of Europe Landscape Convention defines inter-

---

[1204] Bartel et al 346.

national law's stance on landscapes, by placing people at the centre of the planning process, while the Convention on Biological Diversity's Akwé: Kon Guidelines recommends involvement of indigenous and local communities in the EIA process.

It is the human rights field that has advanced the furthest, at times bypassing the State in the face of abuse or inaction. Human rights law recognises the cultural rights dimension to landscape, or rights of access to enjoy landscape as cultural heritage as well as the associated rights of customary rights or collective property, in addition to affording communities the opportunities to be heard and protected where their interaction with the environment is critical to their quality of life (the human rights dimension to landscape as framed in the rights to a healthy environment).

The Inter-American Court system in particular has taken an innovative approach to developing landscape rights, although only in the context of indigenous communities thus far. Nevertheless, human rights law also has the potential to offer cultural rights protection to everyone, which would include the right to enjoy access to the cultural heritage as part of the right to a cultural identity. All communities have intimate connections with public spaces as the settings for their lives, and depend on the continuation of these spaces for human existence. Innovative, participatory and sustainable approaches to natural and cultural resources are therefore necessary for protecting these dynamic spaces. The Inter-American Court of Human Rights' approach has influenced the drafting of the first regionally binding environmental treaty in Latin America and the Caribbean, the Escazú Agreement.

Should it enter into force, and be ratified by states in the Lesser Antilles, the Escazú Agreement may provide a regional framework for integrating community concerns and place-based considerations in the law via the use of participatory mechanisms. Escazú aims for full implementation of the rights to environmental information, to participate in environmental decision-making, and to access environmental justice in the courts. Procedural rights can strengthen the capacity of communities to engage more effectively in heritage governance through access to environmental information, use of participatory mechanisms to strengthen the duty to consult the public in decision-making, and access to justice, such as extending the standing to make claims to individuals, communities and groups, even where they lack title to property, should they be affected by any proposed development that would negatively impact the environment. Communities will therefore have the enabling mechanisms to contest landscape use.

Escazú has acknowledged that specific social, geographic, cultural and environmental circumstances must be factored into strategies for enhancing participatory governance of the environment. This opens the door to accommodating locally specific needs of communities where natural resources are concerned, and by extension, secures the protection of the landscapes they live in. In lieu of a regional framework for landscape protection, this may be the appropriate option for the Lesser Antilles to meet the needs of these communities.

Law configures space in such a way that has implications for heritage protection in the Lesser Antilles, entrenching power dynamics that disregard local communities and privatise public space. Yet local resources have local limits, are informed by local needs and practices, and so-called 'universal' principles that underpin the law are neither neutral in formation nor purpose. A sense of belonging, identity, and memory, the building blocks of heritage, all have spatial references. In order to sustain heritage resources that are rooted in the land, any approach to heritage protection must therefore contend with issues of land access and ownership for excluded cultural groups, by recognising community definition of public spaces. Ironically, international law's progressive stance on heritage has created an arena for local communities to advocate for protection of their resources. Lawmaking at the international level is contributing to the crystallisation of law by recognising local custom as an important source of law, which has implications for the protection of human rights, landscape and heritage in the Caribbean.

This dissertation has argued that landscapes, as the dwelling places of communities, are important to local livelihoods, practices, memory and identity, and so ultimately act as the cradle of cultural heritage. Legal protection of cultural heritage will not be effective unless it is based on an understanding of this symbiotic relationship. Landscape as an approach emphasises the importance of the relationship between local communities and their environments in the creation of place, and spatial justice as the objective, focuses on the relevance of space to delivering effective legal services. As a complement to one another, they create opportunities for reforming the legislative framework for heritage protection by integrating local conditions and circumstances found in the Lesser Antilles when drafting, implementing and enforcing the law.

This research has made a number of contributions. It has produced the first overview of cultural heritage law in the Lesser Antilles. It has presented an innovative approach to heritage protection via a legal geographical analysis of cultural heritage law. In exposing the colonial origins of these laws, I demonstrated how these doctrinal foundations suppress local definitions of space, which has impacted modern attitudes towards landscape, by treating heritage resources as simply scenic in value. This has implications for the sustainable development and survival of these small island states. A spatial justice lens was employed to demonstrate how prioritising placelessness can marginalise communities and undermine the protection of heritage resources, while legal geographical and legal anthropological perspectives enhance the understanding of law beyond its formalist textual presence, to embrace non-formal but locally relevant norm-setting behaviours that are critical for the sustainability of these resources, and decolonise the imposed common law tradition.

I suggested that 'where' heritage is located can be as important as what heritage is and why it serves a purpose. When place is narrowly or selectively defined in the law, heritage is controllable and even disposable. Place must be recognised as a specific geographic location, while acknowledging the mutability of identity and social relationships associated with that place. Landscape shines a spotlight on the deficiencies of property law and how it affects heritage governance. As cultural nature, it contextualises heritage, importing sustainability, spatial justice and respect for communities into a framework for heritage protection. For the Lesser Antilles, cultural heritage cannot be appreciated in a vacuum, held apart from the painful, oppressive past that created it. That past is recorded in the landscape, and is obscured by the law via its allocation of land and power to private interests. Revealing these connections between land, law and people is thus critical for achieving sustainable heritage protection.

Bibliography

Secondary sources

Abramson A and D Theodossopoulos (eds), *Land, Law and the Environment: Mythical Land, Legal Boundaries* (Pluto Press 2000).

Accenture/National Trust, *Demonstrating the Public Value of Heritage* (National Trust 2006).

Ahmad Y, 'The Scope and Definition of Heritage: From Tangible to Intangible.' *International Journal of Heritage Studies*, 12(3) (2006): 292-300.

Alexander E, *Museums in Motion: An Introduction to the History and Function of Museums* (Nashville: American Association for State and Local History 1979).

Alexander ER, *Approaches to Planning: Introducing Current Planning Theories, Concepts and Issues* (Taylor and Francis 1992).

Anderson W, 'Multilateral Environmental Agreements (MEA) Implementation in the Caribbean: Report and Guidelines' (UNEP 2000).

―――, *Principles of Caribbean Environmental Law* (Environmental Law Institute 2012).

Anderson-Córdova KF, *Surviving Spanish Conquest: Indian Fight, Flight, and Cultural Transformation in Hispaniola and Puerto Rico* (University of Alabama Press 2017).

Aplin G, 'World Heritage Cultural Landscapes.' *International Journal of Heritage Studies* 13(6) (2007): 427-446.

Ariese-Vandemeulebroucke C, *The Social Museum in the Caribbean: Grassroots Heritage Initiatives and Community Engagement* (Sidestone Press 2018).

Armitage D, *The Ideological Origins of the British Empire* (Cambridge University Press 2000).

Arranz Márquez L, *Repartimientos y Encomiendas en la Isla Española* (Fundación García Arévalo, 1991).

Avrami E, 'Making Historic Preservation Sustainable.' *Journal of the American Planning Association*, 82(2) (2016): 104-112.

Barral V, 'Sustainable Development in International Law: Nature and Operation of an Evolutive Norm.' *European Journal of International Law* 23(2) (2012): 377-400.

Bartel R and N Graham, 'Property and Place Attachment: A Legal Geographical Analysis of Biodiversity Law Reform in New South Wales.' *Geographical Research* 54(3) (August 2016): 267-284.

Bartel R, N Graham, S Jackson, JH Prior, DF Robinson, M Sherval and S Williams, 'Legal Geography: An Australian Perspective.' *Geographical Research* 51(4) (November 2013): 339-353.

Beattie J, E Melillo, and E O'Gorman (eds), *Eco-Cultural Networks and the British Empire: New Views on Environmental History* (Bloomsbury Academic 2015).

Beckford GL, 'Institutional Foundations of Resource Underdevelopment in the Caribbean.' *The Review of Black Political Economy* 2, 3 (Spring 1972): 81-101.

_____, *Persistent Poverty: Underdevelopment of Plantation Economies in the Third World* (Oxford University Press 1972).

Beinart W and L Hughes, *Environment and Empire* (Oxford University Press 2009).

Belder L, *The Legal Protection of Cultural Heritage in International Law* (Delex 2014).

Bengsten P, 'Just Gardens? On the Struggle for Space and Spatial Justice.' *Australian Feminist Law Journal* 39 (2013): 79-92.

Bennett L and A Layard, 'Legal Geography: Becoming Spatial Detectives.' *Geography Compass* 9 (7) (July 2015): 406-422.

Bennett L, 'How does Law make Place? Localisation, Translocalisation and Thing-law at the World's First Factory.' *Geoforum* 74 (2016): 182-191.

Benton L, 'Colonial Law and Cultural Difference: Jurisdictional Politics and the Formation of the Colonial State.' *Comparative Studies in Society and History* 4(3) (July 1999): 563-588.

Besson J, 'History, Culture and Land in the English-speaking Caribbean.' In AN Williams (ed), *Proceedings of the Conference on Land in the Caribbean: Policy, Administration and Management in the English-speaking Caribbean* (University of Wisconsin-Madison 2003).

Blake J, 'On Defining the Cultural Heritage.' *ICLQ* 49 (2000): 61-85.

_____, 'UNESCO/World Heritage Convention – Towards a More Integrated Approach.' *Environmental Policy and Law* 43(1) (2013): 8-17.

_____, *International Cultural Heritage Law* (Oxford University Press 2015).

Blomley N, *Law, Space, and the Geographies of Power* (Guilford Press 1994).

_____, 'Landscapes of Property.' *Law & Society Review* 32 (1998): 567-612.

_____ and GL Clark, 'Law, Theory and Geography.' *Urban Geography* 11(5) (1990): 433-446.

_____ and JC Bakan, 'Spacing Out: Towards a Critical Geography of Law.' *Osgoode Hall Law Journal* 30(3) (Fall 1992): 661-690.

Boast R, 'Neocolonial Collaboration: Museum as Contact Zone Revisited.' *Museum Anthropology* 34(1) (March 2011): 56-70.

Boer B and G Wiffen, *Heritage Law in Australia* (Oxford University Press 2006).

_____ and S Gruber, 'Heritage Discourses' in B Jessup and K Rubenstein (eds), *Environmental Discourses in Public International Law* (Cambridge University Press 2012).

Boomert A, 'From Cayo to Kalinago: Aspects of Island Carib Archaeology' in CL Hofman and A van Duijvenbode (eds), *Communities in Contact: Essays in Archaeology, Ethnohistory & Ethnography of the Amerindian Circum-Caribbean* (Sidestone Press 2011).

Bonnell VE and L Hunt, *Beyond the Cultural Turn* (University of California Press, 1999).

Bonyhady T, *The Law and the Countryside: the Rights of the Public* (Butterworths Law 1987).

Braverman I, D Delaney, N Blomley, and A Kedar (eds), *The Expanding Spaces of Law: A Timely Legal Geography* (Stanford University Press 2014).

Bright AJ, "Removed from off the Face of the Island': Late Pre-Colonial and Early Colonial Amerindian Society in the Lesser Antilles' in CL Hofman and A van Duijvenbode (eds), *Communities in Contact: Essays in Archaeology, Ethnohistory & Ethnography of the Amerindian Circum-Caribbean* (Sidestone Press 2011).

Brion Davis D, *Inhuman Bondage: the Rise and Fall of Slavery in the New World* (Oxford University Press 2008).

Brodie N and M Kersel, *Archaeology, Cultural Heritage and the Antiquities Trade* (University Press of Florida 2006).

Browne RM, *Surviving Slavery in the British Caribbean* (University of Pennsylvania Press 2017).

Buffery CA, 'Changing Landscapes: A Legal Geography of the River Severn.' PhD diss., University of Birmingham 2015.

Bulkan A, 'From Instrument of Empire to Vehicle for Change: The Potential of Emerging International Standards for Indigenous Peoples of the Commonwealth Caribbean.' *Commw L Bull* 37(3) (2011): 463-489.

Burke S, 'The Evolution of the Cultural Policy Regime in the Anglophone Caribbean.' *International Journal of Cultural Policy* 13:2 (2007): 169-184.

Cane P and J Conaghan, *The New Oxford Companion to Law* (Oxford University Press 2008).

Carman J, *Valuing Ancient Things: Archaeology and the Law* (Leicester University Press 1996).

_____, *Archaeology and Heritage: An Introduction* (Continuum 2002).

_____, *Archaeological Resource Management: An International Perspective* (Cambridge University Press 2015).

Casid J, *Sowing Empire: Landscape and Colonization* (University of Minnesota Press 2004).

Castilla-Beltrán A, Hooghiemstra H, Hoogland MLP, Pagan Jimenez JR, Geel B van, Field MH, Prins M, Donders T, Herrera Malatesta EN, Ulloa Hung J, McMichael CH, Gosling WD and Hofman CL, 'Columbus' Footprint in Hispaniola: A Paleo-environmental record of Indigenous and Colonial Impacts on the Landscape of the Central Cibao Valley, Northern Dominican Republic.' *Anthropocene* 22 (2018): 66-80.

Christman B, 'A Brief History of Environmental Law in the UK'. *Environmental Scientist* (November 2013): 4-8.

Clark K, *Informed Conservation; Understanding Historic Buildings and their Landscapes* (English Heritage 2001).

_____, Heritage Lottery Fund (Great Britain), English Heritage, National Trust (Great Britain), *Capturing the Public Value of Heritage: the Proceedings of the London Conference*, 25-26 January 2006 (English Heritage 2006).

Clark K, 'From Regulation to Participation: Cultural Heritage, Sustainable Development and Citizenship', in D Therond (ed), *Council of Europe, Forward Planning: the Function of Cultural Heritage in a Changing Europe* (Council of Europe, 2000).

Cleere H, 'The Uneasy Bedfellows: Universality and Cultural Heritage' in R Layton, J Thomas and P Stone (eds), *Destruction and Conservation of Cultural Property* (Routledge 2001).

Con Aguilar E, *Heritage Education – Memories of the Past in the Present Caribbean Social Studies Curriculum: A View from Teacher Practices* (Sidestone Press 2020).

Conley, JM and WM O'Barr, 'Legal Anthropology Comes Home: A Brief History of the Ethnographic Study of Law.' *Loyola of Los Angeles Law Review* 27(1) (1993): 41-64.

Cookson NA, *Archaeological Heritage Law* (Barry Rose Law Publishers Ltd 2000).

Cosgrove D, *Social Formation and Symbolic Landscape* (Croom Helm 1984).

Costonis JJ, *Icons and Aliens: Law, Aesthetics and Environmental Change* (University of Illinois Press 1989).

Council of Europe, *Heritage and Beyond* (Council of Europe Publishing 2009).

Creutzfeldt N, M Mason and K McConnachie (eds), *Routledge Handbook of Socio-Legal Theory and Methods* (Routledge 2019).

Crooke E, 'An Exploration of the Connections among Museums, Community and Heritage' in BJ Graham & P Howard (eds), *The Ashgate Research Companion to Heritage and Identity* (Ashgate 2008).

Crosby A, *The Columbian Exchange: Biological and Cultural Consequences of 1492* (Greenwood Press 1972).

_____, *Ecological Imperialism: the Biological Expansion of Europe, 900-1900* (Cambridge University Press 1986).

Cullingworth B and V Nadin, *Town and Country Planning in the UK* (Routledge 2006).

Cummins A, 'Caribbean Museums and National Identity.' *History Workshop Journal* (2004) 58: 224-245.

Cummins A, K Farmer and R Russell (eds), *Plantation to Nation: Caribbean Museums and National Identity* (Common Ground Publishers 2013).

Dahlberg A, R Rohde and K Sandell, 'National Parks and Environmental Justice: Comparing Access Rights and Ideological Legacies in Three Countries.' *Conservation and Society* 8(3) (2010): 209-224.

Damodaran V, 'Environment and Empire: A Major Theme in Environmental History' in MN Harris and C Lévai (eds), *Europe and its Empires* (Plus-Pisa University Press 2008).

Daniels S, 'Marxism, Culture and the Duplicity of Landscape' in R Peet and N Thrift (eds), *New Models in Geography* Vol. II: 196-220 (Unwin and Hyman 1989).

Davis P, 'Places, 'Cultural Touchstones' and the Ecomuseum' in G Corsane (ed), *Heritage, Museums and Galleries* (Routledge 2005).

Delaney D, *The Spatial, the Legal and the Pragmatics of Place-making: Nomospheric Investigations* (Routledge 2010).

_____, 'Legal Geography I: Constitutivities, Complexities, and Contingencies.' *Progress in Human Geography* 39(1) (2015): 96-102.

_____, 'Legal Geography II: Discerning Justice.' *Progress in Human Geography* 40(2) (2016): 267-274.

_____, 'Legal Geography III: New Worlds, New Convergences.' *Progress in Human Geography* 41(5) (2017): 1-9.

Delle JA, MW Hauser, DV Armstrong, and A Henriques, *Out of Many, One People: The Historical Archaeology of Colonial Jamaica* (1st edn, The University of Alabama Press 2011).

De Silva L, 'Escazú Agreement 2018: A Landmark for the LAC Region.' *Chinese Journal of Environmental Law* 2 (2018): 93-98.

Dillman J, *Colonizing Paradise: Landscape and Empire in the British West Indies* (University of Alabama Press 2015).

Donders Y, *Towards a Right to Cultural Identity* (Intersentia 2002).

Donovan JM, *Legal Anthropology: An Introduction* (AltaMira Press 2008).

Drayton R, 'Imperial Science and a Scientific Empire: Kew Gardens and the Uses of Nature, 1772-1903.' PhD diss., Yale University, 1993.

_____, *Nature's Government: Science, Imperial Britain, and the 'Improvement' of the World* (Yale University Press 2000).

Dwyer-Amussen S, *Caribbean Exchanges: Slavery and the Transformation of English Society, 1640-1700* (The University of North Carolina Press 2007).

Economides K, M Blacksell and C Watkins, 'The Spatial Analysis of Legal Systems.' *Journal of Law and Society*. 13(2) (1986): 161-181.

Esteban Deive C, *La Española y La Esclavitud del Indio* (Fundación García Arévalo 1995).

Evans M, *Principles of Environmental & Heritage Law* (Prospect Publishing 2000).

Fairclough G, 'New Heritage Frontiers', in *Launching Colloquy of Heritage and Beyond: A Publication on the Contribution of the Council of Europe Framework Convention on the Value of Cultural Heritage for Society*, Lisbon, 20 November 2009, 31, available at: <http://www.coe.int/t/dg4/culutreheritage/heritage/identities/SpeechesLisbon/>

Falk Moore S, 'Certainties Undone: Fifty Turbulent Years of Legal Anthropology, 1949-1999.' *The Journal of the Royal Anthropological Institute* 7(1) (March 2001): 95-116.

Fechner FG, 'The Fundamental Aims of Cultural Property Law.' *International Journal of Cultural Property* 7(2) (1998): 376-394.

Ferdinand M, 'Ecology, Identity, and Colonialism in Martinique: The Discourse of an Ecological NGO (1980-2011)' in C Campbell and M Niblett (eds), *The Caribbean: Aesthetics, World-Ecology, Politics* (Liverpool University Press, 2016).

Fitzpatrick SM and AH Ross, (eds), *Island Shores, Distant Pasts: Archaeological and Biological Approaches to the Pre-Columbian Settlement of the Caribbean* (University Press of Florida 2010).

Fitzpatrick SM and WF Keegan, 'Human impacts and adaptations in the Caribbean Islands: an historical ecology approach', (2007) *Earth and Environmental Science Transactions of the Royal Society of Edinburgh*, 98, 29-45.

Floy JA, 'Sustainable Heritage Tourism, Climate Change and the National Trust.' PhD diss., University of Birmingham, 2015.

Fog Olwig K, 'National Parks, Tourism and Local Development: A West Indian Case.' *Human Organization* 39(1) (1980): 22-30.

_____, 'The Burden of Heritage: Claiming a Place for a West Indian Culture.' *American Ethologist* 26(2) (May 1999): 370-388.

Fonseca MJ, 'The Colonization of American Nature and the Early Development of International Law.' *Journal of the History of International Law* 12 (2010): 189-225.

Forrest C, *International Law and the Protection of Cultural Heritage* (Routledge 2010).

Forsyth, M (ed), *Understanding Historic Building Conservation* (Blackwell 2007).

Francioni F, 'Thirty Years On: Is the World Heritage Convention Ready for the 21st Century.' *The Italian Yearbook of International Law Online* 12 (1) (01/01/2002): 13-38.

_____, 'The Human Dimension of International Cultural Heritage Law: An Introduction.' *European Journal of International Law* 22(1) (2011): 9-16.

Francioni F and F Lenzerini (eds), *The 1972 World Heritage Convention: A Commentary* (Oxford University Press 2006).

Francioni F, 'Culture, Heritage and Human Rights: An Introduction,' in F Francioni, and M Scheinin (eds), *Cultural Human Rights* (Martinus Nijhoff 2008) 1-15.

Geertz C, *The Interpretation of Cultures: Selected Essays* (Basic Books 1973).

Gibson C, *Empire's Crossroads: A New History of the Caribbean* (Macmillan 2014).

Gillman D, *The Idea of Cultural Heritage* (Cambridge University Press 2010).

Gillespie A, *Protected Areas in International Law* (Martinus Nijhoff 2007).

Gould EH, 'Zones of Law, Zones of Violence: The Legal Geography of the British Atlantic, circa 1772.' *The William and Mary Quarterly* 60(3) (July 2003): 471-510.

Government of Grenada, *Grenada Protected Areas System Plan Part 1: Identification and Designation of Protected Areas.* Prepared by OECS/Mel Turner, 2009.

Government of Grenada, *Grenada Cultural Policy 2012.*

Government of Grenada, *Climate Change Adaptation (Disaster Management) Plan for Lower Sauteurs.* Grenada. Prepared by OECS/Geotechnical Investigative Services, 2013.

Government of St Vincent and the Grenadines, *National Parks and Protected Areas System Plan 2009-2014.*

Goy RHM, 'The International Protection of the Cultural and Natural Heritage.' *Netherlands Yearbook of International Law* 4 (1973): 117-141.

Graham N, *Lawscape: Property, Environment, Law* (Routledge-Cavendish, 2010).

Grove R, *Green Imperialism: Colonial Expansion, Tropical Island Edens and the Origins of Environmentalism, 1600-1860* (Cambridge University Press 2005).

Green PE, 'Caribbean Cultural Landscape: the English Caribbean potential in the journey from 'tentative listing' to being 'inscribed'.' *Journal of Heritage Tourism*, 8(1) (2013): 63-79, DOI: 10.1080/1743873X.2013.765749

Halikowski Smith S, 'The Mid-Atlantic Islands: A Theatre of Early Modern Ecocide.' *International Review of Social History* 55 (2010): 51-77.

Hall CM, and W Frost (eds), *Tourism and National Parks: International Perspectives on Development, Histories and Change* (Routledge 2009).

Hanna JA, 2017 'The Status of Grenada's Prehistoric Sites: Report on the 2016 Survey and an Inventory of Known Sites', manuscript on file at the Grenada National Museum and Ministry of Tourism, Botanical Gardens, Grenada.

Harwood R, *Historic Environment Law: Planning, Listed Buildings, Monuments, Conservation Areas and Objects* (Institute of Art and Law 2012).

Hauser MW, 'The Infrastructure of Nature's Island: Settlements, Networks and Economy of Two Plantations in Colonial Dominica.' *International Journal of Historical Archaeology* 19 (3) (2015): 601-22.

_____, 'The Political Ecology of Water and Enslavement: Waterways in Eighteenth-Century Caribbean Plantations.' *Current Anthropology* 58(2) (2017): 227-256.

_____, and D Hicks, 'Colonialism and Landscape: Power, Materiality and Scales of Analysis in Caribbean Historical Archaeology' in D Hicks, L McAtackney and G Fairclough (eds), *Envisioning Landscape: Situations and Standpoints in Archaeology and Heritage* (Routledge 2007).

Hauser MW and DV Armstrong, 'The Archaeology of Not Being Governed: A Counterpoint to a History of Settlement of Two Colonies in the Eastern Caribbean.' *Journal of Social Archaeology*, 12(3) (2012): 310-333.

Heap D, 'New Developments in British Land Planning Law – 1954 and After.' *Law and Contemporary Problems* 20(1) (1955): 493 -514.

Herzfeld M, 'Spatial Cleansing: Monumental Vacuity and the Idea of the West.' *Journal of Material Culture* 11(1/2) (2006): 127-149.

Hicks D, *The Garden of the World: An Historical Archaeology of Sugar Landscapes in the Eastern Caribbean* (Archaeopress 2007)

Hofman CL, 'Indigenous Caribbean Networks in a Globalizing World' in C De Corse (ed), *Power, Political Economy, and Historical Landscapes of the Modern World* (SUNY Press 2019).

Hofman CL and JB Haviser, 'Into the Future for Archaeological Heritage Management in the Dutch Caribbean' in Hofman CL and JB Haviser (eds), *Managing Our Past into the Future: Archaeological Heritage Management in the Dutch Caribbean* (Sidestone Press 2015).

Hofman CL and MLP Hoogland, 'Caribbean Encounters: Rescue Excavations at the Early Colonial Island Carib Site of Argyle, St. Vincent' in C Bakels and Hans Kamermans (eds), *Analecta Praehistorica Leidensia: The End of Our Fifth Decade*. Publication of the Faculty of Archaeology, Leiden University 2012.

_____, 'Connecting Stakeholders: Collaborative Preventive Archaeology Projects at Sites Affected by Natural and/or Human Impacts.' *Caribbean Connections* 5(1) (2016): 1-31.

_____, 'A Cultural Framework for Caribbean Island Historical Ecology Across the Lesser Antilles in PE Siegel (ed), *Island Historical Ecology: Socionatural Landscapes of the Eastern and Southern Caribbean* (Berghahn Books 2018).

Hofman CL, J Ulloa Hung, EN Malatesta Herrera, JS Jean, TF Sonnemann and MLP Hoogland, 'Indigenous Caribbean Perspectives: Archaeologies and Legacies of the First Colonised Region in the New World.' *Antiquity* 92(361) (2018): 200-216.

Holder J and C Harrison, *Law and Geography* (Oxford University Press 2003).

Hollsten L, 'Controlling Nature and Transforming Landscapes in the Early Modern Caribbean.' *Global Environment* 1(1) (2008): 80-113.

Home R, 'Transferring British Planning Law to the Colonies: The Case of the 1938 Trinidad Town and Planning Regional Ordinance.' *Third World Planning Review* 15(4) (1993): 397-410.

Honychurch L, *Carib to Creole: A History of Contact and Culture Exchange* (The Dominica Institute 2000).

Hooghiemstra H, T Olijhoek, MLP Hoogland, M Prins, B van Geel, T Donders, W Gosling and CL Hofman, 'Columbus' Environmental Impact in the New World: Land Use Change in the Yaque River Valley, Dominican Republic.' *Holocene* 28(11) (2018): 1818-1835.

Hudson BJ, 'Landscape as Resource for National Development: A Caribbean View.' *Journal of the Geographical Association* (April 1, 1986): 116-121.

Hunter J, *Archaeological Resource Management in the UK: An Introduction* (Sutton Publishing Ltd 1997).

Hutt S, *Cultural Property Law: A Practitioner's Guide to the Management, Protection, and Preservation of Heritage Resources* (American Bar Association 2004).

Hyam R, *Understanding the British Empire* (Cambridge University Press 2010).

Ingold T, 'The Temporality of the Landscape.' *World Archaeology* 25(2) (1993): 152-174.

International Council of Museums *Development of the Museum Definition According to ICOM Statutes (1946-2001)* UNESCO, 2009 <http://archives.icom.museum/hist_def_eng.html> accessed May 25, 2018.

International Council of Museums, 'International Council of Museums Statutes', Adopted by The Eleventh General Assembly of ICOM, Copenhagen, Denmark, June 14, 1974.

International Council on Monuments and Sites, *Cultural Landscapes of the Pacific Islands*. (ICOMOS, 2007).

IUCN Commission on National Parks and Protected Areas (CNPPA), *Parks for Life, Action for Protected Areas in Europe* (IUCN, 1994), at: <https://portals.iucn.org/library/sites/library/files/documents/1994-023.pdf>

_____, Management Guidelines for IUCN Category V: Protected Areas Protected Landscapes/Seascapes (IUCN, 2002).

James P, 'Anglo-Australian Law and the Aboriginal Cultural Heritage', *Historic Environment* 11 (2, 3) (1995): 52-56.

Johnson W (ed), *The Chattel Principle: Internal Slave Trades in the Americas* (Yale University Press 2005).

Jones M, 'Landscape, Law and Justice: Concepts and Issues.' *Norwegian Journal of Geography* 60 (2006): 1-14.

Jordan L, 'Managing Built Heritage for Tourism in Trinidad and Tobago: Challenges and Opportunities.' *Journal of Heritage Tourism* 8(1) (February 2013): 49-62. ·

Jørgensen K, M Clemetsen, K Halvorsen Thoren and T Richardson, *Mainstreaming Landscape through the European Landscape Convention* (Routledge 2016).

Keegan WF, and CL Hofman, *The Caribbean before Columbus* (Oxford University Press 2017).

Keehnen FWM, CL Hofman and AT Antczak, 'Material Encounters and Indigenous Transformations in the Early Colonial Americas' in CL Hofman, FWM Keehnen (eds), *Material Encounters and Indigenous Transformations in the Early Colonial Americas. The Early Americas: History and Culture no. 9* (Brill 2019).

Kelly KG, 'Archaeology, Plantations, and Slavery in the French West Indies' in KG Kelly and B Bérard (eds), *Lesser Antilles Plantation Archaeology* (Sidestone Press 2014).

Kelly KG and MD Hardy (eds), *French Colonial Archaeology in the Southeast and Caribbean* (University of Florida Press 2011).

King TF, 'What should be the 'Cultural Resources' Element of the EIA?' *Environmental Impact Assessment Review* 20 (2000): 5-30.

Kotze LJ and L Jansen van Rensburg, 'Legislative Protection of Cultural Heritage Resources: A South African Perspective.' *Queensland University of Technology Law & Justice Journal* 3(1) (2003): 121-141.

Kuruk P, 'Cultural Heritage, Traditional Knowledge and Indigenous Rights: An Analysis of the Convention for the Safeguarding of Intangible Cultural Heritage.' *Macquarie Journal of International & Comparative Environmental Law* 1 (2004): 111-134.

Lansley J, 'Membership Participation and Ideology in Large Voluntary Organisations: The Case of the National Trust.' *Voluntas* 7(3) (1995): 221-240.

Layard A, 'What is Legal Geography?' (University of Bristol Law School Blog, 11 April, 2016), <http://legalresearch.blogs.bris.ac.uk/2016/04/what-is-legal-geography/> accessed 21 June, 2017.

Lenzerini F, 'Intangible Cultural Heritage: The Living Culture of Peoples.' *The European Journal of International Law* 22(1) (2011): 101-120.

Lixinski L, *Intangible Cultural Heritage in International Law* (Oxford University Press 2013).

Lonetree A, *Decolonizing Museums* (University of North Carolina Press 2012).

Lowenthal D, *The Heritage Crusade and the Spoils of History* (Cambridge University Press 1998).

_____, 'Natural and Cultural Heritage'. *International Journal of Heritage Studies* 11(1) (2005): 81-92.

MacDonald S, *A Companion to Museum Studies* (Wiley-Blackwell 2011).

McKibben B, *The End of Nature* (Penguin Books 1990).

McManamon FP, 'Cultural Resources and Protection Under United States Law.' *Connecticut Journal of International Law* 16 (2) (2000-2001): 247-282.

McNeely J, *Coping with Change: People, Forests and Biodiversity.* Gland: IUCN 1994.

Makzouni J and S Egoz (eds), *The Right to Landscape: Contesting Landscape and Human Rights* (Ashgate, 2011).

Marshall, L (ed), *Archaeology of Slavery: Toward a Comparative Global Framework* (Southern Illinois University Press 2015).

Martin DG, and A Scherr, 'Lawyering Landscapes: Lawyers as Constituents of Landscapes.' *Landscape Research* 30(3) (01 July 2005): 379-393.

Martin JA, *Island Caribs and French Settlers in Grenada: 1483-1763* (Grenada National Museum Press, 2013).

_____, *A-Z of Grenada Heritage,* 2nd edn (forthcoming).

Meskell L, 'UNESCO's World Heritage Convention at 40'. *Current Anthropology* 54(4) (August 2013): 483-494.

Mickleburgh HL and JR Pagán-Jiménez, 'New Insights into the Consumption of Maize and Other Food Plants in the pre-Columbian Caribbean from Starch Grains Trapped in Human Dental Calculus.' *Journal of Archaeological Science* 39(7) (2012): 2468-2478.

Mitchell D, 'Cultural Landscapes: Just Landscapes or Landscapes of Justice?' *Progress in Human Geography* 27(6) (2003): 787-796.

_____, 'Go Slow: An Afterword on Landscape and Justice'. *Norwegian Journal of Geography* 60 (1) (2006): 123-27.

Mitchell WJT (ed), *Landscape and Power* (2nd edn, University of Chicago Press 2002).

Mol AAA, *The Connected Caribbean* (Sidestone Press 2014).

Molesworth S, 'Managing Heritage Cities in Asia and Europe: The Role of Public-Private Partnerships'. Delivered at the Public Forum and Experts' Meeting – *International National Trusts Organisation's Network Experiences in Public Private Partnership Approaches towards Management of Heritage Cities*, 12-14 July 2012, Yogyakarta, Indonesia.

Mrozowski SA, 'Colonization and the Commodification of Nature.' *International Journal of Historical Archaeology*, 3(3) (1999): 153-166.

Musitelli J, 'World Heritage: between Universalism and Globalization'. *International Journal of Cultural Property* 11(2) (2002): 323-336.

Naimark NA, *Genocide: A World History* (Oxford University Press 2016).

Newton M, 'The Race Leapt at Sauteurs: Genocide, Narrative and Indigenous Exile from the Caribbean Archipelago.' *Caribbean Quarterly* 60(2) (2014): 5-28.

North MacLaren A, 'Protecting the Past for the Public Good: Archaeology and Australian Heritage Law.' PhD diss., University of Sydney, 2006.

Oas SE and MW Hauser, 'The Political Ecology of Plantations from the Ground Up.' *Environmental Archaeology* 23(1) (2018): 4-12.

OAS, 'Enhancing the Socio-economic Potential of Cultural Heritage in the Caribbean: Caribbean Heritage Survey Analysis – Regional Needs and Opportunities to Support Cultural Heritage Protection.' Prepared by Coherit Associates, 2013.

Odendahl K and M Peters, 'The Significance of Cultural Heritage for State Stability and its Protection by Public International Law' in J Raue and P Sutter (eds), *Facts and Practice of State-building* (Brill 2009).

OECS, 'Grenada Protected Areas System Plan.' Prepared by Mel Turner, 2009.

_____, 'Climate Change Adaptation (Disaster Management) Plan for Lower Sauteurs, Grenada.' Prepared by Geotechnical Investigative Services, 2013.

O'Keefe P, 'Preliminary Study on the Advisability of Preparing an International Instrument for the Protection and Promotion of Museums and Collections (legal and technical aspects)'.

_____ and LV Prott, *Law and the Cultural Heritage. Volume 1: Discovery and Excavation* (Professional Books Ltd. 1984).

O'Keefe R, 'The Right to Take Part in Cultural Life under Article 15 of the ICESCR.' *ICLQ* 47(4) (1998): 904-923.

_____, 'World Cultural Heritage: Obligations to the International Community as a Whole?' *ICLQ* 53(1) (2004): 189-209.

_____, 'Protection of Cultural Property under International Criminal Law.' *Melbourne Journal of International Law* 11(2) (November 2010): 339-392.

Olmos Giupponi B, 'Fostering Environmental Democracy in Latin America and the Caribbean: An Analysis of the Regional Agreement on Environmental Access Rights.' *RECIEL* 28 (2019):136-151.

Olwig K, 'Recovering the Substantive Nature of Landscape.' *Annals of the Association of American Geographers* 86 (4) (December 1996): 630-653.

_____, 'Commons & Landscape', *Landscape, Law & Justice: Proceedings from a Workshop on Old and New Commons,* Centre for Advanced Study, Oslo, 11-13 March 2003.

_____, 'Introduction: the Nature of Cultural Heritage and the Culture of Natural Heritage – Northern Perspectives on a Contested Patrimony.' *International Journal of Heritage Studies* 11(1) (2005): 3-7.

_____, 'The Landscape of 'Customary' Law versus that of 'Natural' Law'. *Landscape Research* 30(3) (2005): 299-320.

_____, 'Representation and Alienation in the Political Landscape.' *Cultural Geographies* 12 (2005): 19-40.

_____, 'Place Contra Space in a Morally Just Landscape'. *Norwegian Journal of Geography* 60(1) (2006): 24-31.

_____, *Landscape, Nature and the Body Politic: From Britain's Renaissance to America's New World* (University of Wisconsin Press 2002).

_____, 'Globalism and the Enclosure of the Landscape Commons' in ID Rotherham (ed), *Cultural Severance and the Environment – the Ending of Traditional and Customary Practice on Commons and Landscapes Managed in Common* (Springer 2013).

_____, 'Landscape', in *International Encyclopedia of the Social & Behavioral Sciences* (2nd edn, 2015): 224-230.

_____, 'Virtual Enclosure, Ecosystem Services, Landscape's Character and the 'Rewilding' of the Commons: the 'Lake District' Case.' *Landscape Research*, 41(2) (2016): 253-264.

Olwig K and K Fog Olwig, 'Underdevelopment and the Development of "Natural" Park Ideology' *Antipode* 11(2) (1979): 16-26.

Olwig K, C Dalglish, G Fairclough and P Herring, 'Introduction to a Special Issue: the Future of Landscape Characterisation, and the Future Character of Landscape – Between Space, Time, History, Place and Nature.' *Landscape Research* 41(2) (2016): 169-174.

Otis G and A Laurent, 'Indigenous Land Claims in Europe: The European Court of Human Rights and the Decolonization of Property.' *Arctic Review on Law and Politics* 4(2) (2013): 156-180.

Pagán-Jiménez JR, 'Human-plant Dynamics in the Precolonial Antilles: A Synthetic Update' in WF Keegan, CL Hofman, and R Rodríguez Ramos (eds), *The Oxford Handbook of Caribbean Archaeology* (Oxford University Press, 2013).

Patterson O, *Slavery and Social Death: A Comparative Study* (Harvard University Press 1982).

Petrie L, 'An Inherently Exclusionary Regime: Heritage Law – The South Australian Experience.' *Macquarie Law Journal* 5 (2005): 177-199.

Phelan M, 'A Synopsis of the Laws Protecting Our Cultural Heritage.' *New England Law Review* 28 (1993-1994): 63-108.

Philippopoulos-Mihalopoulos A (ed), *Law and the City*. (Routledge-Cavendish 2007).

Philippopoulos-Mihalopoulos A, 'Spatial Justice: Law and the Geography of Withdrawal.' 6 *International Journal of Law in Context* (2010): 201-216.

_____, 'Law's Spatial Turn: Geography, Justice and a Certain Fear of Space.' *Law, Culture and the Humanities* 7 (2) (2011): 187-202.

_____ and S FitzGerald 'From Space Immaterial: The Invisibility of Lawscape.' *Griffith L. Rev.* 17 (2008): 438-454.

Phillips A, 'The Nature of Cultural Landscapes – A Nature Conservation Perspective.' *Landscape Research* 23(1) (1998): 21-38.

─────, *Management Guidelines for IUCN Category V Protected Areas Protected Landscapes/Seascapes* (IUCN, 2002).

Pratt M, 'The Arts of the Contact Zone.' *Profession* 91 (1991): 33-40.

Prott L, 'On Comparative Legal Terminology and *Patrimoine Culturel*.' *Journal of Comparative Law*, 8(1) (2013-2014): 305-312.

Prott LV, 'Problems of Private International Law for the Protection of the Cultural Heritage.' *Recueils des Cours* V (1989): 224-317.

───── and PJ O'Keefe, "Cultural Heritage' or 'Cultural Property'?' *International Journal of Cultural Property* 1(2) (1992): 307-320.

Pue WW, 'Wrestling with Law: (Geographical) Specificity vs. (Legal) Abstraction.' *Urban Geography* 11(6) (1990): 566-585.

Pugh J, and J Henshall Momsen (eds), *Environmental Planning in the Caribbean* (Ashgate Publishing 2005).

Randolph J, *Environmental Land Use Planning and Management* (Island Press 2003).

Reid B, *Myths and Realities of Caribbean History* (University of Alabama Press 2009).

Renes H, 'Islandscapes: Isolation and Pressure'. *Landscapes* 15(1) (2014): 44-58.

Richardson B, I Mgbeoji, and F Botchway, 'Environmental Law in Post-colonial Societies: Aspirations, Achievements and Limitations' in B Richardson and S Wood (eds), *Environmental Law for Sustainability* (Hart 2006).

Richardson B, 'Environmental Law in Postcolonial Societies: Straddling the Local-Global Institutional Spectrum'. *Colorado Journal of International Environmental Law and Policy* 11(1) (2000): 1-82.

Richman JR and MP Forsyth (eds), *Legal Perspectives on Cultural Resources* (AltaMira Press 2003).

Riesto, S and A Tietjen, University of Copenhagen, 'Doing Heritage Together – New Heritage Frontiers in Collaborative Planning,' in S Egoz (ed), *Defining Landscape Democracy: Conference Reader*, Norwegian University of Life Sciences : Centre for Landscape Democracy, 2015.

Rodwell D, *Conservation and Sustainability in Historic Cities* (Wiley-Blackwell 2007).

Rogers L, "The Heavens are High and the Emperor is Far Away': Cultural Heritage Law and Management in China.' *Historic Environment* 17(3) (2004): 38-43.

Rojas R Valcárcel, *Archaeology of Early Colonial Interaction at El Chorro de Maíta, Cuba* (University Press of Florida, 2016).

Rössler M, 'World Heritage – Linking Cultural and Biological Diversity,' Paper for the Seventh US/ICOMOS Symposium: Learning from World Heritage, Natchitoches, Louisiana, 25-27 March 2004.

─────, 'World Heritage Cultural Landscapes: A UNESCO Flagship Programme 1992 – 2006.' *Landscape Research* 31(4) (2006): 333-353.

Russell I, 'Heritage, Identities, and Roots: A Critique of Arborescent Models of Heritage and Identity' in GS Smith, P Mauch Messenger and HA Soderland (eds), *Heritage Values in Contemporary Society* (Left Coast Press 2010).

Sankatsing Nava T and CL Hofman, 'Engaging Caribbean Island Communities with Indigenous Heritage and Archaeology Research.' *JCOM: Journal of Science Communication* 17(4)(2018): 1-10.

Sanz C, *The Protection of Historic Properties: A Comparative Study of Administrative Policies* (WIT Press 2009).

Sauer C, 'The Morphology of Landscape.' *University of California Publications in Geography*, no. 2 (1925): 19-53.

Scazzosi, L, 'Reading and Assessing the Landscape as Cultural and Historical Heritage.' *Landscape Research* 29(4) (2004): 335-355.

Schama S, *Landscape and Memory* (Knopf 1995).

Schrijver N and F Weiss, *International Law and Sustainable Development* (Martinus Nijhoff 2004).

Selman P, 'Centenary Paper: Landscape Planning – Preservation, Conservation and Sustainable Development.' *Town Planning Review* 81(4) (2010): 335-355.

Shaw M, *International Law* (5th edn, Cambridge University Press 2003).

Shearing S, 'Reforming Australia's National Heritage Law Framework.' *Macquarie Journal of International and Comparative Environmental Law* 8(1) (2012): 71-95.

Sheller M, *Consuming the Caribbean: From Arawaks to Zombies* (Routledge 2003).

Siegel P and EL Righter, *Protecting Heritage in the Caribbean* (University of Alabama Press 2011).

Siegel PE, Hofman CL, B Bérard, R Murphy, J Ulloa Hung, R Rojas Valcárcel and C White, 'Confronting Caribbean Heritage in an Archipelago of Diversity: Politics, Stakeholders, Climate Change, Natural Disasters, Tourism and Development'. *Journal of Field Archaeology* 38(4) (2013): 376-390.

Smith A and KL Jones, Thematic Study: Cultural Landscapes of the Pacific Islands (ICOMOS 2007).

Smith L, *Archaeological Theory and the Politics of Cultural Heritage* (Routledge 2004).

_____, *The Uses of Heritage* (Routledge 2006).

_____, 'Theorizing Museum and Heritage Visiting' in A Witcomb and K Message (eds), *The International Handbooks of Museum Studies: Museum Theory* (John Wiley & Sons 2015).

Soja EW, 'The City and Spatial Justice.' Paper prepared for presentation at the conference Spatial Justice, Nanterre, Paris, March 12-14, 2008.

Stancioff CE, *Landscape, Land Change and Well-being in Small Island Contexts: Case Studies from St Kitts and the Kalinago Territory, Dominica* (Sidestone Press 2018).

Stancioff CE, R Stojanov, I Kelman, D Nemec, J Landa, R Tichy, D Prochazka, G Brown and CL Hofman, 'Climate Change impacts on Local Populations in the Caribbean and the Indian Ocean: A Synthesis of Perceptions of St. Kitts (Caribbean Sea) and Malé (Indian Ocean).' *Atmosphere* 9(12) (2018): 459-479.

Stavenhagen R, 'Cultural Rights: A Social Science Perspective' in A Eide, C Krause, and A Rosas (eds), *Economic, Social and Cultural Rights: A Textbook* (Springer, 2001).

Stec S and J Jendroska, 'The Escazú Agreement and the Regional Approach to Rio Principle 10: Process, Innovation, and Shortcomings.' *Journal of Environmental Law* 31 (2019): 533-545.

Strecker A, 'The Human Dimension to Landscape Protection in International Law' in F Lenzerini, and S Borelli (eds), *Cultural Heritage, Cultural Rights, Cultural Diversity: New Developments in International Law* (Martinus Nijhoff 2012).

_____, 'Revival, Recognition, Restitution: Indigenous Rights in the Eastern Caribbean.' *International Journal of Cultural Property* 23(2) (2016): 167-190.

_____, 'Indigenous Land Rights and Caribbean Reparations Discourse.' *Leiden Journal of International Law* 30(3) (2017): 629-646.

_____, 'The Law is at Fault? Landscape and Agency in International Law' in T Waterman and E Wall (eds), *Landscape and Agency* (Ashgate 2017).

_____, *Landscape Protection in International Law* (Oxford University Press 2018).

_____, 'Landscape as Cultural Heritage' in F Francioni and A Vrodljak (eds.), *Oxford Handbook on International Cultural Heritage Law* (Oxford University Press 2020).

_____, 'Article 13: Respecting Customary Practices' in L Lixinski and J Blake (eds.), *Commentary on the 2003 Convention on Safeguarding the Intangible Cultural Heritage* (Oxford University Press 2020).

Sundin B, 'Nature as Heritage: the Swedish Case.' *International Journal of Heritage Studies* 11(1) (2005): 9-20.

Sutter P and J Raue, *Facets and Practices of State-building* (Brill 2009).

Talbot J and R Buddley, 'Postcolonial Town Planning in Commonwealth nations: A Case Study of the Solomon Islands – an Agenda for Change.' *The Round Table* 96(390) (June 2007): 319-329.

Tallack M, *The Un-Discovered Islands* (Polygon 2016).

Taylor K and J Lennon, 'Cultural Landscapes: A Bridge Between Culture and Nature?' *International Journal of Heritage Studies* 17(6) (2011): 537-554.

Taylor N, *Urban Planning Theory since 1945* (Sage Publications 1998).

Taylor, W (ed), *The Geography of Law: Landscape, Identity and Regulation* (Hart 2006).

Techera EJ, 'Safeguarding Cultural Heritage: Law and Policy in Fiji.' *Journal of Cultural Heritage* 12 (2011): 329-334.

Teich M, R Porter, and B Gustafsson (eds), *Nature and Society in Historical Context* (Cambridge University Press 1997).

Throsby D, 'The Value of Heritage.' Paper delivered at Heritage Economics Workshop, 11-12 October 2007, Australia National University.

Toppin Allahar C, "De Beach Belong to We!' Socio-economic Disparity and Islanders' Rights of Access to the Coast in a Tourist Paradise.' *Oñati Socio-legal Series* 5 (1) (2015): 298-317.

Ulloa Hung J and R Rojas Valcárcel (eds) *Indígenas Indios en el Caribe: Presencia, Legado y Estudio* (Instituto Tecnológico de Santo Domingo 2016).

UNESCO/World Heritage Centre, 'Cultural Landscapes: The Challenges of Conservation.' World Heritage Papers 7. UNESCO 2003.

_____, 'Management of Caribbean Cultural Resources in a Natural Environment: Sites of Memory and Participation of Local Communities' Concept Note, Barbados, 11-15 March 2013.

_____, Report of the Workshop: Management of Caribbean Cultural Resources in a Natural Environment: Sites of Memory and Participation of Local Communities, Barbados, 11-15 March 2013.

_____, 'Safeguarding Precious Resources for Island Communities.' World Heritage Papers 38. UNESCO 2014.

_____, 'Caribbean Action Plan for World Heritage 2015-2019.' Adopted in Havana on 28 November 2014.

Vecco M, 'A Definition of Cultural Heritage: From the tangible to the intangible.' *Journal of Cultural Heritage* 11 (2010): 321-324.

Waterton E, L Smith and G Campbell, 'The Utility of Discourse Analysis to Heritage Studies: The Burra Charter and Social Inclusion.' *International Journal of Heritage Studies* 12(4) (2006): 339-355.

Watts D, *The West Indies: Patterns of Development Culture and Environmental Change since 1492* (Cambridge University Press 1990).

Whiting J, *Museum Focussed Heritage in the English-speaking Caribbean*. Paris: UNESCO, 1983.

Whitt L, *Science, Colonialism and Indigenous Peoples: The Cultural Politics of Law and Knowledge* (Cambridge University Press 2009).

Wigen K, R Bridenthal, and JH Bentley (eds), *Seascapes: Maritime Histories, Littoral Cultures, and Transoceanic Exchanges* (University of Hawaii Press 2007).

Wilson S, *The Indigenous People of the Caribbean* (University Press of Florida 1997).

Wiltshire KD, and LA Wallis, 'A History of Aboriginal Protection Legislation in South Australia.' *Environmental and Planning Law Journal* 25(2) (2008): 98-114.

Wiltshire K, *Heritage, Federalism and the Environment*. R. L. Matthews. Canberra, Centre for Research on Federal Financial Relations, Australian National University, 1985.

World Commission on Environment and Development, *Our Common Future* (Oxford University Press 1987).

News Sources

Allen Agostini L, 'No surprise here' (*Trinidad and Tobago Guardian*, 2 December 2014) <http://www.guardian.co.tt/article-6.2.391123.c15833cc9e> accessed 30 July 2018.

BBC News, 'Australia drops Tasmanian Wilderness logging campaign'. 20 March 2016 < http://www.bbc.com/news/world-australia-35854980> accessed 28 October 2019. 'Bid to settle Greyfriars out of court' (*Trinidad Express*, 5 January, 2015) <https://www.trinidadexpress.com/news/local/bid-to-settle-greyfriars-demolition-out-of-court/article_857e6357-3494-502e-a423-c29ae55b42d3.html> accessed 30 July 2018.

Boodram K, 'National Trust to take legal action' (*Trinidad Express*, 1 September 2015) <https://www.trinidadexpress.com/news/local/national-trust-to-take-legal-action/article_95ccba41-68d0-575b-8755-6a1e933f5da2.html> accessed 30 July 2018.

Bubb K, 'Camerhogne Debate reaches Brooklyn' (*Now Grenada*, 17 March 2016) <http://www.nowgrenada.com/2016/03/camerhogne-park-debate-reaches-brooklyn/> accessed 8 February 2018.

Campbell C, 'Amerindian burial site under siege' (*Now Grenada*, 1 March 2018) <https://www.nowgrenada.com/2018/03/archaeologists-saving-amerindian-burial-site-under-siege/> accessed 15 November 2018.

Charan R, 'Too late for Greyfriars' (*Trinidad Express*, 24 August 2015) <https://www.trinidadexpress.com/news/local/too-late-for-greyfriars/article_3560b-1be-c9e3-5c7f-a1ee-ca2e7224edc9.html> accessed 30 July 2018.

_____, 'Historic church falls' (*Trinidad Express*, 30 August 2015) <https://www.trinidadexpress.com/news/local/historic-church-falls/article_e571c8db-4468-5467-a683-f3c282a36481.html> accessed 30 July 2018.

Clarke M, 'Save our heritage for future generations' (*Trinidad Express*, 2 December 2014) <https://www.trinidadexpress.com/news/local/save-our-heritage-for-future-generations/article_d6dacaab-75c0-5b9d-bad1-de8b4a266f28.html> accessed 30 July 2018.

Clyne K, 'Owner of Greyfriars: Toxic roof removed from church hall' (*Trinidad and Tobago Guardian*, 13 November 2014) <http://www.guardian.co.tt/article-6.2.390342.7e91ca0fce> accessed 30 July 2018.

———, 'State moves to save Greyfriars' (*Trinidad and Tobago Guardian*, 25 November 2014) <http://www4.guardian.co.tt/news/2014-11-25/state-moves-save-greyfriars> accessed 30 July 2018.

Dart T, 'Derek Walcott museum closes amid row over Caribbean tourist developments' (*The Guardian*, 21 June 2017) <https://www.theguardian.com/books/2017/jun/21/derek-walcott-museum-st-lucia-caribbean-tourism> accessed 30 July 2018.

Fraser J, 'A Heritage Building lives on in Trinidad' (*The New York Times*, 26 March 2015) <https://www.nytimes.com/2015/03/27/greathomesanddestinations/a-heritage-building-lives-on-in-trinidad.html> accessed 30 July 2018.

Fraser M, 'Greyfriars Church sold' (*Trinidad Express*, 12 August 2014) <https://www.trinidadexpress.com/news/local/greyfriars-church-sold/article_2b81668a-e44a-5bee-b54f-7738c63cb660.html> accessed 30 July 2018.

———, 'Protesters block demolition crew: confrontation at Greyfriars Church' (*Trinidad Express*, 10 November 2014) <https://www.trinidadexpress.com/news/local/protesters-block-demolition-crew/article_80a66872-36ba-54c8-865b-7b54aa1ab2c3.html> accessed 30 July 2018.

———, 'Greyfriars owner hires engineer' (*Trinidad Express*, 5 December 2014) <https://www.trinidadexpress.com/news/local/greyfriars-owner-hires-engineers/article_dac1ab5f-3c5f-5a37-8144-39f664e96470.html> accessed 30 July 2018.

———, 'I felt compelled to buy Greyfriars' (*Trinidad Express*, 17 August, 2015) <https://www.trinidadexpress.com/news/local/i-felt-compelled-to-buy-greyfriars/article_058b9f52-a7bc-53ba-8f27-80833b74137d.html> accessed 30 July 2018.

Gill A, 'Relocate park and build hotel' (*Now Grenada*, 14 March 2016) <http://www.nowgrenada.com/2016/03/relocate-park-build-the-hotel/> accessed 8 February, 2018.

'Government to work along with critics on Camerhogne Park' (*Now Grenada*, 15 January 2016) <http://www.nowgrenada.com/2016/01/government-work-along-critics-camerhogne-park/> accessed 8 February 2018.

'Government consultations on Camerhogne Park' (*Now Grenada*, 5 March 2016) <http://www.nowgrenada.com/2016/03/government-consultations-on-camerhogne-park/> accessed 8 February 2018.

Horne K, 'Indigenous people await Village restoration' (*The Vincentian,* 9 August 2019) <http://thevincentian.com/indigenous-people-await-village-restoration-p17710-135.htm> accessed 4 December 2019.

'IADC National Trust working on petroglyphs solution' (*Searchlight*, 12 October 2007) <https://searchlight.vc/searchlight/news/2007/10/12/iadc-national-trust-working-on-petroglyphs-solution/> accessed 30 July 2018.

Joseph L, 'Camerhogne Park and the national interest' (*Now Grenada*, 7 March 2016) <http://www.nowgrenada.com/2016/03/camerhogne-park-and-the-national-interest/> accessed 8 February, 2018.

Loubon M, 'Galy defends demolition: Church a danger to the public' (*Trinidad Express*, 31 August 2015) <https://www.trinidadexpress.com/news/local/galy-defends-demolition-church-a-danger-to-the-public/article_14008d6d-bafa-5a4c-8451-65936f0345dc.html> accessed 30 July 2018.

Mead L, 'Escazú Agreement on Rio Principle 10 Gains Signatures, Ratifications <http://sdg.iisd.org/news/escazu-agreement-on-rio-principle-10-gains-signatures-ratifications/> accessed 9 October 2019.

'National Trust moves to protect historic Greyfriars Church' (*Trinidad Express,* August 2014) <https://www.trinidadexpress.com/news/local/national-trust-moves-to-protect-historic-greyfriars-church/article_75b7d56d-c75a-5320-8e9a-f9e476137a98.html> accessed 30 July 2018. 'No decision on Camerhogne Park' (*Now Grenada*, 13 January 2016) <http://www.nowgrenada.com/2016/01/no-decision-camerhogne-park/> accessed 8 February 2018.

Pidduck A, 'Historic church in dire need of repairs and assistance' (*Trinidad and Tobago Newsday*, 3 October 2010) <https://archives.newsday.co.tt/2010/10/03/historic-church-in-dire-need-of-repairs-and-assistance/> accessed 30 July 2018.

Paul A, 'Greyfriars owner submits demolition plan', (*Trinidad and Tobago Guardian*, 22 February 2015) <http://www.guardian.co.tt/news/greyfriars-owner-submits-demolition-plan-6.2.375536.45d102b5ce> accessed 30 July 2018.

Press release: 'NDC Statement on Town Hall Meeting for Camerhogne Park' (*Now Grenada*, 16 January 2016) <http://www.nowgrenada.com/2016/01/22054/> accessed 8 February 2018.

'Press release: 'The Save Camerhogne Park Committee finalises resolution for signing by political parties' (*Now Grenada*, 11 January 2018) <http://www.nowgrenada.com/2018/01/the-save-camerhogne-park-committee-finalises-resolution-for-signing-by-political-parties/> accessed 8 February, 2018.

'Repurposing of Woodford Square' (*Trinidad and Tobago Guardian*, 23 November 2014) <http://www.guardian.co.tt/article-6.2.390758.5a110e2900>accessed 30 July 2018.

'Save Greyfriars Church' (*Trinidad Express*, 14 August 2014) <https://www.trinidadexpress.com/news/local/save-greyfriars-church/article_b04f74c8-f023-5fe8-9741-c64a96d-5b47e.html> accessed 30 July 2018.

'St Lucia Prime Minister cuts funding for National Trust' (*Antigua Observer*, 26 April 2017) <https://antiguaobserver.com/st-lucia-pm-cuts-funding-for-national-trust/> accessed 3 July 2018.

Straker L, 'Camerhogne Park to be relocated' (*Now Grenada*, 6 January 2016) <http://www.nowgrenada.com/2016/01/camerhogne-park-relocated/> accessed 8 February 2018.

Surtees J, 'Trinidad's forgotten architectural gems' (*The Guardian*, 16 February 2015) <https://www.theguardian.com/travel/2015/feb/16/trinidad-port-of-spain-architecture-tour> accessed 30 July 2018.

'SVG National Trust saves petroglyphs at Argyle' <https://searchlight.vc/searchlight/news/2007/06/29/svg-national-trust-saves-petroglyphs-at-argyle/> (*Searchlight,* 29 June 2007) accessed 30 July 2018.

Summary

In the introductory chapter, the theoretical and methodological context for the research is laid out and key concepts defined. The scope of the study area is demarcated, comprising the independent English speaking islands of the Lesser Antilles (Antigua and Barbuda, Barbados, Dominica, Grenada, Saint Lucia, St Kitts and Nevis, St Vincent and the Grenadines, and Trinidad and Tobago). The significance of an integrated definition of heritage resources to small landmasses is underscored. This cultural nature is known as landscape and is the source of a people's heritage. Valuing heritage via the protection of landscape supports the survival of local livelihoods and community cohesion, which has implications for the future sustainability of culturally diverse small island economies. This approach to heritage protection benefits from new socio-legal methodologies such as legal geography and legal anthropology, which look at the particular space (geographic location or place) heritage emanates from to determine successful protection strategies for the local community (spatial justice), and consider norms beyond textual legislation to determine the effectiveness of regulating heritage resources. With this in mind, the laws examined relate to museum and national trusts, antiquities, land use planning, and parks and protected areas. The chapter summarises the research questions, and outlines the layout and structure of the dissertation.

Chapter Two develops the theoretical framework as it relates to the Caribbean landscape and spatial justice, applying Kenneth Olwig's landscape theory to reveal the law's role in defining and ultimately erasing landscape, and the implications for heritage protection. Landscape as it exists in common law countries is traced to its roots in England, and an overview is provided of the reduction of the communal landscape in its dynamic form to its aestheticised shadow today, as a landscape garden. This was achieved through enclosure, and enclosure laws helped transform landscapes into private property for elite interests, under the guise of avoiding 'waste' of land and promoting efficiency of agriculture, while displacing commoners and their local way of life. This practice was so successful that it was transplanted throughout the British Empire, resulting in the imperial landscape. The implications for heritage protection are illustrated by way of examining the transformation of the Amerindian landscape in the Lesser Antilles to the plantationscape. Amerindian genocide was justified by framing indigenous peoples as primitive and dangerous, unhygienic occupiers of space. Expelling these peoples facilitated the conversion of their clan approach to land into private property. This suppression of community identity and humanity continued via the importation of enslaved African labour for the purpose of exploitative monoculture. The law as an instrument of empire enabled these practices – the earliest conservation laws such as the King's Hill Reserve Act in St Vincent and the Grenadines created colonial reserves to maintain the plantation economy. By denying local and enslaved peoples access to space exclusively in favour of the plantocracy, spatial injustice was embedded in the legal framework and the heritage of local communities was expunged. This practice set the tone for the relationship between landscape, law and heritage.

Confronting this legacy begins in Chapter Three, which explores the development of landscape protection in international law with reference to the Lesser Antilles. Amy Strecker's seminal work on the subject is discussed, highlighting landscape's origins as visual background in soft law instruments such as UNESCO recommendations, to its emergence as a heritage category in the World Heritage Convention, as well as its treatment in environmental law and human rights law, before finally it becomes a subject in its own right in the European Landscape Convention (ELC). The ELC places people at the centre of landscape and by recognising the value of community relationships with the land to sustainable development, no longer dismisses landscape as an aesthetic backdrop. Both the EU and Inter-American court systems are examined to assess interpretation of landscape protection. The Inter-American system is more progressive but restricts landscape rights to indigenous communities only. While there is no counterpart to the ELC in the Caribbean, the future for landscape protection with the newly adopted Escazú Agreement on Access to Information, Public Participation and Justice in Environmental Matters in Latin America and the Caribbean is speculated upon, given the Escazú Agreement's requirements for the procedural environmental rights of communities to be respected where there is proposed land use change, which potentially demonstrates recognition of the diversity of land uses reflective of landscape, in spite of the absence of communal rights to landscape in the common law. Ultimately, this chapter acknowledges that international law has taken a progressive stance in protecting local communities and their rights.

Chapter Four is the first of three chapters to examine contemporary domestic legislation, in this case antiquities and heritage legislation. National trusts of the Lesser Antilles, which are the main bodies responsible for heritage, evolve out of the National Trust of England and Wales, so their development is compared and contrasted with this model institution. National trusts prioritise colonial heritage as they were originally designed to uphold the interests of the elite. Museum law is not well developed, but three examples from Barbados, Grenada and Trinidad and Tobago are discussed. Laws in draft, namely the Antiquities bills of Antigua and Barbados, are examined with an eye to the future development of heritage law in those countries. While there are attempts to become progressive, underlying assumptions remain embedded in antiquities law and continue to influence its drafting and enforcement. These demand an object-or site- based approach to heritage, detached from the integrated relationships with communities and the environment which imbue that heritage with value and sustain its existence.

Chapter Five is dedicated to planning law, which is based on English town and country planning legislation. The chapter makes a distinction between those countries that have retained town and country legislation (Barbados, St Vincent and the Grenadines, and Trinidad and Tobago) and the remaining Lesser Antilles countries, which have developed modern physical planning and development control legislation. Town and country legislation from the UK reflects the needs of Postwar Britain, rather than the Lesser Antilles. Because this law was originally designed to promote development, often at the expense of heritage, heritage itself is not considered a legitimate land use in the Lesser Antilles, and is relegated to an aesthetic consideration. Procedural mechanisms, such as a duty to consult the community and the environmental impact assessment are hampered by this narrow definition of land and are underutilised where heritage is concerned. Even where model legislation has been developed for the sub-region, underlying planning objectives continue to treat heritage as an obstacle to development, and often frame it as a threat to public health in need of removal, this 'spatial cleansing' thus serving to reinforce the accepted spatial definition of land as private property.

Chapter Six discusses landscape as public space, which is regulated by parks and protected areas legislation. The park ideal as first defined in English legislation disguised the forcible enclosure of communal land, a practice that was extended when park law was transported to the Americas. In the Lesser Antilles, these proto-parks took the form of colonial reserves for the purpose of supporting plantation agriculture, and excluded Amerindian peoples from these lands. Review of park law reveals that this dynamic of exclusive conservation continues, whether through the design of parks, their prioritisation as tourism assets, or the use of fees. The underlying aim is to curtail public access and land use and suppress local community relationships that are responsible for the nurturing of heritage resources. This reduces the multiplicity of spatial definitions associated with common land in favour of entrenching private interests as property. This reinforces the premise that the inherited eco-imperialist framework was designed to extinguish local customary practices. Spatial justice is therefore relevant for challenging formal legal approaches to protecting public spaces.

In the absence of caselaw, Chapter Seven highlights some examples of public space disputes in the Lesser Antilles that illustrate the inadequacy of current heritage legislation. Conflicts represent community action to protect landscape (and by extension their heritage) where the legislation fails them. In some instances, poor administration is an indicator of deficiencies in the law, such as in Saint Lucia, where the National Trust was expected to develop heritage as tourism assets in spite of its protective mandate. Indeed, a common theme, as Greyfriars Church in Trinidad and Tobago also reveals, concerns the challenges of protecting public spaces where heritage law and planning law come into conflict. Despite the existence of a specific law for protecting Amerindian heritage, Grenada's first example in Lower Sauteurs emphasises the shortcomings of the EIA process in planning where communities and heritage protection are concerned, while the EIA process in Argyle, St Vincent and the Grenadines serves as a valuable counterpoint because a contemporary indigenous community was able to challenge this process. Finally, the second example from Grenada, Camerhogne Park, demonstrates the degree to which implementation of parks law can become a springboard for spatial justice issues in that island, particularly as it relates to use and access, with the public challenging the government's proposed sale of the park. These examples affirm that where public spaces are not recognised within the law and are undermined to reinforce private property interests, land is ascribed fixed spatial definitions that are colonial in character. Yet landscapes by their very nature are contested, with multiple interests and uses that differ from community to community, as the conflicts reveal. The law does not accommodate the range of communal interests that landscape represents, so these uses are unrecognised, resulting in spatial injustice and potential loss of heritage unless communities challenge these practices.

Chapter Eight concludes by observing that these challenges arising across the Lesser Antilles support the argument that decolonising the legal framework requires moving away from the universalist eco-imperialist forces that disrupted community bonds in the land, erased local knowledge of resource use and stifled associated cultural traditions. By drawing on perspectives from legal geography and legal anthropology, new insights have been revealed concerning the inadequacies of the legal framework for heritage protection. Deploying the landscape lens has exposed the ways in which community relationships with the land are essential for sustaining heritage. A spatially just analysis of the law highlights how the narrow and abstract definition of land as property rights erases the specificity of place. Property fails to represent those diverse interests in land that vary from location to location and generate heritage. This makes heritage controllable and even disposable according to the law, an object, a building or a view to be preserved or removed at whim. Thus landscape as cultural nature contextualises heritage, importing sustainability, spatial justice and respect for communities into a framework for heritage protection. Yet a right to landscape is not recognised in the common law. One way to translate these considerations into domestic law is to emulate the emancipatory trend in international law, which empowers local communities by equipping them with procedural environmental rights that enhance their collective capacity to participate in and challenge decisions about landscape use. Ratifying the Escazú Agreement may thus be seen as a vehicle for implementing landscape protection and localising the law in the long term.

Curriculum Vitae

Amanda Byer is an environmental lawyer from the island of Grenada. She obtained her Bachelor of Arts degree in Economics from Sarah Lawrence College, New York, and her Bachelor of Laws from the University of the West Indies (UWI). She holds Master's degrees in Environmental Law (with distinction) from University College London, and in Natural Resource Management (with distinction) from the UWI. Amanda has worked as an environmental legal consultant throughout the Lesser Antilles, specifically on the implementation of international environmental treaties such as the UN Framework Convention on Climate Change, UNESCO Convention on World Heritage, Convention on Biodiversity and the Land Degradation Convention; as well as on the analysis of laws pertaining to protected areas, heritage tourism and public participation.

Amanda's interest in law as an instrument for promoting sustainability in small island states has led her research towards the role of communities and their relationship with heritage resources (both natural and cultural). This formed the subject of her doctoral dissertation at Leiden University (2015-2020) within the ERC Synergy NEXUS1492 project.